CRITICAL ISSUES IN CRIME AND SOCIETY
Raymond J. Michalowski, Series Editor

Critical Issues in Crime and Society is oriented toward critical analysis of contemporary problems in crime and justice. The series is open to a broad range of topics including specific types of crime, wrongful behavior by economically or politically powerful actors, controversies over justice system practices, and issues related to the intersection of identity, crime, and justice. It is committed to offering thoughtful works that will be accessible to scholars and professional criminologists, general readers, and students.

For a list of titles in the series, see the last page of the book.

Life after Death Row

Exonerees' Search for Community and Identity

Saundra D. Westervelt
Kimberly J. Cook

Rutgers University Press
New Brunswick, New Jersey, and London

Library of Congress Cataloging-in-Publication Data

Westervelt, Saundra Davis, 1968–
    Life after death row : exonerees' search for community and identity / Saundra D.
Westervelt, Kimberly J. Cook.
        p. cm. — (Critical issues in crime and society)
    Includes bibliographical references and index.
    ISBN 978–0–8135–5383–2 (hbk. : alk. paper) — ISBN 978–0–8135–5382–5
(pbk. : alk. paper) — ISBN 978–0–8135–5339–9 (e-book)
    1. Death row inmates—United States.   2. False imprisonment—United
States.   3. Prisoners—Deinstitutionalization—United States.   4. Ex-convicts—
United States—Psychology.   5. Ex-convicts—United States—Social conditions.
6. Ex-convicts—Services for—United States.   7. Judicial error—United States.
I. Cook, Kimberly J., 1961–   II. Title.
    HV8699.U5W47   2012
    364.660973—dc23
                                                                        2011046943

A British Cataloging-in-Publication record for this book is available from the
British Library.

Chapter 2, "Researching the Innocent," contains excerpts and modifications of
"Feminist Research Methods in Theory and Action: Learning from Death Row
Exonerees," by S. Westervelt and K. J. Cook, in *Criminal Justice Research and
Practice*, ed. S. Miller (Lebanon, NH: University Press of New England, 2007).
© University Press of New England, Lebanon, NH; reprinted with permission.

Visit our website: http://rutgerspress.rutgers.edu

Manufactured in the United States of America

For Gary Beeman, Kirk Bloodsworth, Shabaka Brown, Sabrina Butler, Perry Cobb, Charles Fain, Gary Gauger, Alan Gell, Tim Howard, Gary James, Dave Keaton, Ray Krone, Walter McMillian, Juan Melendez, Alfred Rivera, Scott Taylor, Delbert Tibbs, Greg Wilhoit, and their families, and all of the innocent, in and out of prison, who continue to search for freedom, acknowledgment, and acceptance

Contents

TABLES AND FIGURES

Preface

THE IDEA FOR THIS PROJECT was born in November 2000 at the American Society of Criminology conference in San Francisco, California. I (Saundra) had organized a panel on wrongful conviction issues and asked Michael Radelet to serve as a discussant. Kim, a former student of Mike's and good friend, attended to see Mike and hear some of the papers presented. Kim and I had never met. During his few minutes of discussion, Mike reeled off a list of topics related to wrongful conviction issues that had not been undertaken and that desperately needed attention. One of those topics was about life after exoneration: what is life like for exonerees once they leave prison? I immediately gravitated toward that particular topic among those Mike offered up. Having just finished work on my first project related to wrongful convictions, I was casting about for something new to work on, and this particular topic seemed intriguing. It combined my interests in wrongful convictions with my methodological preference for qualitative research. Unbeknownst to me, Kim was thinking exactly the same thing. Having completed work on some projects related to capital punishment, she found compelling the idea of combining her interests on the death penalty with a new area she did not know much about, wrongful conviction—a project on life after release for death row exonerees might be just the ticket. But, again, we did not know each other, so we had no way to know we were contemplating the same project.

That all changed later that afternoon when I was staffing the outreach table for the Division on Women and Crime, and Kim arrived to take the next shift. Kim recognized me from the earlier panel and told me how much she had gotten out of the papers, but in particular, how interesting she had found Mike's discussant portion. We swapped funny stories about how we each had come to know Mike Radelet. I picked up on Kim's earlier comment about his discussion and offered that my interest also had been piqued by a particular topic he had mentioned.

We soon discovered that we had landed on the same idea. We eagerly began thinking out loud about how we could pursue this project. Kim even had a title already in mind—"Life after Death." Within thirty minutes, we had crafted the outline of this research and forged the beginnings of a productive and deeply meaningful friendship.

It would take, however, almost two years before we could begin serious work on the project. The following semester and summer, Kim headed off to Australia on a Fulbright fellowship to pursue her interests in restorative justice. In July, I headed off on a new adventure of my own when my son, Drew, was born. So it was not until sometime in 2002 when both of our lives settled back down to a place where we could begin work on this project. Since then, our interviews with exonerees have taken us around the United States, remembering that when we first began, conferences regularly attended by exonerees were not frequent occurrences. If you wanted to talk to an exoneree, and a death row exoneree at that, you had to go to him or her. So we did. In the process, we have shared many meaningful moments with each other and with them. For a project spanning nearly a decade, the number of people we must thank is voluminous. No doubt, we will inadvertently forget to thank someone. We hope that you know who you are and that you have felt our appreciation in other ways.

We, of course, first must thank Mike Radelet. Without his compelling idea and subsequent unwavering support, we would have never met, become friends, and embarked on this fascinating work that has enriched our lives. The gratitude we have for the eighteen exonerated death row survivors who participated in our research is truly too deep to fully express. We thank each of them and their families—Gary B., Kirk, Shabaka, Sabrina, Perry, Charles, Gary G., Alan, Tim, Gary J., Dave, Ray, Walter, Juan, Alfred, Scott, Delbert, and Greg—for their openness, their trust, and their patience. We had no idea it would take us this long to complete this project, and we know they have been waiting. We hope we have done justice to their experiences and have rendered their journeys more visible to others. We want to assure them that our original commitment to them still stands. We pledge not to profit from their stories and plan to donate all net proceeds from this book to organizations dedicated to serving the wrongly convicted.

We would like to thank our two funding sources for providing the resources necessary to travel to exonerees for interviews and to transcribe those interviews after returning home: the External Proposal Development Incentive Program, Office of the Associate Provost for Research at the University of North Carolina at Greensboro and the American Sociological Association's Fund for Advancement of the Discipline Award supported by the American Sociological Association and the National Science Foundation.

The primary hurdle to overcome in doing this research was that of locating death row exonerees willing to talk with us and share their stories. Many people assisted us in contacting and staying in touch with exonerees over the years. We appreciate their trust in us. They include Peter Neufeld, Naomi Fein, Sarah Tofte, Rob Warden, Edwin Colfax, Ali Flaum, Bryan Stevenson, Angie Setzer, Jim McCloskey, Dick Dieter, Jim Marcus, David Atwood, Jeff Garis, Nancy Vollertsen, Susan Sharp, Debra Crandall, Clive Stafford Smith, Terry Rumsey, Kurt Rosenberg, Andrea Lyon, Jim Owen, and Jeanette Johnson. We also are grateful to other death row exonerees we have met during the course of this project, though our funding limitations prevented us from including them in the study: Ron Keine, Harold Wilson, Gary Drinkard, and Randy Steidl.

We could not have completed this project without the assistance of graduate students and administrative office staff who worked on tables and charts, kept track of funding, and transcribed data. We are truly grateful to the following for their help: Jean Holliday, Chardon Murray, Kateri Bruno, Rachael Patterson, Kristen Hefner, Alma Quinn, Hannah Bridges, Meredith Fraser, Katie Gay, Holli Reeves, and Kayla Picotte. The biographical summaries in chapter 3 were written with the assistance of Casey Strange, a graduate student in sociology at the University of North Carolina at Greensboro.

We would like to thank all of those at Rutgers University Press for sticking with us throughout the development of the book, in particular Marlie Wasserman, Adi Hovav (our former editor), Peter Mickulas (our current editor), and series editor Ray Michalowski (our dear friend and colleague). We appreciate the helpful comments of two anonymous reviewers whose insights strengthened the manuscript in numerous ways. Additional colleagues and friends we thank include Lynn Chancer, Michael Jacobson, Mona Danner, Cathleen Burnett, Claire Renzetti, Susan Caringella, Kai Erikson, Richard Leo, Bill Chambliss, Jim Ptacek, Valerie Braithwaite, John Braithwaite, Stephen Mugford, Kathleen

Daly, Kirk Williams, Ron Huff, Jim Coleman, Theresa Newman, Rich Rosen, Jon Powell, Robert Norris, Jim Acker, Matt Robinson, Ada Haynes, Liesel Ritchie, Mark Rabil, Darryl Hunt, and Jennifer Thompson.

Finally, we each have a few personal thank-yous to extend. Saundra would like to thank Jack Humphrey for introducing her to the wrongful conviction issue and Steve Kroll-Smith for thoughts on earlier versions of the project, in particular his suggestion that we investigate the literature on trauma for useful analytical tools in better explaining the experiences of our participants. She wishes to acknowledge the patience and support of her colleagues at UNCG, in particular Julie Brown and Tim Johnston, who have been so helpful in providing time away from service obligations and teaching to allow this project finally to come fully to fruition. As always, she is so grateful to her husband, Van, for liking a smart girl. His support made it okay for her to pursue this project because she knew that he was there even when she mentally and physically was not. She wants to thank her son, Drew, for his patience and understanding every time Mom said that she had to work on "the book" rather than chase turtles. She hopes that one day he will be proud of her accomplishment.

Saundra also would like to thank Kim, who is no longer "just" her coauthor but now her dearest friend. One does not anticipate finding a best friend during investigations of some of life's most horrible events, but this is the case here. She would like to thank Kim for being smart and for having a heart, for making the hard work fun, for always reminding her not to take herself too seriously, and for forcing her out of her own head.

Kim would like to thank her colleagues and friends at UNCW in the Department of Sociology and Criminology, especially Diane Levy, Gary Faulkner, John Rice, Randy LaGrange, Steve McNamee, Jean-Anne Sutherland, Christy Lanier, Leslie Hossfeld, and Mike Maume (for taking on important service roles). Others to thank at UNCW include David Cordle, David Webster, Carrie Clements, Matt Ten Huisen, Jimmy Reeves, Carol Pilgrim, Kim Sawrey, Lee Prete, and Kathleen Berkeley. She wishes to thank her family members Freda and Everett Cook, outstanding parents for fifty years. Kim is eternally grateful that they fetched her from the bus station in Bangor one cold and bitter night in December 1980. Kim also wants to thank her son, Greg Cook, who was about twenty when this project started and is now thirty; she loves him more than she can say. He has grown into an honorable, kind, and generous man. And Kim thanks her sister, Carolee White, and her brothers, Rick and Brian Cook. Big brothers teach you how to be tough; big sisters teach you how to have fun: thanks!

Finally, Kim expresses how much she appreciates Saundra, Van, and Drew. There was no way to predict that during the course of this project the two would become best friends. Saundra has helped Kim to learn how fun clothes shopping, ice cream, chasing turtles and raising frogs, world travel, and playing board games can be as "down time." It is comforting to find a best friend whose brain is practically interchangeable with her own and whose heart and soul is a place of comfort and safety, always. Van and Drew also are delightful discoveries on this adventure. She looks forward to many more years of fun and family time with the Westervelts.

Saundra D. Westervelt
Kimberly J. Cook
September 2011

PART ONE

 Setting the Stage

WE BEGAN INTERVIEWS with death row exonerees across the country in August 2003. For the next four years, we traveled from eastern North Carolina west to California and from the panhandle of Florida north to Chicago. We interviewed exonerees who had been out of prison for a little over a year and those out for over twenty years. Several had spent one-third to one-half of their lives incarcerated for a crime they did not commit. All had been convicted of capital crimes and told they were no longer worthy of life. All struggled with the ongoing impacts of their wrongful convictions for themselves and their loved ones and to rebuild lives based on acceptance, connection, and innocence. While we asked about their wrongful convictions, we focused much more on their transitions when they left prison free and innocent people.

Part one sets the stage for the description and analysis of the obstacles they encounter in the challenge to rebuild their lives and strategies they use to cope along the way. Although the book is written to be as accessible as possible to lay audiences, we emphasize that it is a social scientific study of the postexoneration experiences of death row exonerees in the United States. It is not an anecdotal or journalistic account or an account based on practitioners' work with this population. Our analysis is grounded in sociological methods. We cannot claim that this is better, more accurate, or better informed than others that have addressed similar issues, only that we focus less on each individual's experience and more on illuminating patterns of struggle and coping that link together the experiences of our eighteen participants. Chapter 1 identifies the research questions that structure the study and situates the research in the broader wrongful conviction literature and other literatures on which we rely throughout the study. Chapter 2 explains the methodology used to access and interview our participants and to analyze the sixteen hundred pages of transcript that resulted. Chapter 3 introduces the eighteen death row exonerees who participated in the study. It begins with descriptive information about the participants and their cases and then provides a brief overview of each participant's case. These case reviews give context to the experiences discussed over the course of the book and introduce many of the people, places, and basic case facts mentioned. Part one lays the sociological foundation for the analysis to come.

CHAPTER 1

Living the Aftermath of a
Wrongful Conviction

THESE DATA OFTEN are used to characterize "the innocent" in the United States, people who have been wrongly convicted of crimes and released from prison because of ample evidence of their factual innocence (as of September 2011).

138—the number of people exonerated of capital crimes and released from death row since 1973; 9.8—the average number of years they spent in prison awaiting exoneration (www.deathpenaltyinfo.org)

273—the number of DNA-based exonerations; 13—the average number of years they spent in prison awaiting exoneration (www.innocenceproject.org)

340—the number of wrongful (mostly rape and murder) convictions uncovered between 1989 and 2003 (Gross et al. 2005)

27—the number of states that provide monetary compensation to the wrongly convicted; 10—the number of states that provide services such as help with housing, employment, and education; 0—the number of states that provide postrelease assistance to exonerees in accord with the model proposed by the Innocence Project (www.innocenceproject.org)

10—the number of nonprofit organizations that provide social services to exonerees

43—the number of states served by an innocence project; 11—the number of states with an Innocence or Criminal Justice Reform Commission (www.innocenceproject.org)

0.027 percent–5 percent—estimates of the percentages of cases (of various types) resulting in a wrongful conviction (0.027 percent in *Kansas v. Marsh* 2006; 0.5 percent in Huff et al. 1996 and Zalman et al. 2008; 1.4 percent in Poveda 2001; 2.3 percent in Gross and O'Brien 2008; 3.3 percent–5 percent in Risinger 2007).

These numbers represent substantial change in identifying and assisting those wrongly convicted of crimes in the United States in just ten years. Nevertheless, the numbers mask the flesh-and-blood reality for the wrongly convicted. While they outline the contours of "innocence" in the United States, they obscure nuances and human experiences. Capturing the human dimensions of "innocence" is the primary focus of this book. To do so requires getting behind and underneath the numbers to the people whose lives they represent, whose lives have been disrupted, uprooted, and turned upside down by their convictions and incarceration for crimes they did not commit. The numbers alone cannot convey the losses they have suffered, the opportunities they have lost, or the emotional turmoil they confront, all as a result of their wrongful convictions. The numbers obscure . . .

The overwhelming grief felt by Kirk Bloodsworth at the death of his mother, his staunchest supporter, just five months before his exoneration and release after almost ten years of wrongful incarceration;

The unspeakable pain confronted by Perry Cobb when he learned of the rape of his young daughter while he was wrongfully incarcerated and, thus, unavailable to protect her;

The disorienting trauma persistently endured by Gary Gauger over the discovery of his murdered parents and his subsequent interrogation and arrest for their brutal deaths;

The utter helplessness felt by Sabrina Butler on the day she thought she was to be taken to her execution for her wrongful conviction for killing her infant son;

The irreplaceable years of fatherhood snatched from Greg Wilhoit whose small children were raised in a foster home

while he wasted away on death row for killing their
mother, his wife;

The bitterness and anger experienced by Shabaka Brown over
the death of his brother when he was denied the right to
give him a life-saving kidney donation while on death row.

The numbers, while important, are merely placeholders for the
people whose voices vividly render what it means to be wrongly convicted and condemned.

Many have shared their stories of innocence through biographical
and autobiographical books or vignettes of their stories published by
others (see Leo 2005). But most of these focus on their lives leading up
to their arrests and the legal wrangles resulting in their wrongful convictions, usually including detailed accounts of the legal missteps that landed
them in prison for crimes they did not commit (Leo 2005). Thus, these
stories demonstrate how the wrongful conviction happened: eyewitness
misidentification, police and prosecutorial misconduct, rush to judgment, false confessions, jailhouse snitches, informant mishandling, tunnel
vision, and inadequate defense services, to name a few (Huff et al. 1996;
Leo 2005; Radelet et al. 1994; Scheck et al. 2000; Westervelt and
Humphrey 2001).

Yet these accounts paint an incomplete picture of what it means to
be wrongly convicted. The story of the innocent does not end the day
they are incarcerated for the crime or even the day their innocence is
revealed and they are released. The impact of their wrongful conviction
includes more than their struggle to survive prison while fighting for
their freedom. Their story, and their struggle, continues after they leave
prison. For their stories to be more completely told, they must include
what life is like the day *after* the day of their release, when their new life
begins, as they begin to confront and reconcile the impact of their
wrongful conviction. Until this part of the journey of the innocent is
examined and explained, the true meaning of what it is to be wrongly
convicted is incomplete.

Counting the number of wrongly convicted—the number of
"exonerees"—can easily mislead people into thinking that the day of
release or exoneration is the end game, the end of this long journey
to innocence reclaimed. And, of course, it is difficult to overstate the

significance of exoneration for someone who has been wrongly convicted of a heinous crime. But the day an innocent person gets counted as an exoneree is not the end of his or her journey at all. In a way, the day he or she becomes an exoneree is rather the beginning of another stage in his or her journey, another chapter in his or her story, a chapter that has yet to be fully written. What happens when the exoneree begins anew?

Beginning in 2003, we set out to explore this part of the story of the innocent. At that point, very little was known about life after exoneration. The voices of the innocent were usually heard from for a few days after release but not much thereafter. We knew little about what life was like when they returned to their communities, their families, and their homes. Were they welcomed home as triumphant heroes who finally bettered the system? Were they rejected as misfits who were probably guilty (if not of this then something else) no doubt damaged by their years of incarceration? Whatever their welcome, what problems did they confront as they tackled the business of life? How did they manage the problems they faced? What made adjusting easier? What made it harder? How often did they encounter people who still believed that they really did do it? Little was known about the answers to these questions; thus, we aimed to find out as best we could by asking these questions of eighteen individuals who had been wrongly convicted of crimes so heinous that they had been slated for execution. Here, we give them an opportunity to explain what life after death row is really like.

EXONEREES, PAROLEES, PRISONERS, AND TRAUMA SURVIVORS

A few stories of the lives exonerees confront after release have been told in the years since we began this work, but not that many. This is still not part of the story of the innocent that gets the most attention. But, no doubt, it gets more focus than it did when we first began in 2003. For example, more of the auto/biographies of the wrongly convicted include descriptions of life after release and clearly reveal how difficult the journey after exoneration often is (see, e.g., K. M. Cook 2008 and Grisham 2006). Lawyers, activists, and service providers have initiated discussions about the struggles their clients face after release based on their own firsthand accounts of watching them navigate life after exoneration. These include reports by both the Northwestern Center on Wrongful Convictions and the Innocence Project that highlight the barriers to reintegration faced by exonerees, relying heavily on the experiences of those with whom they work (Illinois Criminal Justice Information Authority 2002 and Innocence Project 2009, respectively). Service providers for the Life After Exoneration Program (LAEP), the first nonprofit organization established to assist exonerees with reintegration, also have published accounts that discuss, at least in part, the struggles their clients face after release (Vollen and Eggers 2005; Weigand 2009).[1] The media have picked up on this part of the story and provided some coverage of what happens to the innocent when they return home (see, e.g., Coen 2004; Cohen and Hastings 2002; K. Davis 2011; Locke 2011; Roberts and Stanton 2007; Slevin and Lydersen 2008).

Similarly, more academic analyses of life after exoneration have begun to appear. Much of this work (the majority, in fact) focuses on the issue of what exonerees should get after release rather than on what life is actually like, though obviously these two intertwine. Specifically, much of the academic attention has focused on the issue of compensation for the wrongly convicted or other services that could assist the transition back into society (Bernhard 2004, 2009; Kahn 2010; Lawrence 2009; Lonergan 2008; Norris 2011). Two analytical works that stand out as more focused examinations of what life is truly like for exonerees after release are Kathryn Campbell and Myriam Denov's (2004) examination of five Canadian exonerees and Adrian Grounds's (2004) evaluations of eighteen British exonerees. Both reveal many of the same struggles with reintegration and adjustment found in our own research, and we cite these similarities throughout. Our work builds on their findings but broadens the scope of their work to include the United States and individuals wrongly convicted of capital crimes and housed on death row.

A major contribution of our examination of life after exoneration is that it draws on these other works to provide a comprehensive and analytical examination of life after death row that relies most heavily on the actual voices of exonerees themselves. While much of the work on life after release has relied primarily on third-party descriptions of exonerees' struggles, our goal is to provide a framework through which exonerees explain these struggles themselves, in their own words.[2] Given the degree to which they previously have been robbed of opportunities to speak for themselves and be heard, we believe this to be an essential component of understanding what life after exoneration is truly like. Additional goals are to describe the difficulties commonly faced by exonerees and provide an analytical structure for illuminating how they manage those difficulties, the techniques they use to cope with the life they find waiting for them. By pursuing these goals, we expect to confirm what others have contributed but also extend what is known about life after exoneration in new directions and provide new tools for understanding that push the discussion forward.

Part of the challenge of providing this analytical framework has been weaving together the various literatures relevant to understanding the experiences of exonerees. In particular, we draw on literatures related to trauma recovery and management, the impact of long-term incarceration on prisoners, and parolee reentry. Each contributes something that helps us better understand and explain life after exoneration, and we borrow heavily from each of these literatures as appropriate throughout the research.

It is obvious after spending any amount of time with death row exonerees that their lives have been traumatized by the experience of their wrongful capital conviction and incarceration. This does not mean they live in a traumatized state indefinitely or that the trauma is paralyzing and debilitating. That is not the case. Some we met said they were doing quite well, in fact, while others revealed their persistent and severe struggles with depression, anger, and guilt. Still, even within this variation in their own ideas about how well they were doing, they all agree that they have struggled to build their lives after their exoneration and release. They manage and experience those struggles in different ways, but they all agree on the struggle itself. Therefore, we argue that exonerees are much like other types of trauma survivors and that the effects of their trauma and recovery processes are similar to those of trauma survivors in kind and scope.

We are not alone in recognizing this similarity between exonerees and survivors of other forms of life-threatening trauma, such as natural disasters, severe abuse or torture, and terminal illness. Adrian Grounds (2004, 175) came to a similar conclusion after his psychiatric assessment of eighteen wrongly convicted individuals, noting "the clinical syndromes and adjustment problems I observed in the wrongfully convicted men . . . are described in the psychiatric literature on trauma, particularly the literature on war veterans." Heather Weigand (2009, 430) agrees based on her work with exonerees through LAEP: "Many suffer from mental health symptoms that resemble those suffered by veterans of war and torture survivors. . . . I will not argue that the exonerated are torture victims, but their symptoms upon reentry are those of torture survivors." Our own decision, however, to rely on the trauma literature to better understand life after exoneration actually came from neither of these sources but instead from the suggestion of a colleague whose specialty is disaster research. After reading a draft of an earlier paper of ours, he noted commonalities between our participants and the victims of Hurricane Katrina with whom he had been working. It was his recognition of similarities between our participants and his own that initially prompted us to examine this literature more deeply. In doing so, we found that the aftereffects of trauma described by survivors closely parallel experiences described by exonerees: feelings of dislocation and disconnection, grief over losses, damage to relationships, and bouts with anger, guilt, and distrust. Interestingly, many researchers from different traditions have come to the same conclusion—trauma is at the core of the experience of a wrongful conviction.

So we adopted this as a primary explanatory framework for better understanding life after exoneration and use it to examine the traumatic effects of a wrongful conviction and incarceration as well as the coping strategies exonerees use to manage their trauma. Key components of the trauma management literature include how survivors deal with the stigmatization and other assaults on their identity associated with being a trauma survivor. Thus, we also examine the impact of stigma on exonerees and the difficulty they face in rebuilding identity after release. The trauma management literature is central to our analysis of the difficulties exonerees confront and more particularly how they reconcile their new lives and new beliefs about themselves and those around them.

Exonerees also share similarities with prisoners and parolees. However, this should not be surprising as prisoners and parolees are certainly impacted by their experiences with incarceration, life disruption, and difficult reentry. Exonerees share the experience of incarceration with the rightly convicted and thus experience many of the same effects of incarceration. The fact that their incarceration is undeserved and wrongful does not insulate them from the negative impact of the prison environment. We can only speculate, short of additional research, that the "wrongfulness" of their incarceration exacerbates rather than attenuates the effects of living in prison. Whether this is true or not, exonerees need to manage life in prison, including life on death row, and experience many of the aftereffects commonly attributed to long-term incarceration. We use this literature repeatedly to give insight into their coping while incarcerated and their struggles after release.

The problems exonerees have with reentry discussed throughout these pages are in many ways shared by parolees after release, and we draw attention to those similarities when relevant. Housing, employment, health care, family disruption—these are common barriers to reintegration faced by parolees and exonerees alike. In fact, the situation for exonerees often is made worse because they are ineligible for the limited reentry services often provided to parolees. And, like parolees, some face a community hostile to them and unwilling to accept or assist them as they rebuild. Still, without additional research, we can only speculate about similarities and differences, though we draw from the literature on parolee experiences to understand the obstacles faced by exonerees after release.

These literatures provide important analytical tools to examine fully the experience of life after death row. Together, they create a framework for understanding what exonerees have to say about life after exoneration. Our hope is that this framework is the structure, the canvas, on which exonerees' words paint a multihued picture of life after release. We find that the picture is unsettling and even disappointing, that in the aftermath of the grave injustice done to them by the state, they are abandoned to face the challenges of rebuilding a life alone. They reveal that the experience of a wrongful capital conviction and incarceration is deeply disorienting. It displaces the innocent from their families and communities and even from their beliefs about who they are and their place in the world. It uproots them from their moorings; it disconnects them from their own emotional selves and from the relationships on which their lives are centered. It disrupts their plans and goals for the future. It expels them from humanity to a place where they face extermination. It does all of this, and then at the moment of release they are forced to confront repairing, reconnecting, reestablishing themselves in their own lives and in the lives of those to whom they return. Typically without acknowledgment of the wrong done to them nor the resources to understand how it has transformed them, they are simply let go with no assistance or direction to find out where they fit in the world they enter, a world also transformed from the one they left. They struggle to find a place in the midst of this torrent of change and their own invisibility.

The Story of Life after Death Row

We begin the story of life after death row in the chapters in part 1 that explain the research process and introduce the research participants. Chapter 2 of part 1 explains the guiding principles of feminist methodology that inform our choices of research methods and describes the methods we used to locate and interview eighteen death row exonerees and analyze their interviews. In chapter 3, we introduce the participants in our research, beginning with basic analyses of the social and legal characteristics of their cases. The bulk of the chapter includes short case summaries of each participant's wrongful conviction to provide basic events, people, and places to which we and they refer throughout the rest of the book. These case summaries might best be used as references for readers as they encounter the voices of our participants in the pages that follow.

The chapters in part 2 focus on the multidimensional array of problems confronting exonerees in the months and years after their exoneration and release. Chapter 4 tackles the more practical matters of finding housing, employment, and health care and their struggles to relearn how to live freely in a world very different from the one they left. Chapter 5 examines their overwhelming grief and loss, losses of loved ones and time, relationships, and feelings of security. These are losses they could not mourn while incarcerated and must find a way to manage in order to move forward in their new lives. Chapter 6 explains the broader web of impact of their wrongful conviction and the damage inflicted on their relationships with family and friends. Chapter 7 reveals the deep emotional wounds left open after release and the rocky emotional terrain they face in their daily lives. Together, the chapters in part 2 make clear the problem of fit faced by exonerees—where do they fit? Where do they fit in their families, in their relationships, in their communities, and even within their own skin? Having been uprooted and dislodged from their lives, where now do they go to find rootedness and connection?

Part 3 examines the various pathways they take to managing the struggles explored in part 2. Given the obstacles they face, how do they choose to cope? This coping actually begins before they even step out of prison as they must find ways to survive and negotiate life in prison and on death row, all while continuing the battle for their exoneration. This is the focus of chapter 8. In chapter 9, we address the issue of coping after they leave death row and examine two primary approaches exonerees use to manage the struggles they confront. For some, coping means embracing their wrongful conviction and incorporating it into their ways of making meaning about their new place in the world. For others, coping means leaving the experience of their wrongful conviction out of the new lives they hope to build. This discussion of coping is continued in chapter 10 as we examine how they rebuild their own sense of self while at the same time managing the false stigma with which they often are burdened. The chapters in part 3 reveal the ways exonerees attempt to make meaning of their wrongful conviction for themselves and their communities and reestablish connections to those around them.

The chapters in part 4 discuss the invisibility and lack of acknowledgment that so often characterize their lives after release. Chapter 11 discusses what exonerees believe they need after release to assist in reintegrating with family and community but also which forms of assistance they actually got, or more accurately did not get. Exonerees reveal deep hostilities over the lack of acceptance and acknowledgment they received by state officials and, often, their communities, more so than the lack of services provided to them after release. They make clear that doing justice for the wrongly convicted means helping them rebuild their lives as well as creating opportunities for restoration and reintegration. Finally, chapter 12 examines reform initiatives, proposed by others and ourselves, that would provide the practical assistance exonerees so often need after release while recognizing the injustice done to them and our collective responsibility to help them rebuild, reconnect, and find a new place in this world.

IT IS PROBABLY not possible to ever paint the complete picture of the experience of "the innocent" or what it is like to be wrongly convicted of a crime, more so a capital crime, and incarcerated for years. The stories of the wrongly convicted continue to unfold years, even decades, after their exoneration and release from prison. But any story of the innocent must include at least some understanding that the wrongful conviction experience does not end the day of exoneration and release. That day is only the beginning of a new chapter of their journey, a journey not yet widely acknowledged and rife with challenges. In the pages that follow, eighteen survivors of wrongful capital convictions provide a glimpse into their journey.

Chapter 2

Researching the Innocent

Historically, feminist methodology has emerged within a context of women scholars studying women subjects. Our project expands qualitative feminist methods to women scholars studying (predominantly) men subjects, in this case death row exonerees, by utilizing a life history technique (Atkinson 1998; Lewis 2008; Patton 2002; Tierney 1998). Life history methods, guided by feminist principles, allow the researcher and participants to dialogue as whole persons, to form meaningful and holistic relationships, while mutually aiming to tell participants' stories with integrity. David Lewis (2008, 560) suggests that using life history techniques reveals "hidden narratives" where researchers can empower participants to tell their stories. Furthermore, "life history methods and feminist narrative analysis techniques can be used to reach beyond pathologized conceptions of identity and adjustment" among marginalized people (Sosulski et al. 2010, 30). We have been explicit in our attempts to maintain our feminist integrity in the research process while studying a group of people whose lived experiences have not been central to most feminists' concerns. Thus, we ask, how do we accomplish feminist methodology in the process of interviewing mostly male innocent individuals who have been exonerated of capital crimes?

Feminist Methods in Theory and Practice

Since classics by Shulamit Reinharz (1979) and Sandra Harding (1986) revolutionized how social science can and must incorporate gender considerations into theory, analysis, and methodological development, feminist scholars have expanded sociology from a "value-free" social science into a socially relevant, activist-oriented, and grounded theoretical approach. According to Reinharz (1992, 6), feminist methods are "used . . . by people who identify themselves as feminist or as part of the women's movement." We identify ourselves as feminist and are concerned that our approach to research maintains certain principles emerging from feminist theory, methodology, and ethics. We discuss four central principles of feminist method and how we engage these in our study of death row exonerees: the belief that research is a collaborative process, the centrality of trust and openness in this collaborative process, the role of the "ethic of care" in research, and the necessity of bringing issues of gender, race, and class to the forefront of research.

Each research project requires idiosyncratic adaptations of method, especially qualitative projects, in order to learn about and analyze the described phenomenon. Our project is no exception. We have chosen to examine unusual and traumatic events and to combine our established expertise in wrongful convictions (Westervelt) and the death penalty (Cook) with our convictions as feminists committed to ethical research that illuminates and enhances people's lived realities, while avoiding exploitation (Pittaway et al. 2010). Thus, we "mix and match" from the best practices and principles of qualitative research methods to meet the goals of our project—to record, analyze, and learn about the aftermath of a wrongful capital conviction directly from exonerated death row survivors.

Fundamentally, social research is best conducted within a collaborative setting between the scholars and participants in the research (Ely 1991). Feminist research can create "a sense of connectedness and equality between researcher and researched" (Patton 2002, 129). Our role in the collaborative process is to facilitate participants, in this case exonerees, telling their own stories that have consequences for modern society and criminological and sociological theory (Patton 2002). As facilitators, we are guided by the principle that we neither criticize nor categorize the participants or their experiences. Bringing their voices to the public issues of capital punishment and wrongful convictions requires their voices to be heard as authentically as possible, in their own words (K. J. Cook 1998) without "filtering" by our own interpretations or categorizations into psychological "disorders" or social (mal)adaptations. Because we hope to explore and understand the flesh-and-blood realism of their experiences, we cannot reduce their stories to only statistical patterns or disengaged numerical measures of various aspects of their stories. Thus, our feminist methods are inductive rather than reductive.

Furthermore, as individuals who have been talked about, classified, categorized, and legally processed as if they were murderers, these participants have rarely been granted an opportunity to speak for themselves. Their lawyers talked for them (with varying degrees of effectiveness); prosecutors spoke against them with lethal intent; witnesses spoke against them; journalists spoke with authority about their cases; jurors and judges convicted and condemned them. All the while, the participants in this study felt powerless to respond effectively in their own words and rarely believed they were truly heard. Our project provides an opportunity for exonerees' authentic voices to be heard, thus affirming the value and meaning of their lived experiences.

We made a number of choices in our research process to increase the level of collaboration between us and our participants. They chose the location of the interview to ensure their comfort. We asked only that the interviews be in quiet places with no phones and/or children, to protect the quality of audio recording for transcription purposes. We provided all participants with a copy of the final transcript and invited them to make corrections to ensure as much input into the final "product" as possible. We did not subject participants to psychological evaluation and/or survey before the interview, though some scholars might have preferred we do that. Exonerees view their reintegration and coping as a process, and they frequently compare their current states of mind with their memories of times past. So while they may "objectively" suffer from depression or posttraumatic stress disorder if tested, they see themselves as more psychologically, socially, and emotionally sound (or damaged) at the time we met them than they were several months or years previously. Thus, it was essential to allow them the opportunity to speak for themselves and claim their own stories, free from the labels or prefabricated categories placed on them by others (Goldman and Whalen 1990; Goodley 1996; Hones 1998).

Unfortunately, the power of labeling can never fully be escaped, and their stories are powerful testimonies to the enduring consequences of stigma, sociolegal classifications that render a human being "worthy" of capital punishment, as well as the capacity of hope, faith, and fortitude.

Part of our feminist epistemological framework draws from Patricia Hill Collins (1991), who teaches that dualistic approaches employing mutually exclusive categories are less helpful than "both/and" frameworks that recognize complexities of identity and ownership of authentic selves. So while on the one hand our participants have been frightfully traumatized, stigmatized, and bereaved, at the same time they have survived on hope, dreams, and desires for vindication.

We chose a life history technique because it sees an interview as a collaborative event (Atkinson 1998; Goodley 1996; Hones 1998). Interviewing participants has an important legacy in feminist methodology. Hilary Graham (cited in Reinharz 1992, 18) refers to interviewing as "the principle means by which feminists have sought to achieve the active involvement of their respondents in the construction of data about their lives." The life history technique emphasizes this "active involvement" of all research participants (scholar and subject) and allows participants to dictate the direction of interviews as much as the researchers. For example, we found that more than one participant created opportunities to discuss at length the adequacy (or inadequacy) of the Bush administration's handling of current events, including those not directly related to criminal justice or death penalty issues. No matter which direction we took with the interview, several exonerees returned to politics. Ray Krone spent quite a bit of time discussing how he adapted to prison life itself, and life on death row in particular, even though our primary focus was on his life once he was released from prison. When participants took these directions in our discussion, we followed their lead, believing that we can learn as much by discussing what they deem important as we can from following our own interview schedule. This interview process allows for unexpected tangents to emerge into full-blown themes that might be unanticipated by the researcher, as is typical when using this type of grounded theory approach (Charmaz 2005; Glaser and Strauss 1967).

As William Tierney (1998) notes, a collaborative interview process is particularly important for marginalized peoples and those who have experienced powerlessness and exploitation because it increases the level of trust between researchers and participants and reduces the possibility that the interview itself will become another form of exploitation as viewed by the participants. More than one exoneree has told us that researchers came to interview them and were never heard from again, leaving the exonerees feeling used and exploited. This brings us to the second principle of feminist methodology essential to our research—the establishment of trust.

The process of conducting interviews with death row exonerees has been an exercise in trust, respect, and relationship building. These are guiding principles of qualitative and feminist methods (Patton 2002). Because the people we interviewed have been so terribly treated (wrongly accused, convicted, and sentenced to death), the degree to which they are able to trust us, or anyone, varies. We did not assume that they should or would want to talk to us. We began the process of building trust with decisions about how first to contact them. Our access to exonerees came through networks of scholars, attorneys, and activists who work with and are trusted by them. Some of these individuals we knew and some we did not. For those we did not know, we provided references to allow them to check our credibility as researchers before they put us into contact with exonerees with whom they work. We avoided cold calling exonerees as much as possible, preferring instead to have these other trusted individuals contact them on our behalf. At the very least, we initiated contact through an introductory letter. This approach worked well for us, such as when we contacted Shabaka Brown: "To be honest with you, the only reason I'm sittin' at this table is because of Mike Radelet [a close friend of Brown's and colleague of ours]. I mean, that's the truth. . . . I trust [his] judgment. We talk a lot. We talk when I'm at work or at home. We email each other. I trust his judgment. He said y'all was cool people." We hoped to relay to exonerees that we were interested in hearing about their experiences but that any contact with us was up to them; they have control over their own stories.

We also attempted to build trust by following up with exonerees on any requests made of us. Two specific examples come to mind. First, while traveling in North Carolina, the son of one of our participants needed some immediate help in an emergency situation. The participant called one of us to ask for advice about how best to negotiate the situation for his son. We made some inquiries of colleagues and provided as much information as possible to help them better address their problem. Sabrina Butler also made a request of us to help her get a copy of the transcript of her second trial at which she had been acquitted. According to Butler, during this retrial, her former husband testified that he had been the last person to see her baby alive. This testimony had stunned her because, though she knew that she did not kill her child, she did not, to that point, know what had happened to her son. She wanted the transcript in order to reread that portion of his testimony. However, because she was acquitted at this trial and thus the transcript was not needed for a possible appeal, the court did not automatically produce it. She asked us to help her get a copy. We pursued every angle possible to locate the transcript, including finding the name of the court stenographer on duty during her trial (over ten years earlier) and attempting to make contact with this person. Although we were unable to produce the trial transcript, we did provide Butler with copies of all legal documents we had in our files, and she seemed to appreciate our extended efforts on her behalf.

Trust also is enhanced, we believe, by an up-front acknowledgment and exploration of the identity of all participants; therefore, if anyone was interested in our lives or asked personal questions, we replied as fully as possible. We could not hope to gain openness and honesty from people if we were closed and guarded about ourselves. In principle, this is considered by some to be sound feminist practice (Oakley 1981). For us, it is essential in helping bridge the gap between our experience and theirs. This is even more so the case given that we are two middle-class white women interviewing working-class and poor men (mostly), many of whom are African American or Hispanic. Thus, we engaged in self-disclosure when asked or appropriate as long as it did not silence or infringe upon the participants telling their own stories.

Another element of the establishment of trust is that the listener believes the speaker. Crowden (cited in Reinharz 1992, 3) suggests that understanding someone comes from "seeing with a loving eye" and, we would add, hearing with compassion (Presser 2005; Scully 1988). We do not argue that "believing the speaker" means relying on the speaker as the sole source of information. We collected extensive documentation on each exoneree before our interviews, including all publicly available legal documents, newspaper articles, scholarly books or articles, and even film clips. We used these materials to become intimately familiar with the details of each case and as a reference to check exonerees' own memories of such details. For us, "believing the speaker" means giving credence to the story being told by the participant, giving it weight and accepting his or her experiences, feelings, beliefs, and claims.

In this project, the participants had fruitlessly proclaimed their innocence for decades, having not been heard or believed by powerful entities (prosecutors, judges, juries) and the public, a deafness to their voices that nearly resulted in their deaths. Thus, to believe the participants in this research is essential for their truths to be illuminated, understood, and perhaps compensated and affirmed. We are not "studying" them so much as we are learning from them about the nature of personal fortitude, faith, forgiveness, anger, obstacles, frustrations, racism, sexism, dislocation, debilitation, hope, and despair. Doing so is an essential foundation of trust.

A third guiding principle of our methodology, borrowed and adapted from Carol Gilligan (1982), is an "ethic of care" for ourselves and participants, recognizing and honoring the relational dynamics involved in research collaboration. We apply this to our care for each other and our families, and it begins with our mutual trust. We have full lives; we are both busy women with families, careers, and a multitude of responsibilities. This research was time-consuming and required extensive travel, taking us away from responsibilities at home and work. We have both been overwhelmed with various aspects of our lives such that our capacity to focus on research has vacillated. Fortunately, when one of us is stressed out, the other pulls more of the load. We care for and about each other and our quality of life.

Our ethic of care also applies to the participants in the project. Since we typically interview them once, and live long distances away from them, we maintain contact in a variety of ways. We send holiday gifts to each person, we call and write to them regularly to inquire as to their general well-being, we share their joys and provide advice/support when asked. We try to keep them in contact with each other by filling them in on each other's lives whenever they ask about someone. Once during an interview trip to Chicago, we took one exoneree, Delbert Tibbs, on a day trip to visit another exoneree and close friend, Gary Gauger. We realize, also, that what we can provide is limited; we are not lawyers, and our resources are finite. But our concern for each is real. This guiding principle helps us to remember that these collaborations are ongoing relationships that enhance our lives and our understandings of broader social justice issues.

The final guiding principle of our research drawn from feminist concern is the necessity of bringing issues of gender, race, and class to the forefront of the interview process (Collins 1991; Donnelly et al. 2005). As noted earlier, we are two white, middle-class, well-educated women interviewing mostly males who are predominantly working or lower class and who have varying levels of education. Over half of our participants are African American or Hispanic. Rather than approach our participants with a "color-blind" demeanor (Donnelly et al. 2005), we openly problematize the complexities of class and racial/ethnic structures in our interviews. For many of the participants, negative racial stereotypes significantly impacted the circumstances leading up to their wrongful convictions. Delbert Tibbs, for example, was convicted on the basis of false cross-racial eyewitness identification. Walter McMillian, a black man, was convicted of killing a white woman in Alabama in a trial where the (white) judge was named for Confederate general Robert E. Lee. Sabrina Butler was a young mother of two small children, black, poor, and on welfare in Mississippi, and was portrayed in the media as an unfit mother and "welfare queen" in the early 1990s. We cannot be blind to these gendered, racialized, and class-based patterns of structural oppression if we are serious in our efforts to understand and fully analyze exonerees' experiences. Rather, we concur that these can be "tools for understanding rather than factors that get in the way of understanding" (Reinharz 2011, 8).

IMPLICATIONS FOR FEMINIST THEORY AND METHODS

Our experience in learning from death row exonerees over the past several years teaches us that the gender of research "subjects" should not determine whether feminist methods should be used in a research project. The guiding principles emerging from feminist methodology can apply equally well to an examination of the lives of men as women (Messerschmidt 2000, 2004). The use of feminist methods should be determined by the nature of the project, the convictions of the scholars, and not merely the gender of the participants. Feminist methods are particularly well suited if the researcher seeks an understanding of participants as whole people with often conflicting beliefs and feelings who exist within a larger web of obligations, relationships, and structures of power.

This is especially true if one seeks to understand participants who have been marginalized, disenfranchised, or exploited. By defining research as collaborative and "subjects" as active participants, feminist methods allow participants agency and an opportunity to own their stories and be heard and accepted in a way denied to them in other settings. By recognizing from the outset the class, racial, and gendered structures of oppression that may be at work in their lives, this method gives voice to the larger structural processes that shape their experiences and that often go unseen and unheard by others. Thus, this method provides a framework for building trust with participants who may be unsure about the research process and creates opportunities for understanding individuals and groups who may very well be inaccessible when approached in other ways.

Finally, we add that a feminist approach is unique in that it treats both participants and researchers as whole persons. We refer to the people in our research as "participants" rather than as "subjects" in order to convey their collaborative input into this process. Our participants are more than "just" death row exonerees. They are fathers, mothers, sons, daughters. They have jobs and dreams for the future that often do not revolve around their status as "exoneree." We try to interact with the whole person as much as possible, even though our contact was initiated because of their "exoneree" status. When we write or talk on the phone, we as often ask about their children as we do about the most recent activities related to their cases. Greg Wilhoit called us when he became a grandfather for the first time. We sent Sabrina Butler information about an eye disease when she told us of some ongoing headaches she was experiencing. We listen to a CD that Perry Cobb gave us of him singing, his occupation before his wrongful conviction.

This same principle applies to us as researchers as well. As researchers, we go into the field with what Shulamit Reinharz (2011, 5) calls a "tripartite division among selves": the "research selves, personal selves, and situational selves." We live within larger webs of obligations, relationships, and structures of power that impact on how we approach research, how we approach a research participant or even a particular interview. Detachment from one's topic or research participant may sound effective in theory and may be appropriate in other research projects but often prevents connection and deeper understanding in practice. As researchers, we bring experiences and authentic emotions to the table. To the extent that sharing those pieces of one's self with the participant can aid in achieving a better understanding of the participant's own story, feminist principles recognize its value. Therefore, we find that feminist methods are adaptable, are flexible, and promote unifying themes of analytical and ethical importance allowing equitable exchanges among research participants and a more complete picture of the lived experiences, in this case, of death row exonerees.

INTERVIEWS WITH DEATH ROW EXONEREES

Since 1973, 137 men and 1 woman have been released from prison after having been exonerated of capital crimes. These individuals had been wrongfully convicted of crimes they did not commit, sentenced to death, and eventually exonerated based on substantial evidence of their actual innocence. From August 2003 to September 2006, we interviewed 18 of these 138 death row exonerees. Our study does not include individuals who were erroneously convicted of noncapital crimes or those who eventually were released due to legal error, though evidence of their guilt may be substantial. We focus solely on individuals sentenced to death who have been exonerated based on evidence of actual innocence.

At the time we began our research, only two lists of exonerees existed—the list of death row exonerees maintained by the Death Penalty Information Center (DPIC) and the growing list of DNA exonerees produced by the Innocence Project at the Cardozo School of Law in New York City.[1] We chose to focus on the death row exonerees identified by the DPIC for two reasons. First, this was an inclusive list of exonerees extending back to 1973, before the advent of DNA technology, and it thus included both DNA and non–DNA exonerees. Second, because of the common feature of their wrongful death sentence, all exonerees on this list had the shared experiences of being wrongly convicted for crimes they did not commit and devalued to the extent of being condemned to death. Thus, our eighteen participants were chosen from the list of death row exonerees maintained by the DPIC, which includes all individuals exonerated of capital crimes since 1973 based on one of the following criteria: (1) the original conviction was overturned on appeal with acquittal at retrial, (2) the original conviction was overturned on appeal and charges were dropped by the prosecutor or dismissed by a judge, and/or (3) an absolute pardon was granted by a governor based on new evidence of innocence.[2]

We chose individuals who varied by race, state in which convicted, length of time in prison, length of time on death row, length of time since exoneration, and reason for exoneration. Among the 138 exonerees listed on the DPIC list, only 1 is a woman, and we have interviewed her; thus, variability with respect to gender is limited to her one case. All of our participants had been exonerated for at least a year, giving them time to experience life after release. We employed a four-pronged approach to studying their experiences. First, we collected as many relevant legal documents as we could about their cases: appellate reviews in state and federal courts, motions or briefs available in the public domain, and documents provided by our participants and/or their attorneys. Second, we searched local, state, and national news outlets to read as much press coverage as possible about each of their cases, including the original trial, the years of appellate review, and ultimately the exoneration and release. The amount of news coverage varied widely by case. Furthermore, we searched for academic books and popular press books where their cases might have been discussed. Third, we conducted in-depth life history interviews with them. And fourth, we recorded field notes about our visit with each participant and, in some cases, with their family members or friends with whom we also spent time.

We traveled to all participants and interviewed them in their home or somewhere nearby of their choosing. With Alfred Rivera, we were denied access to him in federal prison and thus completed our interview through written correspondence. The interviews lasted from two hours to two days. Each interview was audiotaped and transcribed, producing transcripts ranging from 55 to 180 single-spaced pages and resulting in over 1,600 pages of transcript in total. All but one exoneree gave us permission to use his or her real name in the research. Each person received compensation of $125 as well as a small and appropriate thank-you gift. In most interviews, we shared meals together and chatted informally. Since these initial meetings, we have maintained periodic contact with all participants to see how they are doing, although the amount of contact with each has varied. We have remained closer to some than others, as some have chosen over the years to remain more distant. Chapter 3 describes in more detail the participants in our research and the details of their cases.

CODING AND ANALYSIS

Once the data were transcribed, we coded them for emerging themes and compared experiences across cases. We employed open coding to identify the broadest themes expressed by our participants and axial coding to identify the similarities and differences within those open coding themes (Charmaz 2005; Patton 2002). One such theme discussed by all of our participants was the practical problems they faced during the immediate postrelease period. They also described in great detail the challenges of confronting the many losses endured while also grappling with the grief of those losses. They shared the difficulties of rebuilding relationships that had been profoundly altered by their imprisonment and the comforts of having significant relationships in their lives when they were released from prison. They talked about how they managed to negotiate difficult emotional terrain in the aftermath of their release. Many described in harrowing detail their experiences in prison and on death row—their own execution dates (real and perceived), the executions of other inmates, and the impacts of all of it on their families. They shared how the trauma of their wrongful convictions and death sentences continues to haunt them in everyday life. They often expressed their frustrations with and commitments to being heard and turning their experiences into impetus for social policy reform. These are the "open coding" themes that frame the chapters presented in our book.

During the coding process, we divided transcripts between us, and each took the lead coding a set. We then shared these initial coding passes with the other, who rechecked them by the transcripts to ensure consistency and completeness. We identify a "theme" as any category about which four or more of our participants described similar experiences or shared similar views (accounting for approximately 20 percent of our total sample). If an idea or experience was mentioned by fewer than four of our participants, we considered it an idiosyncratic experience that, while interesting to the unique experiences of the individuals who mentioned it, did not rise to the classification of a "theme." Within those open coding thematic categories, we captured many axial coding similarities and differences. These axial coding categories frame the details offered in each of the chapters. This resulted in 436 single-spaced pages of coded data into open and axial coded themes.

Our approach is to identify and describe the themes and categories that lie at the heart of exonerees' concerns and allow their words to convey the true essence of their thoughts and beliefs. In using quotations directly from interviews, we have edited for the sole purpose of ensuring readability. We have taken out "ums" and "uhs" and the repetitive use of phrases such as "you know" but have retained colloquial idiosyncrasies and most dialect to maintain authenticity of voice. While some filtering is inevitable in the process of presenting these data, our aim remains intact: to present exonerees' experiences in their own words, to offer rich detail of their experiences of wrongful capital convictions, and to reveal how they make meaning of their experiences as people whose stories matter to the broader public debates about crime, justice, injustice, imprisonment, and the death penalty.

Similar to all qualitative in-depth studies in sociology, this study is limited in its generalizability. Our findings and analysis are not meant to be applicable to other groups of exonerees. We do find commonalities between the experiences of our participants and those of other death row exonerees, and exonerees more generally, based on comparisons of our findings to the limited literature available on the exoneree experience (see Campbell and Denov 2004; Grounds 2004; Illinois Criminal Justice Information Authority 2002; Weigand 2009). However, we cannot be scientifically sure of generalizability.

Furthermore, we cannot definitively assert that in contrast to parolees, death row exonerees are any worse or better off, as we do not have a comparison group of parolees from which to draw such conclusions. Based on the literature on prisoner reentry, we recognize that many of the struggles with reintegration noted by our participants are shared by the rightly convicted after their release from prison.[3] For example, prisoner reentry and reintegration is characterized by protracted problems finding housing and meaningful employment (Apel and Sweeten 2010; Bahr et al. 2010; Gaes and Kendig 2003;

Grounds and Jamieson 2003; Metraux and Culhane 2004; Petersilia 2003; Shivy et al. 2007; Stoll and Bushway 2008; Travis and Waul 2003; Uggen et al. 2006). Ex-prisoners suffer long-term health problems associated with their incarceration at the same time that they lack access to health insurance and substantive care (Appleton 2010; Gaes and Kendig 2003; Petersilia 2003; Schnittker and John 2007). They recount sadness over losses of time, relationships, and people close to them (either through death or ruptured relationships) as well as problems developing and maintaining relationships (Grounds and Jamieson 2003; Jamieson and Grounds 2005; Travis and Waul 2003). Their imprisonment exacts a severe emotional toll on them as they report struggling with distrust, depression, withdrawal, and survivor guilt (Grounds and Jamieson 2003; Irwin and Owen 2005).

We also cannot be sure whether the experiences exonerees describe result from their *wrongful* conviction and incarceration or the incarceration experience alone. As Adrian Grounds (2004, 178) explains, "[I]t appears that the miscarriage of justice itself probably cannot account for the full range of outcomes (for the wrongly convicted). Some of the effects are a product of long-term imprisonment per se." However, without a comparison group of parolees, it is not possible to tease out the effects of the wrongful conviction from that of their incarceration. We note similarities between the experiences of exonerees and parolees throughout whenever they apply.

HARROWING EXPERIENCES ripple through the pages of the transcripts from our interviews. Our participants relate that their losses are profound and multiple, their recovery hampered by social and economic obstacles, their feelings of injustice inflamed, their dislocation and displacement continuing for years, and their stigma at times overbearing. Our challenge has been to gain access to our participants and their stories and experiences—their feelings of loss and injustice, their experiences in prison and surviving the death sentence, their fears about and hopes for the future. These individuals have had their words twisted and used against them; they have been manipulated and misrepresented; they have been used and forgotten by politicians, criminal justice officials, and even other researchers. They do not trust with ease, and this was a reality we had to acknowledge to conduct this research.

We tried to establish ourselves as worthy of listening to their stories, as worthy of their trust. We employed a feminist methodological approach because its legacy of integrity and collaboration with research participants provided authentic mechanisms to meet the challenges posed by this research process (Sosulski et al. 2010). We offer a detailed account and analysis of the experiences of the participants in this project and, on the basis of these findings, make recommendations toward social and legal reform for exonerees yet to be released, for surely there will be more.

CHAPTER 3

Introducing the Exonerees

To give context to our analyses, it is important first to introduce the lives and wrongful convictions of our participants. Because the true population of wrongful conviction cases is not known, we cannot generalize the characteristics of these cases to the characteristics of wrongful conviction cases overall. The cases in our study are distinctive in two main respects. First, our eighteen participants have all been convicted of capital crimes and sentenced to death. While to date the Death Penalty Information Center (DPIC) identifies 138 such cases, the majority of known wrongful conviction cases do not involve capital crimes. For example, of the 273 known DNA exonerations, only 17 were for capital offenses (www.innocenceproject.org). Of the 340 mostly rape and murder wrongful convictions identified by Samuel Gross et al. (2005) between 1989 and 2003, about one-quarter involved death sentences. Thus, the participants in our study represent a smaller subset of wrongful conviction cases. Second, a minority (17 percent) of our participants were exonerated using DNA evidence. Of the 340 exonerations noted by Gross et al. (2005), 42 percent resulted from the use of DNA, and no doubt an even larger percentage might account for exonerations today given the continued work of the Innocence Project and wider acceptance of this technology by police, prosecutors, and courts. Our participants, instead, often benefited from the discovery of new evidence, the recantation of witnesses who had perjured themselves at trial, and the revelation of police and/or prosecutorial misconduct that tainted their original convictions. Although these issues also are prevalent in DNA cases, the use of DNA often provides a degree of certainty that courts (and the public) seek for claims of innocence (Leo 2005). Aside from these two primary differences, the case characteristics of our participants are similar to those of other known exonerees.

CASE CHARACTERISTICS

Table 3.1 displays a summary of biographical and case-related details of the participants in our study. Seventeen participants are men; one—Sabrina Butler—is a woman. Of the 138 death row exonerees identified by the DPIC, Butler is the only woman. We thought it essential, therefore, to include her in the research. Female exonerees are few and far between, even within the other two primary groups of known wrongful convictions: the Innocence Project includes only 3 women among their 273 DNA exonerees, and Gross et al. (2005) include only 13 women among their 340 exonerees. Nine (50 percent) of our participants are black, seven (39 percent) are white, and two (11 percent) are Latino. This racial breakdown is close to the racial composition of all death row exonerees. According to the DPIC, 51 percent of the 138 death row exonerees are black, 38 percent are white, and 9 percent are Latino. The racial configuration of our participants also is in line with other known groups of exonerees. Of the Innocence Project's exonerees, 61 percent are black, 30 percent white, and 7 percent Latino (2 percent are of another ethnicity or their race/ethnicity is unknown). Gross et al. (2005) reveal a similar composition of 55 percent black, 32 percent white, and 13 percent Latino.

The average length of time our participants were incarcerated was 9.5 years, though this masks variation in time served by exonerees, ranging from 2 to 26 years. The DPIC indicates that the average length of time between death sentence and exoneration for all death row exonerees is 9.8 years, and the Innocence Project notes a 13-year average length of time served for DNA exonerees. Though all of our participants were originally convicted of capital crimes and sentenced to death, some received retrials at which they were reconvicted but sentenced to life in prison and, as a result, moved from death row into the general population of prison. In these cases, the average length of time served in prison is not equivalent to the average time spent on death row, which is a lesser period of 5 years with a range of no time on death row to 17.5 years. At the time of our interview, the amount of time that had passed since participants' exonerations ranged from 1.5 to 32 years. Their average age at the time of their original conviction was twenty-nine. The eighteen participants represented ten different states in which their wrongful convictions and exonerations occurred.

TABLE 3.1
Biographical Details of Participants

Name	Sex	Race	Age at conviction	State where tried	Years in prison[a]	Years on death row[b]	Year of exoneration	DNA?	Actual offender(s) identified?[c]	Compensation received?[d]
Beeman	M	W	23	OH	3	2.5	1979	No	Yes	No
Bloodsworth	M	W	24	MD	8	1.5	1993	Yes	Yes	Yes
Brown	M	B	24	FL	13	13	1987	No	No	No
Butler	F	B	19	MS	5.5	2.5	1995	No	No	No
Cobb	M	B	37	IL	7	4	1987	No	Yes	Yes
Fain	M	W	35	ID	18	17.5	2001	Yes	No	No
Gauger	M	W	41	IL	3	0	1996	No	Yes	No
Gell	M	W	23	NC	6	4.5	2004	No	Yes	Yes
Howard	M	B	23	OH	26	1	2003	No	No	Yes
James	M	B	23	OH	26	1	2003	No	No	Yes
Keaton	M	B	19	FL	2	1	1973	No	Yes	No
Krone	M	W	35	AZ	9.5	2.5	2002	Yes	Yes	Yes
McMillian	M	B	47	AL	5	5	1993	No	No	Yes
Melendez	M	L	33	FL	17.5	17.5	2002	No	Yes	No
Rivera	M	L	25	NC	2	1.5	1999	No	Yes	No

(continued)

Table 3.1. Biographical Details of Participants (continued)

Name	Sex	Race	Age at conviction	State where tried	Years in prison[a]	Years on death row[b]	Year of exoneration	DNA?	Actual offender(s) identified?[c]	Compensation received?[d]
Taylor[e]	M	B	29	IL	13	10	2003	No	No	Yes
Tibbs	M	B	35	FL	2	1.5	1982	No	No	No
Wilhoit	M	W	32	OK	4	4	1993	No	No	No

[a]This category includes only the years in prison for this wrongful conviction and does not include any prior years of incarceration on other charges. In addition, several participants were not released from prison immediately after exoneration as they completed sentences on other, unrelated charges. That time is not included here. This category also does not include any time they spent in jail or prison awaiting trial, which in some instances was two to three additional years. Numbers (for years in prison and years on death row) are not exact and may have been rounded slightly up or down by one to three months.

[b]The number of years spent on death row may not equal the years spent in prison. Several exonerees received retrials after appellate review, were reconvicted on the same charges, but were sentenced to life in prison rather than death. At that point, they were moved from death row into the general population of prison until their eventual exonerations.

[c]This category includes cases in which the actual perpetrator of the crime for which the exoneree was wrongfully convicted either has been tried and convicted for that crime or has been publicly acknowledged in some way as the actual offender, even if not convicted.

[d]Of those receiving compensation, only two—Bloodsworth and Cobb—were provided compensation via compensation statutes in their states. The others were compensated as a result of litigation pursued against local, county, and/or state officials and agencies.

[e]This exoneree prefers to remain anonymous. We have assigned this pseudonym to him.

For three (17 percent) of our participants, DNA was instrumental in securing their exoneration and release, DNA testing that was not available at the time of their original trials and convictions. For two of these three participants, DNA results identified the actual offenders in their cases, who were later tried and convicted for those crimes. In seven other cases (for a total of nine, or 50 percent of our total), the actual offender has been identified to date. Eight (44 percent) of our participants have received some form of compensation for their wrongful convictions and incarceration. Two of these eight—Kirk Bloodsworth ($300,000) and Perry Cobb ($140,000)—received compensation according to statutory provisions provided in their states. In order to be eligible for this compensation, each had to apply for and receive a gubernatorial pardon after their exoneration and release. In Bloodsworth's case, compensation was made available within about a year of his release; however, Cobb did not receive compensation until almost fourteen years later. The remaining six participants were awarded compensation only after protracted and costly legal battles with the state, although they did, on average, receive substantially more than the two who were compensated via statute. Because it took time to successfully litigate their claims, these participants did not receive compensation for an average of four years after release. These data are similar to those provided by the Innocence Project, which notes that about 50 to 60 percent of DNA exonerees have been financially compensated, and they waited, on average, four years for their awards (Innocence Project 2009).

Because their cases were tried as capital crimes, all of our participants' wrongful convictions rested on charges of murder (see figure 3.1). Most involved a single victim, though four cases did have multiple homicide victims (Cobb, Gauger, Rivera, and Taylor). In addition to murder charges, most involved convictions for additional felonies, including primarily robbery and/or rape or sexual assault. Four of our participants were convicted of killing family members: Gary Gauger, his elderly parents; Sabrina Butler, her nine-month-old son; Greg Wilhoit, his wife; and Scott Taylor, his wife and young son (along with five others). As a result, they suffered the loss of their family members at the same time they were accused, convicted, and sentenced to death for those murders. Kirk Bloodsworth and Charles Fain were accused of

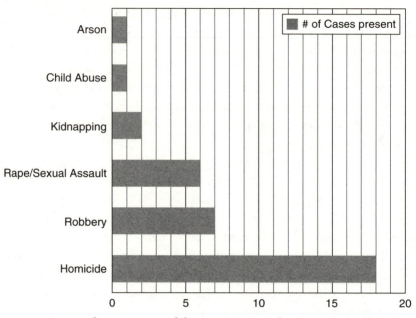

3.1. Charges in wrongful conviction cases for participants

killing young girls who also were sexually assaulted, thus subjecting them to vile treatments by other inmates in prison as well as passionate public hatred. Delbert Tibbs, Walter McMillian, and Shabaka Brown are black men accused of raping and/or killing white victims in the Deep South. Dave Keaton was convicted for killing an off-duty police officer, and Tim Howard and Gary James, codefendants, for killing a bank security guard.

Reinvestigation and appellate review of these cases reveal a host of problems that contributed to their wrongful capital convictions (see figure 3.2), including prosecutorial, police, and judicial misconduct, problems with witnesses, informants, and jailhouse snitches, eyewitness misidentification, false confessions, faulty forensic evidence, and inadequate defense services. Of our nine black participants, seven were convicted by an all-white or mostly white jury. Although other sources cite eyewitness misidentification as the primary cause of wrongful convictions (Gross et al. 2005; Scheck et al. 2000), prosecutorial misconduct is the most frequently occurring error among our eighteen cases. It is important to note that rarely is only one error the cause of a wrongful conviction, but instead many of these problems co-occur in each case.

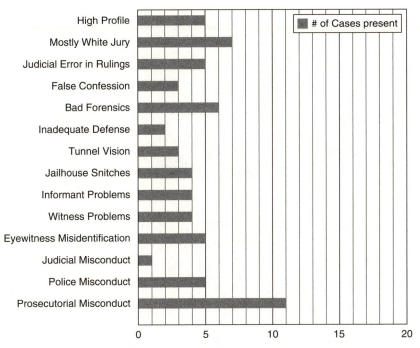

3.2. Errors contributing to wrongful convictions for participants

This list of errors reflects the mistakes and problems most often cited by experts as contributing to the wrongful conviction of the innocent (Huff et al. 1996; Radelet et al. 1994; Scheck et al. 2000; Westervelt and Humphrey 2001).

As to the mechanism through which our participants were able to secure their freedom, the most common exoneration process, used in eleven cases (61 percent), involved a conviction being overturned on appeal with a decision by the district attorney or state's attorney to drop the charges. In many cases, the evidence used at the original trial either was thrown out by the court as wholly unreliable or was so tainted as to be unusable (see figure 3.3). Six cases (33 percent) hinged on participants receiving a not guilty verdict at retrial after their case was overturned on appeal. In one case—that of Scott Taylor—the participant was released pursuant to a gubernatorial pardon. Although three other participants eventually received pardons, this was not the process that eventuated their release but came after their exonerations.

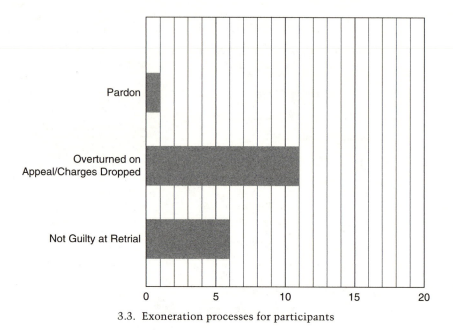

3.3. Exoneration processes for participants

Further analysis of the racial composition of the cases in our study reveals interesting differences between the exoneree–victim racial patterns for our white participants as compared to our black and Latino participants, patterns similarly reflected in other studies of race and wrongful conviction and the death penalty (Gross et al. 2005; Gross and O'Brien 2008; www.innocenceproject.org; K. Parker et al. 2001; E. Smith and Hattery 2011). In this analysis, we exempted those cases in which the victim in the case and the exoneree convicted of his or her homicide were family members, given that, in most circumstances, family members are of the same race. Including family cases, then, might not result in a true reflection of how the race of the victim influences the potential risk of wrongful conviction for white and black defendants. Excluding three family cases leaves a final sample of fifteen for this analysis. (The case of Scott Taylor was left in the analysis. Although two of the victims in his case were related to Taylor, five were not. All five, and Taylor, were of the same race.)

All five of the cases of our white participants were intraracial cases in which the victim(s) in the case also were white (see figure 3.4).

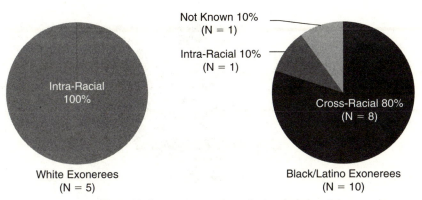

Not Known 10%
(N = 1)

Intra-Racial 10%
(N = 1)

Intra-Racial
100%

Cross-Racial 80%
(N = 8)

White Exonerees
(N = 5)

Black/Latino Exonerees
(N = 10)

3.4. Racial/ethnic composition of cases (nonfamily)

However, this pattern reverses for the majority of our black and Latino exonerees. In eight of the ten (80 percent) nonfamily cases of our black and Latino participants, the victim(s) were white. One, the case of Scott Taylor, involved an intraracial pattern in which Taylor is black as were the five nonfamily victims. In Dave Keaton's case, we were unable to make a determination of the race of the off-duty police officer killed and, therefore, marked the race of the victim as unknown. However, in reading all of the materials linked to Keaton's case, we did notice that while the race of the officer killed is never mentioned, the race of the alleged offenders (Keaton and four others) is emphasized repeatedly. Given this in addition to the time and place of this crime (early 1970s in Florida), we think it quite possible that the victim in the Keaton case also is white. If so, this would mean that nine of the ten (90 percent) black participants in our study were wrongly convicted for cross-racial/ethnic homicides. This confirms findings from other studies that black defendants are at high risk of wrongful conviction when their cases involve white victims and that, in fact, the race of the victim is a dominant factor in who gets convicted and sentenced to death in the United States, both wrongfully and otherwise (www.deathpenaltyinfo.org; Gross et al. 2005; Gross and O'Brien 2008; Persky 2011; Pierce and Radelet 2002; Radelet and Pierce 1985, 1991).

Finally, an analysis of the gender composition of the nonfamily cases in our study reveals that a little over half (53 percent) are cases where both the exoneree and the victim are the same gender and about

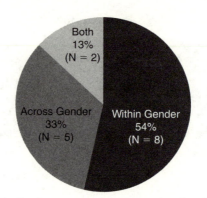

3.5. Gender composition of cases (nonfamily)

one-third (33 percent) are across gender (see figure 3.5). Two cases involved multiple homicide victims who were both male and female. (Note that one case involved the homicide of a male and rape of a female. Only the homicide was counted here for analytical purposes.) Given that only one of our participants is a woman and hers is a family case, all remaining participants in this analysis are men. Thus, approximately half of all wrongful homicide convictions in this study are male on male while one-third are male on female. Of the five male participants convicted of killing females, four also were convicted of sexual assault, two of which involved nine-year-old girls.

These analyses reveal that the eighteen cases of wrongful capital conviction included in our study reflect patterns found in other wrongful convictions, both capital and noncapital. Although our small sample prevents generalizability to all wrongful capital convictions, and even more so to all wrongful convictions, we suspect that our findings resonate with wrongful convictions more generally. The experiences of our participants, thus, illuminate life after death row and exoneration for wrongly convicted people in the United States.

Biographical Summaries

What follows are synopses of the cases of the eighteen participants in our research.[1] Though greatly abbreviated, they provide context for the chapters that follow and elucidate the events that shaped the lives of our participants as they moved ever closer to death row.

Gary Beeman (convicted 1976, Ohio)

At age twenty-three, Gary Beeman was falsely convicted of the murder of Robert Perrin during a robbery and home invasion.[2] Beeman had previous run-ins with authorities, including a robbery conviction for which he had served three years in Ohio State Mansfield Reformatory. The state's star witness against Beeman, a prison escapee named Clair Luizzo, was later thought to be the actual killer. The judge presiding over the trial barred extensive cross-examination of Luizzo and prohibited the defense from calling an additional witness, Robert Westfall, who would have testified that he had heard Luizzo say that he was the actual killer and was pinning the crime on Beeman. Beeman was convicted of capital murder on June 4, 1976, and sentenced to death.

On appeal, Beeman was granted a retrial based on two points of error: (1) the misuse of discretion on the part of the trial judge to prohibit the cross-examination of Luizzo and Westfall and (2) the potential biasing effect of a photo shown to the jury. At retrial, Beeman represented himself for much of the trial, making him the only person to defend himself successfully on a capital charge. After three days on the witness stand undergoing intense questioning, Clair Luizzo was picked up by local police for drunken and disorderly conduct. While in jail, a drunken Luizzo bragged about pinning the murder of Perrin on Beeman: five of his fellow jailees later testified to this during the retrial. As all other evidence against Beeman was circumstantial, the jury subsequently returned a not guilty verdict. Beeman remained in prison for another year on unrelated charges, and in 1980 he was released.

Kirk Bloodsworth (convicted 1985, Maryland)

In 1984, Bloodsworth was a former star discus thrower and honorably discharged marine with no criminal history. Based on a composite sketch of a young blond man with a mustache and eyewitness identification by two young boys, he was misidentified as the man who went into the woods with nine-year-old Dawn Hamilton on July 25 where she was raped and murdered. After a lengthy trial process, Bloodsworth was convicted on March 8, 1985. On March 22, at age twenty-four, he was sentenced to death.[3]

The investigation of Dawn Hamilton's murder received substantial media attention because of the heinous nature of the crime. Possibly due to pressure to find her assailant, several alternative suspects were discarded after Bloodsworth came to police attention through an anonymous tip. In addition to the eyewitness identifications, evidence against Bloodsworth included statements by acquaintances saying he had discussed a bloody rock used in the crime and had indicated he had done something for which his wife would be angry (which turned out to be forgetting to make a purchase for her). The original vote for conviction was eleven to one; however, within two hours, the vote was unanimous.

Bloodsworth's original conviction was overturned on appeal because of the prosecution's failure to reveal a second suspect on whom police had developed information. Bloodsworth was retried, convicted, and given two life sentences. In 1993, DNA testing of semen found on the young girl's clothing revealed that Bloodsworth's DNA was not a match for that found at the crime scene. On June 28, 1993, after eight years in prison with one and a half spent on death row, Bloodsworth was released and became the first person on death row in the United States exonerated by DNA evidence. In December 1993, he received a gubernatorial pardon.

Joseph Green "Shabaka" Brown (convicted 1974, Florida)

At age twenty-four, Brown, a black man, was convicted of the rape and murder of Earlene Treva Barksdale, a white woman, local entrepreneur, and wife of a prominent attorney.[4] The primary witness against Brown was Ronald Floyd, who claimed that Brown and another person had gone into the victim's store to rob it, while Floyd waited outside. Floyd told police that Brown admitted to killing Mrs. Barksdale. In exchange for his testimony against Brown, Floyd received leniency on unrelated robbery charges, though this was not revealed during Brown's trial. Although the FBI found the alleged murder weapon was incompatible with the bullet that killed Mrs. Barksdale, the prosecutor knowingly misled the jury to believe that the gun was a ballistics match. Although Brown's girlfriend and her mother confirmed Brown's alibi, the all-white jury found him guilty of murder and rape and sentenced him to death.

Without an attorney, Brown was forced to represent himself through the appellate process for over four years. In 1981, Richard Blumenthal, at the prodding of an NAACP member, took on Brown's case pro bono. In 1983, his state appeal was denied, and Brown came within fifteen hours of being executed, before a federal judge issued a stay of execution. In March 1985, the U.S. Court of Appeals for the Eleventh Circuit granted his writ of habeas corpus, based on the original prosecution knowingly allowing and exploiting the false testimony of Ronald Floyd. Floyd later recanted his testimony. Based on Floyd's recantation and new information uncovered in a reinvestigation by Centurion Ministries (the nation's first innocence project), the Hillsborough prosecutor's office decided against a new trial, and Brown was released on March 5, 1987.

Sabrina Butler (convicted 1990, Mississippi)

As of July 2011, Sabrina Butler remains the only woman death row exoneree among the 138 exonerees identified by the DPIC. In the evening of April 12, 1989, Sabrina Butler, an eighteen-year-old black single mother of two, rushed her baby boy, Walter Dean, to the emergency room because he had stopped breathing. Butler had returned to her apartment that evening after a short jog to find the baby in distress. She sought help from others in her apartment complex who assisted her in giving the baby CPR in attempts to revive him. However, Walter Dean died soon after reaching the hospital. Butler immediately fell under suspicion, in part because medical staff members claimed that the baby appeared to have been abused. Butler maintained that any bruising was sustained during the process of giving CPR, not from abuse. She readily admits that she and those assisting her used adult-style CPR on the child, unaware that CPR procedures were different for infants.

Butler was questioned at the hospital and later that night interrogated at police headquarters. Butler claims that she tried repeatedly to explain what had happened but that investigators failed to record her version of events and instead wrote their own account of what happened. Based on that manufactured account, Butler was convicted on March 13, 1990, by an all-white jury under a new felonious child abuse statute that provided for the death penalty in cases where abuse resulted in the death of the child.[5] At trial, medical experts testified that the bruises on the baby's body could not have come from a failed CPR attempt. The district attorney, Forest Allgood, insinuated repeatedly that Butler's failure to take the stand was evidence of her guilt. The judge instructed the jury that they were not to return a manslaughter verdict, that the only options were guilty or not guilty of capital murder.

In August 1992, Butler's conviction was overturned by the Mississippi Supreme Court based on Allgood's violation of her Fifth Amendment rights against self-incrimination and the trial judge's failure to instruct on manslaughter statutes. Butler was relocated to the county jail to await retrial, a three-year wait. She was acquitted at retrial in December 1995, when her neighbor, who had tried to help resuscitate the child, came forward to testify and a medical expert from the first trial admitted that his work on the autopsy had been inadequate.

Perry Cobb (convicted 1979, Illinois)

At age thirty-five, Perry Cobb was arrested in December 1977 and charged with armed robbery and two counts of first-degree murder of Melvin Kanter, owner of Mel's Red Hots in Chicago, and a customer, Charles Guccion. Two others were arrested along with Cobb—Darby Tillis and Earl "Frenchie" Grant. Grant's case was eventually severed from that of Cobb and Tillis when he agreed to plead guilty to armed robbery. Until becoming codefendants in their ten-year ordeal, Cobb and Tillis had met only in passing. The primary evidence against Cobb was testimony by Phyllis Santini, the state's star witness and alleged getaway driver. In addition, at the time of Cobb's arrest, police found a wristwatch belonging to Charles Guccion in his apartment that he had recently purchased for ten dollars from Phyllis Santini's boyfriend. Early on, Santini and her boyfriend were suspects until she told police that she drove the actual murderers—Cobb and Tillis—away from the crime scene. Documents later revealed that Santini was paid $1,200 by the prosecution for her testimony against Cobb and Tillis.[6]

From December 1977 to October 1979, Cobb and Tillis were tried three times, twice resulting in hung juries. In the third trial, a witness changed his story about the involvement of Cobb and Tillis in the crime. Arthur Shields, the bartender at the bar across the street from Mel's Red Hots, had testified in the first two trials that he had seen two black men (whom he could not identify) outside Mel's at the time of the crime. In the third trial, he testified that he could identify Cobb and Tillis as the gunmen. On October 5, 1979, Cobb and Tillis were convicted by an all-white jury and later sentenced to death.

The conviction was reversed by the State Supreme Court in October 1983 for two reasons. First, the judge had refused to instruct the jury on "accomplice instructions" regarding Santini's involvement, which would have informed the jury that Santini was an accomplice to the crime and stood to gain from implicating Cobb and Tillis. Second, the judge had disallowed the testimony of two women who had told police that Santini admitted to committing the crime with her boyfriend and that she would be paid for her testimony against Cobb and Tillis.

Their fourth trial resulted in a third hung jury. At the fifth trial, a bench trial, evidence surfaced that the bartender originally had told police that Tillis was not the man he saw across the street at Mel's. The two women to whom Santini had confessed also were allowed to testify. Most surprising was the defense testimony of Michael Falconer, Illinois assistant state attorney. He testified that he had worked with Santini in a factory before beginning law school. During this time, Santini admitted that her boyfriend had robbed a restaurant and shot someone during the robbery; neither was ever charged in the case. In January 1987, Cobb and Tillis were acquitted and released. At the time, they had been tried more times for the same crime than any other defendants in the history of American jurisprudence.

Charles Fain (convicted 1983, Idaho)

In 1983, at age thirty-five, Charles Fain, an honorably discharged Vietnam veteran, was convicted and sentenced to death for the kidnapping, rape, and murder of nine-year-old Daralyn Johnson in Nampa, Idaho.[7] The crime occurred on February 24, 1982, when Johnson was kidnapped while walking to school. Her body was found a few days later near the Snake River by fishermen. Fain had been a garbage collector in Nampa until he was laid off in 1981, after which he moved to Redmond, Oregon, some 360 miles away, to live with his parents. A month after the crime, Fain returned to Nampa to look for work and moved in with a woman who lived just a block from the Johnson home. In September 1982, seven months after the crime, he was stopped by police and asked for a hair sample based on his physical resemblance to a witness's description of the kidnapper.

Fain's conviction rested primarily on microscopic hair analysis, which, according to the FBI's forensic expert, revealed similarities between Fain's hair and three pubic hairs found on the victim. Other evidence included similarities between Fain's car and descriptions of a car seen at the scene of the abduction and a tennis shoe found in his home and a washed-out shoe print found near the crime scene. Two jailhouse snitches testified that Fain told them he had committed the crime, one of whom received a sentence reduction from 230 years to 3 for his testimony. Although Fain passed a polygraph test administered by the police, the judge did not allow the polygraph evidence at trial. Fain had prior convictions for burglary, but no history of sex crimes or crimes against minors, and had maintained a clean record since his successful completion of alcohol rehabilitation. In 2001, the DNA in his case was submitted for testing and revealed that the pubic hairs found on Johnson's body were not his. He was released in August of that year, just shy of his fifty-third birthday.

Gary Gauger (convicted 1993, Illinois)

In 1993, Gary Gauger was in his early forties and living with his parents on the family farm while recovering from problems with alcoholism. Morris and Ruth Gauger ran a motorcycle shop on their farm. On April 9, Gauger found his father murdered in a back room of the garage. He called the police immediately, and after a search of the farm, they found his mother dead in a trailer beside the main farmhouse. Gauger became the prime suspect when he revealed that he had been asleep during the time they apparently were killed on April 8. The police began questioning Gauger in the squad car at the time they arrived and continued interrogating him at the police station from late in the afternoon of April 9 until midmorning the next day. The police claimed that during the interrogation Gauger confessed to slitting his parents' throats. Gauger denied that he confessed. One police officer tried to convince him that he could have committed the crimes during a drunken blackout.

In October 1993, Gauger was convicted of murdering his parents and sentenced to death based on his alleged confession and testimony from two forensic experts.[8] In September 1994, his death sentence was commuted to life in prison without parole based on evidence of his minimal prior record and other mitigating factors. Thus, Gauger never actually lived on death row in Illinois. On appeal in March 1996, the appellate court reversed Gauger's conviction, stating that the police had no probable cause for his arrest and the alleged confession was inadmissible. Within days, the state appealed to the Illinois State Supreme Court to reinstate Gauger's conviction and sentence.

At the time they appealed, the prosecutors in Gauger's case knew of other evidence from a federal investigation, revealing that two Outlaw motorcycle gang members had actually murdered the Gaugers. The prosecutors knew this information in January 1996, but continued to pursue the reinstatement of Gauger's conviction in March. In July, the prosecutors finally revealed the identity of the two actual offenders to Gauger's defense counsel and agreed to release him on home leg monitoring in August 1996, pending their appeal. In early October 1996, the Illinois Supreme Court upheld the lower court decision to reverse Gauger's conviction, and Gauger was released from monitoring on October 4. The prosecutor dropped all charges.

Alan Gell (convicted 1998, North Carolina)

At twenty-one, Alan Gell was a known, minor drug offender in his small hometown in rural North Carolina when fifty-six-year-old retired trucker Allen Ray Jenkins was found robbed and murdered in his home. The exact date of Jenkins's murder remains unknown, but most recent forensic analysis puts his death between April 7 and 9, 1995. However, early in the case, analysis (now discredited) by a forensic pathologist indicated that Jenkins could have been killed as early as April 3, an important choice of date since Gell was in jail immediately prior to that date and left the state the day after, making April 3 the only day that Gell could possibly have killed Jenkins.

No physical evidence linked Gell to the murder. At the scene, police found evidence (i.e., open wine coolers, cigarettes, and an unwrapped tampon) that Jenkins was entertaining women prior to his death. Jenkins was known to entertain teen girls at his home and had been incarcerated previously for one count of indecent liberties with a young girl. This knowledge led police to Crystal Morris, a fifteen-year-old local girl who knew Jenkins. Morris eventually admitted to being at the scene of the crime but told six different versions of events to investigators between April and July 1995. Morris's best friend, Shanna Hall, corroborated Morris's version of events. Hall was Alan Gell's ex-girlfriend. It was Morris and Hall who implicated Gell in the homicide.

Gell was arrested in August 1995 and held in solitary confinement until his trial in February 1998. Based primarily on the erroneous testimony of Morris and Hall and the forensic analysis that Jenkins could have been killed as early as April 3, Gell was convicted of robbery and first-degree murder and sentenced to death in late February.[9] On appeal, Gell was assigned new attorneys who thoroughly investigated the case and discovered exculpatory evidence that had been mismanaged by the prosecution. This evidence included statements to police by at least six people who knew Jenkins and had seen him alive after April 3 and a tape recording of Crystal Morris and her boyfriend discussing plans to lie and deflect attention from her own involvement. Defense investigators also submitted the forensic evidence to famed "body farm" expert Murray Marks and other experts on temperature and entomology at North Carolina State University. Together, these experts more accurately pinpointed the date of death as between April 8 and 10, thereby excluding Gell as a suspect. Based on this information, Superior Court Judge Cy Grant vacated Gell's conviction in December 2002. Gell was retried in February 2004 and acquitted. He was released seven days shy of the sixth anniversary of his wrongful capital conviction.

Timothy Howard and Gary James (codefendants, convicted 1977, Ohio)

Howard and James were both twenty-three years old during the Christmas season in 1976. Howard was a father of two young boys with only a minor juvenile offense on his record. James was not married and did not have children. He had been convicted previously on an unarmed robbery for which he spent about a year in prison. Howard and James were acquaintances, though they both say that they had not seen each other for weeks prior to their arrest. On December 23, 1976, Howard and James were arrested on suspicion of involvement in a robbery of the Ohio National Bank on December 21, 1976, during which the security guard, Berne Davis, was killed.

Based primarily on the identifications of several bank customers and owners of two stores across the street from the bank, Howard and James were convicted of aggravated robbery and murder in 1977.[10] Both were sentenced to death and remanded to death row; however, in 1978, Ohio's death penalty statute was deemed unconstitutional, and all death sentences were commuted to life in prison. Howard and James were moved into the prison's general population. After several unsuccessful appeals, Centurion Ministries took the case and worked for seven years reinvestigating the case and uncovering new evidence. Judge Michael Watson reopened the case in December 2002 to evaluate this new evidence, which included fingerprints at the crime scene that did not match either James or Howard (which conflicted with expert testimony at trial that all recovered fingerprints were too smudged to evaluate); revelations that key witnesses had told FBI agents only days after the crime that they did not recognize any of the participants, statements in direct conflict with trial testimony where they identified Howard and James; and the prosecution's failure to reveal that a bank employee who knew James did not pick him out of a lineup.

As a result of this reevaluation, pressure by Centurion Ministries, and investigative articles by the *Columbus Dispatch*, Judge Watson overturned both convictions in April 2003. Howard was released on bail days later, pending the prosecutor's decision to retry him or drop charges. James, however, remained in custody. While still in custody, James took and passed a polygraph test given by a nationally renowned polygraph examiner paid for by Centurion Ministries. With pressure mounting, in July 2003, the district attorney proposed that he would release James and drop all charges against both James and Howard if James took and passed a second polygraph test, this one administered by a state examiner. James did so and passed. James was released on July 17, 2003, and the prosecutor dropped all charges against him and Howard, twenty-six years after their wrongful capital conviction. They were fifty years old.

Dave Keaton (convicted 1971, Florida)

Dave Keaton was an eighteen-year-old high school football star when he was accused of being the gunman in a five-man robbery of a Tallahassee grocery, where an off-duty sheriff's deputy was killed. The defendants became known as the "Quincy Five" (as they were from Quincy, Florida). Keaton was under suspicion for an unrelated robbery (for which he was eventually convicted and sentenced) when officials questioned him about the robbery and homicide in the grocery. Keaton was detained by police and questioned on and off over the course of a week before he was permitted to talk to counsel or his mother, both of whom he had asked for immediately upon questioning. Police claimed that Keaton voluntarily confessed during these interrogation sessions.

Keaton argued from the moment he was released that the confession he gave was physically and psychologically coerced by police.

In spite of his verifiable alibi, Keaton was convicted of murder and robbery on May 6, 1971, and sentenced to death.[11] His conviction rested primarily on his "confession" and eyewitness identifications of several people in the grocery store on the day of the crime. Of the four other young men implicated along with Keaton, one was found incompetent to stand trial and another's charges were dropped due to insufficient evidence. Keaton was tried alongside a third defendant, and although both were convicted, only Keaton was sentenced to death since he was identified as the gunman. The fourth defendant was tried after Keaton, and in the interim period between the two trials, additional evidence surfaced that implicated three other young black men in the crime, who became known as the "Jacksonville Three." This evidence was used in the trial of the final Quincy Five defendant, who was then acquitted. In late 1971 and early 1972, the Jacksonville Three were convicted of the same robbery and homicide as the Quincy Five.

The Florida Supreme Court overturned Keaton's conviction based on evidence that information about the identifications of the eyewitnesses had been withheld by the prosecution and the evidence linking the Jacksonville Three to the crime. By the time Keaton's case was sent back to the prosecutor for retrial, all of the Jacksonville Three had been convicted. As a result, the prosecutor chose not to retry Keaton, and the charges were dropped. He remained in custody until 1979 on the unrelated robbery conviction.

Ray Krone (convicted 1992, Arizona)

In his mid-thirties, an honorably discharged veteran and mail carrier Ray Krone was convicted of kidnapping and murdering Kim Ancona, a bartender at a neighborhood bar he frequented. Ancona was sexually assaulted and killed in the late-night hours of December 28, 1991, as she was closing the bar. During the event, she was stabbed eight times and bitten. Krone knew Ancona as an acquaintance, but they did not have an intimate relationship. However, based on a misidentification from an earlier Christmas party, detectives believed that there was more to the relationship, leading them to Krone's door. Police also had been told by Ancona's coworker that she was expecting someone named Ray to help her close the bar on the night of her homicide. Another Ray's telephone number later was found in her purse. When approached for questioning the day after the crime, Krone was asked to bite into a piece of Styrofoam. Later, a local dentist identified Krone's bite mark as a match for the bite marks found on Ancona's body.

Krone was convicted on August 7, 1992, based on a videotape of the bite-mark evidence and testimony of several witnesses who claimed a romantic relationship between Krone and Ancona.[12] Krone appealed the verdict on the basis that the bite-mark videotape used by the prosecution was disclosed to the defense only one day before trial, leaving them no time to adequately prepare to refute the findings in the tape. In 1995, Krone was granted a retrial. In 1996, he was again convicted based primarily on the bite-mark evidence but sentenced to life in prison because of the judge's "lingering doubt" as to his guilt. Krone's parents and appellate attorney continued to reinvestigate the case and eventually discovered evidence that the bite-mark evidence had initially been submitted by the prosecution for review to a nationally known and board-certified forensic odontologist (bite-mark expert). This odontologist had excluded Krone as the contributor of the bite marks, information never revealed to the defense. During the reinvestigation, Krone's family submitted the evidence to the same odontologist, who informed them that he had previously reviewed that evidence years earlier for the prosecution. In addition, Krone's defense submitted the DNA evidence in the case for testing. The results revealed that Krone was not the source of the hairs found on Ancona's body and identified a sex offender who lived near the bar, Kenneth Phillips, as the source of the hairs. Krone's defense investigator confronted Phillips, who admitted to murdering Ancona.

As the media heard of the DNA exclusion, Krone's defense team began pressing the Maricopa County district attorney to release him. On April 29, 2002, Krone was cleared of murder charges, and the case against him dismissed. He was the one hundredth wrongly convicted individual exonerated from death row.

Walter McMillian (convicted 1988, Alabama)

Walter McMillian, a black man in his mid-forties with no prior felony convictions, was arrested for the murder of a young white college student, Ronda Morrison. Morrison was murdered on November 1, 1986, while working at a local dry cleaner. That same day, Walter McMillian spent the entire day at a fish fry where family and friends were selling sandwiches to raise funds for the church. Despite his solid alibi, McMillian was arrested and charged with murder based on the identification of Ralph Myers, a white man whom McMillian did not know and who was in police custody for a murder in a nearby town. The only link between Myers and McMillian was a white woman with whom McMillian had had an intimate relationship and who had been involved with Myers in the other homicide. McMillian, and others, suspect that it is this relationship with a white woman in Monroeville, Alabama, that truly brought attention to McMillian, providing the impetus for police and prosecutors to overlook and withhold evidence corroborating McMillian's claims of innocence. In addition to Myers's identification, two white informants also claimed they had seen McMillian's truck at the dry cleaner on the morning of the crime. McMillian was held on death row in Alabama for a year *before* his trial, and in August 1988 he was convicted of murder.[13] The jury recommended a sentence of life in prison; however, his trial judge, Robert E. Lee Key Jr., overruled the jury recommendation and sentenced McMillian to death.

McMillian's case caught the attention of Bryan Stevenson, at the Alabama Capital Representation Resource Center. Stevenson's reinvestigation of the case revealed that Ralph Myers had recanted his implication of McMillian on numerous occasions and had told police that McMillian had nothing to do with the crime, but he had been threatened with execution if he did not testify falsely against McMillian. In fact, all three witnesses against McMillian recanted their statements. Stevenson also discovered evidence withheld from the defense that put Morrison as still alive after the time the prosecution claimed the homicide had occurred. Based on this new information, in addition to public awareness brought to the case by a *60 Minutes* special, the Alabama Court of Criminal Appeals unanimously overturned his conviction. McMillian was released on March 3, 1993.

Juan Melendez (convicted 1984, Florida)

In September 1983, Del Baker was robbed and murdered in the back room of his cosmetology school in Auburndale, Florida. Immediately after the crime, Vernon James was questioned by police because he was in possession of some of Baker's jewelry and witnesses saw him entering the beauty school the night of the crime. However, James was released with only minimal investigation. Melendez later learned that James was a police informant. Melendez was implicated in the murder four months later by felon David Luna Falcon, who told investigators Melendez confessed to him. Falcon told others that he implicated Melendez because Melendez refused to help him in other criminal activities. Court documents reveal that investigators then coerced John Berrien, another known felon, to corroborate Falcon's claims in exchange for reduced charges in a separate murder and armed robbery.

No physical evidence linked Melendez to the crime. His conviction rested primarily on the testimonies of Falcon and Berrien. Several witnesses testified on Melendez's behalf. Dorothy Graham provided an alibi for Melendez for the night of the murder, and James's cell mate testified that James confessed the murder to him. In spite of this, Melendez was convicted and sentenced to death in 1984.[14] Melendez appealed to all levels of the Florida appeals courts with no luck until one of his attorneys, Roger Alcott, discovered the transcript of a conversation between James and his former attorney in which James confessed to killing Baker. On appeal to the Florida Supreme Court in 2001, the court noted that Berrien's testimony had been coerced by police and that ineffective assistance of counsel had denied Melendez the ability to present evidence of Berrien's perjury and James's confessions. The court overturned his conviction, and prosecutors decided not to retry his case. Melendez was released on January 3, 2002, after almost eighteen years on death row.

Alfred Rivera (convicted 1997, North Carolina)

In 1996, Alfred "Heavy" Rivera was a twenty-four-year-old known drug dealer in Winston-Salem, North Carolina, who had multiple previous drug convictions. On March 22, 1996, Michael Nicholson and James Smith were shot at close range in their apartment, allegedly during an altercation over repayment of a drug debt. Rivera was arrested and charged with the murders based on the statements of three others—Jahen Marlin, Milton Hauser, and Antonio Bryant—who claimed that they, along with Rivera, went to collect the debt when Rivera shot and killed Nicholson and Smith. The three would go on to testify against

Rivera in exchange for plea bargains and reduced sentences. With only his girlfriend's alibi testimony to counter their charges, Rivera was convicted of the murders and sentenced to death.[15]

On appeal, the defense argued that the judge had improperly excluded evidence favorable to Rivera's claims of innocence at trial, including testimony from several jail inmates who had talked with Bryant, Marlin, and Hauser about having Rivera take the fall for the murders even though he had not been present at the scene. The conviction was overturned, and on retrial, the testimony of these witnesses persuaded the jury that Rivera had been the scapegoat for the other three. He was acquitted on November 23, 1999, and released.

Scott Taylor (convicted 1990, Illinois)

Taylor is the only one of our eighteen participants who has chosen to remain anonymous to the readers. Thus, Scott Taylor is a pseudonym we have chosen for him. Taylor does know that we reveal some details of his case in order to give context to later discussions and quotations by him, and we have explained to him that some people may be able to determine his identity as a result of piecing together these details. However, in a recent conversation, he noted that his main concern is that a photograph of him not be shown, which, of course, we do not include here. At the time of our interview with him, Taylor indicated his intent to move out of state and change his name. He has indeed moved to a different state, and though we are not sure, we have reason to believe that he has changed his name. To respect his desire for privacy, we provide only basic information about his case.

In 1987, Taylor escaped a fire that consumed his apartment building, but sadly claimed the lives of his wife, fifteen-month-old son, and five neighbors. He was twenty-six with no prior convictions. He was convicted on seven counts of felony murder, one count of arson, and seven counts of aggravated arson in 1990.[16] Despite newly discovered evidence withheld by prosecutors and forensic arson analysis that discredited earlier trial testimony about the nature of ignition of the fire, a judge at an evidentiary hearing in 2002 denied him a new trial. Soon after, Taylor's lawyers filed a petition for a full pardon based on innocence. In 2003, just over sixteen years after the fire, the governor granted Taylor a full pardon, and he was released from prison.

Delbert Tibbs (convicted 1974, Florida)

Delbert Tibbs grew up in Chicago and developed a thirst for knowledge and a desire to connect with and better understand the world around him. Initially, this quest took him to seminary with the aim of becoming a minister. But his spirit grew restless there, and in the early 1970s, he struck out on a "walkabout" around the United States, searching for meaning and spiritual growth. In February 1974, his wanderings brought him to Florida, where he found himself the unwitting subject of an investigation of the murder of a white man and rape of his sixteen-year-old female companion. Three days after the crime and many miles away, a police officer stopped Tibbs and questioned him about his recent whereabouts. Convinced that Tibbs was not involved in the rape and murder, the officer wrote him a note to carry with him that stated he had been questioned and cleared by police. However, the officer also took a Polaroid photograph of Tibbs. The photograph eventually made its way to the police in charge of the investigation and was shown to the rape victim, who identified Tibbs as her assailant. Over a month later while hitchhiking through Mississippi, Tibbs was arrested and brought back to Florida to participate in a lineup for the rape victim. Although her initial description of her assailant was of a dark-skinned man with pock marks on his face, out of the lineup she chose Tibbs, a fair-skinned African American man with a clear complexion.

Tibbs was arrested and tried for rape and murder. He was convicted by an all-white jury of both crimes on December 14, 1974, based solely on the eyewitness account of the rape victim who admitted to being high on drugs the day of the crime and who, when asked to account for the change in her description of the attacker's skin, answered that Tibbs must have "changed colors." Tibbs was sentenced to death.[17] He appealed to the Florida Supreme Court, which ruled that the evidence in the case did not support the guilty verdict and that the case should be retried, citing in particular the unreliable identification of the rape victim. Tibbs was released on bail pending retrial on January 8, 1977, but remained in judicial limbo until 1982 as his attorneys and the state debated whether a retrial in his case would constitute double jeopardy. Given the insufficient evidence against him and lack of credibility of the primary witness, the state's attorney decided in August 1982 to drop all charges against Tibbs.

Greg Wilhoit (convicted 1987, Oklahoma)

On May 31, 1985, Kathy Wilhoit was found raped and murdered in her apartment with her two small children sleeping upstairs. Almost a year later, Greg Wilhoit was charged with the crimes. Wilhoit and his wife were separated and living apart at the time. The physical evidence found at the scene, which included a fingerprint and pubic hair, did not match him. Investigators claimed that bite marks found on Kathy Wilhoit's breast matched her husband's teeth. Wilhoit's parents hired attorneys who, according to Wilhoit, did little investigation and pressured him to plead guilty. Only weeks before his capital murder trial, they hired a new attorney they believed to be one of the best in the area, but unknown to them, the attorney was struggling with severe alcoholism and had appeared in court drunk. Unfortunately, because of his insufficient representation, Wilhoit was unable to effectively refute the two dental experts the prosecution called to testify at trial, one of whom had been out of dental school for less than a year. In May 1987, Greg Wilhoit was convicted of raping and murdering his wife and was sentenced to death.[18] He lost his freedom and his daughters, ages four months and fourteen months at the time of the crime, who were placed in foster care. Luckily, the family who took them in was known by Wilhoit through their mutual affiliation with a community church.

On appeal, Wilhoit was able to retain counsel from Mark Barrett through the Oklahoma Indigent Defense System. In 1991, the Oklahoma Court of Criminal Appeals overturned his conviction based on the lack of adequate representation during his first trial. He was released on bail and waited two years for his second trial to begin. At retrial, eleven of the top odontologists (bite-mark experts) from around the country testified that the bite marks on Kathy Wilhoit's body could not have come from her husband. In March 1993, with no other evidence against him, the judge dismissed the case against Wilhoit after the prosecution rested its case.

THESE STORIES PROVIDE the context for all that follows. These are the people whose lives have been irreparably disrupted, and the events out of which the experiences described in the remainder of the book were borne. What happens when innocent people are taken by the state, convicted of a crime, and scheduled for death? They do their best to explain in the pages that follow.

PART TWO

 Struggling with Life after Exoneration

WHEN WE BEGAN this research in 2003, little was known about the lives exonerees led once they left prison. The issue of innocence was emerging in the national spotlight as a significant problem, mainly due to the publicized work on DNA exonerations by the Innocence Project at Cardozo Law School. Wrongful conviction cases began to receive more media attention than they had in the past, including in-depth investigative reports in newspapers and on television shows like *20/20* and *60 Minutes*.[1] Routinely, the attention focused on the causes of the wrongful conviction, especially the investigation and/or adjudication processes that led to an innocent person being convicted of a crime. However, this attention routinely stopped at the exoneration itself, usually on the day of the exoneree's release from prison (with a few notable exceptions, for example, the report "What Jennifer Saw" on the case of Jennifer Thompson and Ronald Cotton).[2] The lingering image was of the joyful and grateful exoneree embracing loved ones and tearfully leaving the courtroom or walking out of prison a free person. This "happy" ending left the impression that all was well, freedom was secured, life was good.

The chapters in part 2 reveal the rest of the story. These chapters reveal that exonerees walk out of prison into a life fraught with challenges and difficulties, many exacerbated by the criminal justice system's ineffective response to their exoneration and release. Chapter 4 outlines the array of short- and long-term practical problems they confront when going about the business of everyday life. From the more mundane skills of learning how to use a bank card or grocery shop to their persistent problems with unemployment and housing, exonerees explain their daily struggles with where and how to live and survive in a world that has, in many ways, passed them by. Chapter 5 reveals the depth of the losses the exonerees have experienced. Clearly, they feel the effects of their loss of freedom. This entire book is in many ways about the impact of that loss of freedom on their lives. But it is not the loss of freedom that most often brings them to tears; it is the loss of the loved ones they never had opportunity to grieve, the loss of time and opportunities missed, the loss of relationships they did not or could not develop, and the loss of the sense of security that most people take for granted as they go about their daily routines. Chapter 6 explores the negative impact of their wrongful conviction on family members and the challenge of remaking those relationships without the benefit of shared history or time together. Finally, chapter 7 underscores the depth of the emotional journey they begin on the day of exoneration, a journey marked by distrust, guilt, depression, and anger.

The chapters in part 2 paint a picture of the reality exonerees confront after release, a picture quite different from the one we are left with on exoneration day.

CHAPTER 4

Facing Practical Problems

> I had to find a job. I had to find people to love and to
> love me. And I had to find a place to stay . . . clothes . . .
> the whole bit. I had to get to know my son again.
>
> —Delbert Tibbs

AFTER RELEASE, OUR PARTICIPANTS encountered many
challenges as they rebuilt their everyday lives, challenges finding housing
and employment, treating medical problems, using new technologies.
As Gary Gauger adeptly summarizes, "It's like God, where will I live?
How will I do it? What will I do for money? What will I do for work?"
They see these challenges as short-term problems confronted immediately upon release and long-term problems lingering continuously since
release. We discuss these short-term and long-term problems separately,
though they often overlap. For example, finding a job most certainly is
both an immediate problem they must confront and a problem that, for
many, never goes away.

SHORT-TERM PRACTICAL PROBLEMS
Where to Go from Here

The most immediate problem facing exonerees when they learn of
their release is the seemingly simple matter of where to go when they
leave prison. Lola Vollen and David Eggers (2005) discuss this as a problem common among exonerees with whom they work in the Life After
Exoneration Program (LAEP) in California. Although several of our
participants had family, friends, and even attorneys to help, others
did not. Many scrambled in the hours immediately before or after release
to find someone to take them in those first days out of prison. Without
money or supporters with means, they had no stable place to live or call
home. Shabaka Brown, for example, lived with his appellate attorney,

Mike Mello, for several months after release, while Delbert Tibbs recalls that he "had absolutely no money" and lived in an apartment that "should have been condemned."

This quandary stems from a structural problem noted by most exonerees—the inability to develop a reintegration plan for life after release. This problem is rooted in the exoneration processes in many cases, which makes planning for life after release difficult to impossible (see also Grounds 2004). Only a few exonerees knew they were likely to be released on a particular day. For example, Walter McMillian's attorney, Bryan Stevenson, arranged a hearing with the court and the Alabama Attorney General's office to present evidence of McMillian's innocence and secure his release. McMillian recalls knowing about his impending release a week or two in advance, which gave him time to adjust to the idea and make basic plans for life on the outside.

The overwhelming majority of our participants, however, knew of their exoneration and release only hours in advance. As Gary Gauger describes, "I didn't know I was going to be released until the day I walked out the door." Five of our participants—Gary Beeman, Sabrina Butler, Perry Cobb, Alan Gell, and Alfred Rivera—were released immediately following an acquittal at a retrial of their case. Greg Wilhoit received a directed verdict for acquittal by the judge at his retrial. In these instances, the participants did not know what to expect going to court the day of their release. Given that they had each been convicted and sentenced to death for these same charges once before, they were far from certain of their exoneration this time around. Although they longed for freedom and often thought about what they would do once released, the abruptness of their release was not something they could truly plan for. Alan Gell explains this experience as follows:

> [While waiting for retrial], I just made all kinds of plans on how wonderful it would be once I was released. What I didn't realize is I had forgotten what it was like to be free. I forgot what reality was to be in a society. You know? A lot of the things that I said I was gonna do took money to do. . . . When [the judge] looked at me and said I was free to go, I had been wanting to hear them words forever. . . . But, it dawned on me when he said I was free to go that there was something missing. He didn't ask where I was going. He didn't ask

did I have anywhere to go. He didn't advise me to not get into any trouble. He didn't tell me he was sorry that I had to go through what I had to go through. He didn't . . . do anything.

Although Gell had thought about where and how he would live if released, the reality of that plan was more difficult to execute than he had anticipated, and he was struck by the extent to which no one in the courtroom seemed interested in his plans for readjustment (or provided assistance for it). He concludes by noting that the judge acted as if "it was just a normal, everyday occurrence for somebody to just suddenly be taken off death row and released ten years later." Alfred Rivera, who was released one hour after his acquittal at retrial, bluntly attributes much of the difficulty he faced after release to the lack of "time to structure a plan or have the resources that would have allowed some success and stability."

Several exonerees were unaware that their release was imminent and had no time to plan for life immediately after they got out. Gary James learned of his release the night before on the eleven o'clock news. Charles Fain found out when a guard slipped a note under his cell door from two journalists requesting an interview when he was released later that day. He was off prison grounds three hours later. Scott Taylor found out by watching his pardon announced on television. The guards took him immediately from his cell to another part of the prison to process his release, although the prison administrators were confused about what paperwork to file. They too had had no time to plan. Juan Melendez learned that he was being released when he was taken from his cell for what he thought was a phone call from his attorney. He found himself sitting across from a woman typing away on a computer asking him about his personal data. She noticed his confusion and only then informed him that he was getting out of prison, that afternoon. Kirk Bloodsworth knew of his impending release on a Friday and had to wait until Monday for the judge to return from vacation to execute the order of release. In most cases, our participants had an hour or two, maybe a day or two, to construct a plan for where they would go and what they would do. After five, ten, or close to twenty years in prison, the abruptness of their freedom was difficult to process and often left them with limited options of where to turn.

This problem is compounded by the fact that, in most cases, the state provided them with little to no resources of any kind the day they walked out the door. This was a concern echoed by the seven exonerees who participated in a panel discussion of postrelease needs hosted by the Center on Wrongful Convictions at Northwestern School of Law in March of 2002 (Illinois Criminal Justice Information Authority 2002) as well as by many exonerees seeking assistance from LAEP (Vollen and Eggers 2005; see also K. Davis 2011; Weigand 2009). When asked if they received any assistance from the state upon release, one-third of our participants responded simply with "Nothing!" Another third mentioned only small items such as a new pair of pants or shoes or bus fare (see chapter 11 for more details). Sabrina Butler sums up the experience most exonerees had on their day of release as follows: "No money. No nothing. They didn't give me jack! They just took the handcuffs off me, and sent me out the door." In her case, a prison official added insult to injury by warning her on her way out, "If I was you, I would get the hell away from Columbus [Mississippi] because you ain't wanted here."

Negotiating the Honeymoon Period

A significant difference between more recent exonerees released after 2000 and those who have been out for many years is the level of attention (and more positive attention) the more recent exonerees have received in the media. Public awareness of innocence issues has risen sharply in the past decade as exonerations, in particular DNA exonerations, have increased and media outlets have become more interested in highlighting innocence cases (Leo 2005; Leo and Gould 2009). Recent exonerees are more likely to have received significant media coverage in their communities and, as a result, to be recognized in public. Exonerees, such as Shabaka Brown and Gary Beeman, were released when cases of innocence were largely unknown and public skepticism as to actual innocence remained high. They were released to no public fanfare at a time when even the most basic services some states now provide for exonerees were nonexistent (Bernhard 2004; Innocence Project 2009). As a result of these social changes in attention to issues of innocence, exonerees reveal sharp differences in their immediate postrelease experiences dependent upon when they were released.

Though not in every case, recent exonerees more often report positive exchanges with people in their communities who recognize them from news coverage. They recount people stopping them in public places to pat them on the back or offer words of encouragement. For example, Gary James and Tim Howard, codefendants released in 2003, both report receiving clothing and money from community members immediately after their very public exonerations. They recount feeling like rock stars as people they did not know wanted to befriend them. Scott Taylor, pardoned in 2003, describes being overwhelmed by attention, even hiring bodyguards to ensure his safety when he was out in public. Kirk Bloodsworth, released in 1993 as the first DNA death row exoneree, got significant media coverage because his exoneration was the first of its kind. He was a recognizable figure in his hometown of Cambridge, Maryland. However, this recognition was not positive as in the cases of James, Howard, and Taylor. Bloodsworth was greeted with deep skepticism by a public that believed he got out of prison on a technicality. Neighbors and childhood friends crossed the street to avoid passing him, and coworkers taunted him with "child killer" written in the dirt on his truck.

Thus, recent exonerees more often experienced a "honeymoon period" immediately after release that buffered them temporarily from the difficulties of finding a job and stable place to live (Weigand and Anderson 2007 refer to this as the "celebrity phase"). This was not the case with those who had been out for ten or twenty years. But even among recent exonerees, they knew their celebrity was fleeting and that the difficult job of rebuilding their lives was ahead of them. As noted by Gary James, "When I first got out, everybody was recognizing me and everybody was saying 'hi,' then it started fading away. . . . I was trying to start adjusting, and that's when things started getting hard."

Relearning Life

Most of the short-term practical problems that participants discuss revolve around the primary issue of relearning—relearning how to sleep, eat, shop, walk, use money, and even dress themselves. These are problems also noted by Adrian Grounds (2004) in his evaluations of eighteen exonerees. In some instances, it is not relearning that stumps them but learning something new for the first time, especially with regard to new technologies that were introduced while they were in prison. These basics of living often frustrate them, and sometimes make them laugh, in those first days and months after release.

Problems with eating, walking, and sleeping are dominant themes in participants' accounts of life immediately postrelease. Given the limited diet provided inmates ("Bologna and cheese, and a hard-boiled egg for lunch for eight years, eleven months, and nineteen days!" [Kirk Bloodsworth]), it probably should not be surprising that food is both friend and foe when they first get out. Tim Howard describes his craving for food: "I had a hard time with food. At one time, I weighed about two hundred pounds. I ate so much. I was eating everything." Juan Melendez describes an opposite reaction to food. He wanted to eat it, but his system was not ready for it yet: "I couldn't eat that much. Every time I eat something, it felt like a rock. . . . So I was eating a lot of soup when I got out, and drinking a lot of coffee."

Walking also posed some problems, especially for exonerees who spent all of their time on death row and thus had quite limited time outdoors. In such circumstances, it was difficult to build stamina for extended physical activity, and several exonerees noted that they could not exert themselves without their legs buckling beneath them or cramping up. Ray Krone recounted a different problem he had readjusting to walking down the street: "I was walking down the sidewalk. . . . I was over there dodging the parking meters . . . walking in and out of the parking meters and car mirrors . . . and I finally realized what was going on. There was a construction zone along that part of the sidewalk, and they had that hurricane fence up that I was used to in prison, and here I was trying to stay away from the fence because . . . you didn't get too close to the fence [in prison] . . . they'd shoot ya." After realizing what he was doing, Krone decided to confront the problem head-on: "So I went over and grabbed it, and shook it, and bounced up and down. And I don't think I noticed it anymore since then."

Sleeping also is problematic in the weeks after release. Exonerees discuss several problems related to sleeping. One is a matter of comfort. Having slept on a wooden slab with little padding for so many years, they simply are not comfortable in a bed. Several slept on the floor their first nights of freedom. Others recall that their sleep is disrupted by dreams, of being taken off to their electrocution or reincarcerated.[1]

Although dreams like these continue sporadically, they appear to be most intense in the days and weeks immediately after release. Sharing a bed with someone also is difficult early on. In prison, having someone in such close proximity was usually cause for alarm and triggered an aggressive response. Adjusting to sleeping with someone does not come easily. While on one level, they may want intimacy; on another, they are afraid of it. Kirk Bloodsworth explains, "I want my little space on this side of the bed, and I just don't feel like hugging you right now. Don't put your hands on me. . . . I've woke up and grabbed her [his wife] before thinking I was somewhere else."

In addition to relearning these basics of eating, walking, and sleeping, participants frequently mention an array of other adjustments they confront early on. They struggle with places that are quiet and dark, which for some relates to their problems sleeping. Alan Gell recounts his first night at home when the darkness and quiet became overwhelming:

> My first night home, I had two new things to experience immediately which was darkness and quietness. On death row, there's always a fan going, and it's a loud, loud fan. . . . The lights never go out, they dim. . . . I went to bed that first night . . . with the light on and basking in how great it was to finally be home. . . . I pulled the [cord] to turn the light off . . . and it's like when my head hit the pillow . . . I was four or five years old again. It's dark. I can feel the darkness. It's closed in on me. I was claustrophobic behind it. I reached and reached and couldn't find the cord. I was frantic. . . . I swung the door open and some light came in and I was [panting]. I turned the TV on and turned the volume all the way down and laid in bed. . . . You hear cars come up that curve and go by, and eighteen wheelers go by, and one minute it can be totally quiet, no sound at all, and the next minute, Whoom! . . . I was like, "Man, shit, I can't sleep," and I didn't want to let Mom know I couldn't sleep . . . scared of the dark and scared of the quietness.

The quiet makes them uncomfortable because it has not been a part of their experience for so long. In the same discussion, Gell also tentatively revealed his difficulties with some of the basics of dressing himself. He admitted sheepishly that zippers in particular gave him trouble since prison jumpsuits do not have zippers. Tim Howard confided a similar difficulty in that he forgot how to tie a necktie. On the day of his release, when dressing in a suit for the first time in over twenty-five years, the prison guard had to help him with his tie.

Another common adjustment noted by many exonerees is how to handle money. They have not used, or even held, money in many years, and as Kirk Bloodsworth recalls, "rollin' a coin in my hand was almost erotic." Many exonerees commented on the sticker shock they experienced when they first went shopping and how overwhelmed they were by all of the options. Scott Taylor explains, "On death row, things are brought to you. You don't have a choice. My attorneys took me to the grocery store and told me to pull out a cereal. I looked up on this shelf at all these different cereals, and I just didn't know. I didn't know what to pick. I had to have somebody pick for me. . . . That was too much." They struggle to manage their bank accounts and pay bills, having not written checks in many years and never used an ATM or debit card.

In most cases, exonerees were released into a world full of new technology they had never seen, except possibly on television. Most of them relayed stories of their first experiences with technology that most people find commonplace—cell phones, computers, bank machines, CD players, self-serve gas pumps. Learning to negotiate these gadgets was among the first early frustrations they confronted, though usually with a smile on their faces: "I had to retrain my whole thinking process because there was a lot of things that I had to adjust to. Things like, seatbelts was one of them. We didn't have no seatbelts when I was arrested [in 1973]" (Shabaka Brown). Some of their descriptions of encountering new technology for the first time are pretty amusing. Juan Melendez recalls,

When I went in, they didn't have no cell phones. When I went in, they didn't have no CDs; the computer was barely [available]. So when I first got out, I'm in the car and they hand me a cell phone. . . . I said "What the hell I'm gonna do with this?" And he say, "Put it to your ear just like a telephone" . . . and sure enough, my mama pick up the phone, and I told her I was out. Then they hand me a CD. I didn't know what the hell it was neither. It looked like a plate to me. I'm like, "What I'm gonna do with this?" They say, "Do like you do a eight track." Now I know what it was, a eight track. So I just play it like a eight track.

In most cases, exonerees confront, and even overcome, many of these short-term problems in the weeks and months after they are released. But they do experience them as a source of frustration and anxiety at a time already rife with both. They do not receive assistance with life skills or new technology, unless they foot the bill themselves. At the same time that they are adapting to everyday life, they also struggle with many problems that are not so easily overcome. The challenges of finding a job and a home, managing untreated health problems, and negotiating a confusing world await them upon release.

LONG-TERM PRACTICAL PROBLEMS

When asked about their transitions, exonerees consistently discuss three vexing problems: finding employment, getting medical care, and negotiating new spaces. They each talk about at least one of these areas as problems they have persistently encountered since release (see also K. Davis 2011; Illinois Criminal Justice Information Authority 2002; Vollen and Eggers 2005; Weigand 2009).

Finding Employment

The obstacles to reintegration and stability that our participants discuss most frequently are related to finding employment (see also Roberts and Stanton 2007; Vollen and Eggers 2005; Weigand 2009), though a few said that they did not have a problem finding a job. For example, Walter McMillian had a successful business before he was arrested, and he was able to step back into it soon after release. Juan Melendez returned home to Puerto Rico, where he was greeted as a hero. An old friend offered him a job that has allowed him flexibility to travel the country speaking about wrongful conviction and death penalty issues, which serves as an additional source of income for him. These stories, though, are the exceptions rather than the rule. Most frequently, our participants discuss persistent frustrations over finding meaningful and stable employment.

They reveal a variety of factors that make employment difficult to obtain and maintain. The first is structural: although they all have been exonerated, the original capital conviction remains on their record. Expungement requires an attorney's assistance, which is an expense many cannot absorb. Those who may have had some resources prior to son have long since exhausted them on attorneys, investigators, and other legal expenses along the way. They generally emerge from prison without money. They need a job to help build those funds, but their record prevents them from getting a job. Without a job and money, they cannot afford to have their records expunged. Without pro bono assistance of an attorney, they are caught in a vicious cycle. For most, the state provides them no assistance finding a job or removing the primary barrier to employment by expunging their records.

Several describe the dilemma they face when applying for jobs: how to answer the question asked on all applications, "Have you ever been convicted of a felony?" Alan Gell angrily describes his frustrations over this process as follows:

> If you pull it [his criminal record] right now, it'll say . . . murder. It'll say first-degree murder, armed robbery, conspiracy to commit murder, conspiracy to commit armed robbery. It'll say conviction date. . . . It'll say death. And unless you scroll down and get more information for history, you'll never get to see exonerated or not guilty or new trial . . . or acquitted. . . . When you go to apply for jobs, I'm having the damnedest time. . . . You go to fill out a job application and it's like, "have you been convicted of a felony?" Yes or no, not please explain. And then it's, "what was it?" And the line to write it in is that long [uses fingers to indicate small space]. Where do you write, how do you write capital murder but I was later exonerated? Or capital murder but I really didn't do it?

Shabaka Brown has found no acceptable way to answer that question; no matter how exonerees answer that question, they will be criticized: "I know two jobs . . . that said I misrepresented myself on my application. And I asked them, 'How?' . . . And they said I had lied on the question of whether I had been convicted of a felony within seven years. And I didn't lie. I just put, 'NA.' I said, 'That's not applicable.' In fact, I was locked up the last damn seven years! How can I commit a felony? But they said I misrepresented myself." Even when providing what he thought was the best answer, the employer said he was lying. Now, almost twenty-five years after his exoneration in 1987, Brown's record still has not been expunged, and as recently as December 2009, a criminal background check prevented him from getting a job for which he had applied.

A second problem regarding employment is the gap on their resume as a result of their incarceration. If their history was not discovered through a background check (as was more often the case for exonerees released in the 1970s and 1980s when such checks were less common), they often were still left with the dilemma of explaining the five-, ten-, or fifteen-year gap between jobs without revealing where they had been during that time. As Gary James explains, "When I was going around looking for jobs, I had to explain that twenty-six-year gap. I had to tell them everything. . . . And they just didn't want to deal with it. . . . They thought, well, you was in there and something might come back [on you]." Exonerees also have lost skills over the course of their incarceration and are not provided vocational or educational opportunities while in prison.

A third problem is that they would prefer to find employment with some flexibility to allow them time to make additional money through speaking engagements. Public speaking is one way that exonerees can make money; however, these opportunities require travel and are not consistent, abundant, or well paying. For most, speaking cannot be their primary source of income. This leaves them in a bind. They need a job to support themselves, but a job with no flexibility prevents them from pursuing one type of work that often is available to them. Although a couple of our participants were able to work full-time as salaried employees for nonprofit organizations focused on justice reform, these positions were temporary, and thus even these exonerees found themselves back in the position of negotiating the balance between a "regular" job and time for public speaking. A few participants also noted that without a job with some flexibility, they would not be able to go back to school to improve their employability.

The primary way that exonerees do get work, for those who do, is through connections within their social networks. As Delbert Tibbs explains, "Most of my jobs have come as a result of friends looking out for me." Old friends come through with temporary, low-paying jobs without benefits, but at least they help pay the rent and other bills. A few participants have been able to get some stability by being self-employed. Walter McMillian ran his own successful auto parts business, and Gary Gauger farms his family farm. But most are not able to find this level of job security, and even McMillian and Gauger scrape to get by.

Three exonerees in our study (Delbert Tibbs, Gary Gauger, and Dave Keaton) were lucky to be included in the play *The Exonerated* (Blank and Jensen 2004), which played off-Broadway for over six hundred perform-ances and toured the country. Each production of the play ended with a collection of donations for the exonerees whose stories were presented in the play. All three participants noted how helpful these funds had been during the limited time the play ran.

With limited and unstable job opportunities, financial problems loom large (see also Illinois Criminal Justice Information Authority 2002). In contrast to public opinion, many exonerees do not receive compensation or multi-million-dollar settlements from the state. According to the Innocence Project (2009), 50 to 60 percent of DNA exonerees have received compensation in some form (see chapter 11). This, we believe, is actually quite high relative to all exonerees, DNA and non-DNA inclusive. Innocence Project exonerees are lucky in that they frequently receive assistance in pursuing compensation claims, a service not available to most other exonerees. Of our participants, eight (44 percent) received compensation of some kind. Two of these eight participants received compensation through statutory provisions in their states—Kirk Bloodsworth and Perry Cobb—and while Bloodsworth's was awarded within a year of his exoneration, Cobb waited almost fourteen years to receive his. The other six received money after suing the state for compensation, which took many years to successfully negotiate. Actual financial awards arrived on average four years after release, leaving exonerees in poverty in those first years out of prison. With the exception of Walter McMillian, our interviews took place dur-ing the gap after release but before their litigation had been successfully concluded. Without stable income, several participants voiced their fear of being able to survive without turning to illegitimate sources of income: "As the months passed by, my only fear was how would I continue to stay afloat financially without having to resort to anything illegal" (Alfred Rivera).

With limited resources, survival is difficult. Delbert Tibbs admits that he occasionally resorted to "dumpster diving" to live because "I'm not gonna allow myself to starve to death." Sabrina Butler lived day to day on social security checks for the first three years of her release. Her husband, a prison guard who was fired soon after they married, has traveled as far as Florida to look for work to keep the family afloat. Even Kirk Bloodsworth, who did receive some compensation, was homeless, living in his truck and trapping and selling nutria (a large rodent) in the backwoods of Maryland to survive. For most, having spent the most productive years of their lives in prison, their financial constraints make it almost impossible to plan for long-term expenses such as college educations for children or grandchildren or their own retirement.

Health Problems

A second theme that consistently emerges when exonerees discuss long-term problems is their struggle with a wide range of health problems (see also Vollen and Eggers 2005). Their list of chronic health concerns includes arthritis, asthma, kidney stones, high blood pressure, hepatitis, skin rashes, dental problems, digestive disorders, and poor vision. In addition, several participants have had serious health crises since release. Perry Cobb and Kirk Bloodsworth have had heart problems. Cobb's heart attack was serious enough to require a triple bypass, after which he had a series of small strokes. Greg Wilhoit's struggle with a chronic illness brought him close to death in the spring of 2010. Delbert Tibbs battles ongoing complications from diabetes.

The exonerees, of course, are convinced that their continuing health problems are a direct result of the poor food, poor conditions, and stress related to their wrongful confinements: "Stress is the worst thing going on. When I was on death row, my health went south on me pretty much. My hair started fallin' out. My eyes, I couldn't see. . . . My teeth aren't that great. . . . And the food! It was just horrible" (Greg Wilhoit). Others may suggest that these were preexisting conditions or outcomes of age or substance abuse. But our participants argue strenuously that they noticed dramatic changes in their health when they arrived to prison, and studies confirm that incarceration has long-term negative impacts on health (Schnittker and John 2007).

These negative effects could be managed if exonerees had access to good health care. But this is not the case. As Juan Melendez points out, any medical issues they had while incarcerated received little attention, only exacerbating the problems upon release: "They not gonna give you the best medicine. You condemned to death. Why give you the best medicine when they probably kill you tomorrow?" And then once they are out, access to health insurance and medical care is conditioned by employment, which is unstable and limited. The state does not provide medical assistance upon release, even in the form of a basic checkup, and most of their problems receive little attention. Alan Gell provides an amusing, yet poignant, anecdote to sum up this frustration:

> I went to the Department of Social Services and I was like, "I had-n't got no money. I hadn't got no job. I was just let out of prison off of death row. There's no health care for me whatsoever and I got these health problems. I got mental problems. I got some physical problems as far as my foot being broken [while in prison] and never set. Is there any way I can get any help from you?" And they refused. They told me that the only way I could do it is if I was a senior citizen or if I was pregnant.

Negotiating Space

A final long-term problem exonerees frequently discuss is their inability to negotiate space. Several share funny stories about being lost in a building or a neighborhood because they simply could not find their way out. Juan Melendez says, "I go to the bathroom in a building, and when I get out, I don't know how to find my way back. I have a hard time to find my way back. I have a hard time finding the directions because I was in a small world, and now I'm in a big world." In addition, they frequently feel uncomfortable in closed-in spaces. Though these problems are sometimes amusing, clearly their confinement has affected their ability to negotiate space.

Getting lost is common for our participants. Even in neighborhoods where they grew up, they get lost. Gary James reports that he gets lost every day. And he and Tim Howard recount a time when they were driving together to an event and got lost in their hometown. They finally pulled into a parking lot to ask for directions. Luckily, before getting out of the car, one of them noticed that they had inadvertently pulled into the parking lot of a branch of the bank they had been convicted of robbing. They decided it was in their best interests *not* to go into the bank to ask for help! Although getting lost is a seemingly simple thing, this clearly frustrates them, and they realize that navigating is a skill that has deteriorated as a result of their many years of close confinement when every move was orchestrated by prison officials.

Similarly, many are uncomfortable in places where they feel confined or restricted. Juan Melendez and Perry Cobb do not like crowds. Alan Gell and Tim Howard did not like the small rooms they lived in when they first got out of prison. Scott Taylor struggled with his first job out of prison because it was in a dark, cold basement of a building: "I felt confined. I didn't like to have to stay there. It's like being in prison to me. . . . It was weird. I was, like, I have to get some air." Kirk Bloodsworth says that in restaurants his chair must face the door, and that even in the shower he tries to stand right up against the wall. When we met to interview him, he rearranged the chairs before he even sat down. We had his chair in the corner of the room with our two chairs facing his, but he moved it out of the corner immediately. We saw something similar in our interview with Juan Melendez, who always chooses a chair facing the exit. In some cases, this discomfort leads them to avoid public places, as, for example, Perry Cobb finds it difficult to sing in public now, even though this was his profession prior to his wrongful conviction. It simply makes him too "uncomfortable." Negotiation of space clearly remains a significant source of stress for exonerees, even many years after release.

THE PROBLEMS of everyday life confront exonerees the moment they walk out of prison. They quickly realize that they are encountering a new world with new challenges and that, much like a child, they must learn how to negotiate that world and overcome the obstacles in their way: "We're [exonerees] in another world now. And the world, it's not people. It's not because people do not understand you. It's more that you do not understand people. This is they world, not yours. You got to put yourself back in *they* world" (Juan Melendez). This might be their most difficult struggle of all, to come back into a world that has, in many ways, left them behind and determine where they fit in.

CHAPTER 5

Managing Grief and Loss

[What if] the state of North Carolina or some high official comes up to me and says, "Alan, I want you to leave your family. Go to death row. Stay there for nine years. And then you can go back home. Here's a check. It don't matter how many zeros you add onto it. . . . You can have it if you'll go do it." . . . I got to thinking to myself, "There's nothing that they can do. It's not money. Money's not gonna fix it. There's nothing that'll fix it." And it dawned on me that what I had lost is gone. . . . [I'll] never ever, ever again be twenty, twenty-one, twenty-two, up to twenty-nine [years old]. I got really depressed . . . and lost ten pounds in total. You know, they took this from me, and I'm never gonna get it back.   —Alan Gell

THE FEELINGS OF LOSS and grief were palpable for our participants. Even many years later, they grieve loved ones who died while they were incarcerated and ruptured personal relationships with children, family, and friends. Adrian Grounds (2004, 170) found similar experiences among the eighteen exonerees he evaluated, noting that "all had strong and unresolved feelings of loss." According to the trauma literature, persistent feelings of grief and mourning over losses and disruptions are common among trauma survivors of all types (Brashers et al. 1999; Erikson 1976; Herman 1997; Williams et al. 2003). Averaging nine and a half years behind bars, our participants are keenly aware of the many missed opportunities during that lost time. They struggle to regain a sense of security and overcome fears of continued surveillance and suspicion. Despite their best efforts, they know they can never regain all that has been lost.

Loss of Loved Ones

Our participants experienced the loss of loved ones in a variety of ways throughout their ordeal. Four of our participants were convicted for killing close family members: Sabrina Butler in the death of her infant son, Gary Gauger for the killing of his parents, Scott Taylor for arson resulting in the deaths of his wife and young son (and five others), and Greg Wilhoit in the rape and murder of his wife. They were faced with grieving the sudden and shocking losses of those closest to them while simultaneously processing the surreal experience of being condemned to death for those crimes. Sabrina Butler, for example, was barraged with questions from hospital personnel and police while holding her child at the hospital the night he died. Eighteen years old, confused, and alone, she could not process his death and their accusations: "When I was at the hospital when my son died, it was about fifteen, twenty different folks asking me questions. . . . And I'm sitting here holding him, and everybody's asking me . . . I could have said I was an elephant! I don't know what I said. . . . Everybody was asking me 'What happened?' 'Who did this?' . . . I don't know what I said, what I didn't say."

Five other participants discuss loved ones who died while they were incarcerated—parents, grandparents, and siblings. In several cases, they were not told of the deaths until many months after the funeral. In no case were they allowed to attend the service. Shabaka Brown was a match as a potential donor for his brother who was experiencing kidney failure. However, the prison refused to move him to the hospital for the transplant surgery, and his brother died a few days after. Brown did not learn of another brother's death for many weeks afterward because someone at the prison forgot to inform him. Gary James lost both parents and a grandparent during his twenty-six years of wrongful incarceration.

Finally, several exonerees describe their grief over the loss of fellow death row inmates who have been or will be executed. This particular experience of loss might be surprising to some, given that most inmates with whom exonerees served time were guilty of quite heinous crimes. However, our participants are quick to point out that they did not find their fellow inmates to be the "monsters" society paints them to be but instead thought of them as people with families and friends, hopes and dreams. In many cases, their fellow death row inmates were a primary support group on whom they relied for friendship. Juan Melendez explains this connection quite well: "That was one of the hardest parts of being there was when they kill somebody. You got to recognize this. You living in a cell. You got a man next door to you for nine years, ten years. You become attached without even knowing it. And he tells you things, and you tell him things. And you tell him things that you won't even tell your own family because nobody understands but you and him. So, he leans on your shoulder and you lean on his shoulder. And now they come; they snatch him—they kill him." He goes on to say that his day of release was a mixed bag of emotions: "I felt happy but I felt sad because I left them in there. . . . If we don't do something about it, they all can get killed."

Exonerees discuss how their grief was postponed during their incarceration. They were unable to grieve in a meaningful way because they were stripped of the rituals that typically mark the passing of a loved one; they were denied the love and support of family and friends; they were isolated from sharing their grief with others and were not allowed to attend the funerals. As Scott Taylor describes, "The whole time I was locked up, I never really actually, uh, it was still hard for me to believe that they were really dead because last time I seen them, they were alive. . . . I never was able to go to the funeral or mourn until I got out and actually visited [their graves] . . . fourteen years later." This thought brings him to tears as he discusses the disarray in which he found their grave sites on his visit the day of his release.

Gary Gauger provides a wrenching example of this postponed grief. Gauger shares the depth of his grief ten years after his parents' murders and seven years after his exoneration:

> The only way I could say I maybe had grieved a little bit was about a month and a half, two months after my arrest. I had a dream. And I was speaking with my mother. And then I realized, I said, "Oh wait a minute, but you were killed." And then she faded away. I asked her for a hug. [He begins to cry and whisper.] Man, I didn't wanna do this . . . um, I asked for a hug and then she faded away, and I started crying. And I woke up crying and that, I suppose, would have been the . . . [Gauger's speech slurs as he releases a deep, mournful sob. He continues whispering.] Oh man, oh man, I don't even wanna come close to that. That was as close as I had come to

mourning their murders, their deaths. . . . I probably had four or five emotional episodes since then. This is pretty close to one right now. *I feel like I'm a plastic barrier holding back the ocean.* [He laughs.] *You know, not much substance and a lot of weight.* (emphasis added)

The literature on grief and mourning provides a way to better understand exonerees' experiences with loss and postponed grief. Freud ([1917] 1984) argued that mourning, while difficult, is a process through which psychologically healthy individuals are expected to move toward resolution. This process is expected in cases of clear-cut loss, such as the death of a close family member where people gather to remember a loved one's life and recognize shared grief.[1] However, mourning is complicated when the loss is less defined and concrete: soldiers missing in action and children of war who have lost contact with family members in their countries of origin. These "ambiguous losses" represent a "unique kind of loss that defies closure, in which the status of a loved one as 'there' or 'not there' remains indefinitely unclear" (Boss 1999, 6).

Pauline Boss (1999) identifies two types of ambiguous loss. The first includes grief experienced over loved ones who are psychologically absent though physically present. She notes examples such as individuals suffering from Alzheimer's disease, various forms of mental illness, or addiction. Research into this type of ambiguous loss includes families of brain-injured ICU patients (Kean 2010), children with autism spectrum disorders (O'Brien 2007), and individuals with mild cognitive impairment (Blieszner et al. 2007). The second type of ambiguous loss includes feelings of grief over loved ones who are thought of as psychologically present though physically absent. Boss notes the type of grief managed by families of missing soldiers and grief for kidnapped children as two examples of this type of ambiguous loss. Research has examined other examples of this type, such as children of prisoners (Bocknek et al. 2009), families separated by war (Luster et al. 2009), and individuals who have disappeared during war (Robins 2010). Some family members may feel both types of loss at once. For example, Susan Sharp (2005) argues that family members of individuals on death row awaiting execution may experience both. The death row inmate may be physically absent though still psychologically present in family interactions, or the family may consider the inmate psychologically removed from daily life though still alive and thus physically present (see also Radelet et al. 1983; Vandiver 1989; Vandiver and Berardo 2000).

Boss argues that ambiguous loss can be particularly painful and difficult to manage because outside factors related to the uncertainty of the loved one's "death" interfere with more normal grieving processes. In many cases, "people are denied the symbolic rituals that ordinarily support a clear loss—such as a funeral after a death in the family. . . . Their experience remains unverified by the community around them, so that there is little validation of what they are experiencing or feeling" (Boss 1999, 8). The uncertainty and lack of validation can result in complicated grieving "in which a person remains stuck on and preoccupied with the lost object [person]," and thus cannot move through the normal grieving process (Boss 1999, 10). This is known as "frozen grief," in which a person becomes unable to resolve the loss because he or she is denied the typical cultural markers of death.

The postponed grief that many exonerees reveal may be best understood as frozen grief. They have, in effect, experienced a form of ambiguous loss. Their loved ones have died; however, they were denied access to the rituals and shared expressions of grief that mark clear-cut loss. In most cases, the last time they saw their loved one, the person was very much alive and involved in the exonerees' lives. Notification of the death is sudden, often unexpected, and sometimes delayed from its actual occurrence. They are not allowed to attend funeral services or participate in family gatherings surrounding the death. Although exonerees intellectually understand that their loved one is no longer physically present, the loved one still feels very much psychologically present in the exonerees' memory and emotional experience. Their grief and sadness become frozen as they are unable to move beyond the mourning process to resolve their feelings of loss.

Kirk Bloodsworth is emblematic of this frozen sadness. His mother, his staunchest supporter throughout his ordeal, died five months before his exoneration and release from prison. He was overwhelmed with emotion when recounting her death, and his anger over being denied access to her in those final moments was palpable:

Five months. That's all it was. Five months. She was gone. I had to view her body in handcuffs, shackles and leg chains for five minutes.

I couldn't even go to the funeral. It had literally killed her, this mess. She wouldn't go see a doctor because it cost too much money. She was always looking out for me. She hadn't bought a dress . . . she hadn't bought nothing. . . . She didn't want to spend the money for looking after me. It was Christmas of 1992, and she came [to the prison to tell me she was dying]. It was the last time I seen her alive.

Bloodsworth remembered when he first returned to his childhood home after his release to find his mother's clothes still hanging in the closet. He nestled into the clothing and surrounded himself with her things and her smell. He recounted days after release walking into the kitchen to find the lingering scent of her cigarette and sound of her voice, as if she had just walked out of the room. Since our interview with Bloodsworth in March 2004, we have seen him on numerous occasions give public talks about his wrongful conviction. Each time he becomes overwhelmed with emotion when discussing the death of his mother and openly weeps, still mourning her loss.

It may be more difficult to understand the feelings of loss exonerees' experience over the execution or pending execution of a death row prisoner, though feelings of frozen sadness characterize those losses as well. Our interview with Greg Wilhoit had many emotional moments, including when he described the night Chuck Coleman was executed. Coleman and another inmate, Roger Dale Stafford, befriended Wilhoit on death row. Wilhoit recounts, "These two guys, they were stone cold killers, but as long as they liked you and you didn't have something they wanted, they were pretty good guys. They liked me, and I didn't have jack shit, so we became fast friends." By Wilhoit's account, Coleman was under four sentences of death, and the time for his execution had finally arrived. Up to that point, Wilhoit had been quite clear to his fellow death row inmates that he was pro–death penalty. As he said, "I knew I didn't belong there but just because I had a death sentence hanging over my head didn't mean I was gonna compromise my convictions." He was the only person on death row in Oklahoma in favor of capital punishment, and he was quite vocal about his views, including to Coleman, whom he thought should be executed in spite of the fact that they were friends.

However, this all changed the night of Coleman's execution. Wilhoit recalls it as follows:

> They came on [the radio] at eleven minutes after midnight and announced that Charles Curry Coleman had been pronounced dead. And, like I said, I really didn't think it'd bother me. So nobody could have been more surprised than I was, I think, when instead of indifference, I was overwhelmed with grief. And this sounds corny, but it really is true. For one brief moment, the world actually stopped turning. It was as if time stood still. I had a moment of clarity such that I had never experienced before or since. Things that I couldn't see before now became glaringly obvious. The world wasn't a safer place to live in and the sun certainly wasn't going to shine any brighter just because my friend Chuck had been put down like a diseased animal. [Wilhoit begins to get emotional.] And I didn't change my mind about the death penalty because of my situation. I changed my mind . . . I'm sorry [crying] . . . I changed my mind because my friend got executed.

The sadness and grief over those they have lost are raw and lurking just below the surface. It takes very little to bring those emotions forward, and they reexperience them as if coping with them for the first time. Unless they have been able to pay for counseling services, they are left to manage these deep losses on their own and with the support of family members.

LOSS OF TIME

A second theme of loss is the time they lost while incarcerated. Our eighteen participants averaged nine and a half years incarcerated after their convictions.[2] This does not include the time many spent in jail awaiting trial, which for some adds another two or three years onto their total time of incarceration for these charges. The time spent in prison ranged from two years each for Alfred Rivera, Delbert Tibbs, and Dave Keaton to the twenty-six years each served by codefendants Gary James and Tim Howard. At the time of their release, several participants had spent as much as one-third to one-half of their entire lifetimes incarcerated for a crime they did not commit. They are keenly aware of the time they have lost. Tim Howard and Gary James were incarcerated at the age of twenty-three for a robbery–homicide. They spent the first year on death row before the Supreme Court of Ohio commuted all death sentences to life in prison. In total, they were incarcerated for twenty-six years. As Howard notes, "At first, they tried to execute me. Then I had to spend a lot of years, over a half my life, in prison." And as Juan Melendez poignantly explains, "I became an old man in there." He went onto death row in Florida as a father at age thirty-three; he came out almost eighteen years later a grandfather. For Greg Wilhoit, this loss makes him relish the little things in life even more: "I'd go to the grocery store . . . didn't have any money to buy anything, but would just browse. Yeah, I've tried to make up for lost time. I enjoy time every fucking day."

Aside from simply being cognizant of the passage of time, they frequently reflect on what they missed: valuable time with family and children and opportunities to build a life—to marry, have children, parent, and build financial security. Two exonerees became fathers soon after they were incarcerated: "Immediately upon my release, the very first thing I did was pick up my son in my arms, who was born while I was in jail. I never had a chance to touch him before then. . . . I had waited so long to feel him and kiss him. It was the greatest thing to me at that moment" (Alfred Rivera). Rivera ponders whether he would have married the mother of his son and started a life with them had his wrongful conviction not occurred. Gary James was convicted at the age of twenty-three and exonerated at nearly fifty. He laments that he missed the opportunity to have children but thinks the time has now passed: "I would like a family, but it's kind of unrealistic. I don't have no kids. And, I don't know, I don't think I'm gonna have none. You know at this point, that's the only thing I want. I would like to have at least one." Perry Cobb recounts a horrific story of how his eleven-year-old daughter was kidnapped and repeatedly raped while he was incarcerated. He was told about this incident after his release. We asked him what he did after finding out, and he replied, exasperated, "What can I do?" He reiterates several times that he feels sadness over not being there to help his daughter deal with what happened to her. He feels robbed of the time to parent his child and now there is "nothing I could do about that. But I'll never forget."

LOSS OF RELATIONSHIPS

Exonerees also regret the lost relationships with family and friends who have drifted out of their lives. In two cases, participants lost custody of their children because of their wrongful convictions. Gary Gauger's ex-wife and new husband adopted his youngest daughter and took away his visitation rights while he was in prison. Upon release, they obtained an order of protection against him to ensure he had no contact with her. Although he did eventually contact his son, he was unable to redevelop a meaningful relationship with him. Sabrina Butler lost custody of her oldest son to his paternal grandmother while she was incarcerated. After her release, she battled for four years to regain custody of him.

In other cases, friends and family believed in the exonerees' guilt and abandoned them. Although Gary Gauger's twin sister was supportive during and after his incarceration, his brother was not: "About two months before trial, he decided I was guilty. Removed himself from my exoneration team. Even when I was scheduled to be released, he was still going around telling relatives that I was guilty. . . . There is no relationship." Several others remain angry about being set adrift by friends when they were needed most. After exonerees' release, their former friends often reappear, wanting to resume previous relationships. But exonerees hesitate because they feel abandoned and forgotten. Scott Taylor recalls that he received Christmas cards from old friends the first Christmas after his release, cards that made him angry because he needed them more when he was on death row than he did once he was released. Thus, while exonerees attempt to make up for lost time by repairing and rebuilding relationships, in many instances these relationships are beyond repair and are lost altogether.

LOSS OF SECURITY

Loss of security refers to the inability of some exonerees to feel safe and free from surveillance and suspicion. This theme emerged early in our interviews and was not a subject we had anticipated uncovering. We then incorporated a question about security into the remainder of the interviews. It is important to note that several participants had not given this much thought or had definite negative reactions to the idea that they felt unsafe in some way. As Juan Melendez emphatically states, "I ain't got time to be worrying about things like that. If they gonna do it [rearrest him for something], do it. If they don't, they don't." So while this is not a fear shared by all participants, it was a recurring theme. Many feared being retried for the same crime or being connected to a new crime in some way. After all, they had been wrongfully convicted once before; they saw no reason to assume it could not happen again.

To manage this fear, they developed strategies to increase their feelings of security when in public. Kirk Bloodsworth explained how he always made sure someone knew where he was, just in case he needed an alibi. Alan Gell recounts that when he first was released and was traveling for public speaking engagements, "I was really paranoid about being falsely accused again." At every hotel, he would have a few drinks and strike up a conversation with the bartender to ensure that he would be remembered. He also would chat with the desk clerk before going to bed and write down the clerk's name on a slip of paper to keep in his pocket. Perry Cobb's father kept a log of his comings and goings in the first months after prison. Ray Krone's description of the precautions he took when traveling back to Arizona (where his wrongful conviction took place) are revealing of his own feelings about loss of security:

> So I have been back to Arizona. I traveled in groups. I didn't drive in a car or get by myself anywhere. I was actually in a bar one night having some drinks and some trouble started. And I got the hell up outta there quick. I didn't wanna be around anywhere that there was anything going on. . . . I was very careful where I went. I took one of these little microphones, a little recorder along with me in my pocket, just in case I ever did get stopped. I was gonna have that thing running.

While some might think such measures are unnecessary and exonerees are simply overreacting, they would disagree. And some evidence indicates they may be accurately perceiving their risk. Two exonerees were approached by police soon after release and asked about other crimes under investigation. The exonerees believed that they were approached simply because of who they were. Alan Gell got the most direct confirmation that his caution was well founded:

> I did find out that I won't just being paranoid. . . . About seven months after my release, [one of my attorneys] called me up, and

he was like . . . "Well, I just wanted to let you know that you got a clean inspection." And I was like, "Clean inspection? What are you talking about?" And he's like, "Well, I got word from the grapevine that the SBI had an agent following you around after you were released. And so far they hadn't saw you drinking and driving or soliciting a prostitute or just anything that might be illegal."

Gell was incensed that he had been the target of investigation, as if officials were just waiting for a reason to rearrest him.

Although the greatest fear participants have is of confrontations with criminal justice officials, two exonerees also noted that they feared other people as well. Perry Cobb eventually left Chicago because of his feelings of insecurity about the criminal justice system and because of encounters he had with family members of the victim in his case. On one occasion, family members cornered Cobb and his date in a movie theater. They were able to escape without injury, but the incident left them shaken and angry. He finally decided to begin a new life in a different city and state where he was not well known or recognizable, and his sense of security increased dramatically after his move. Scott Taylor moved away from the city in which he was exonerated for similar reasons. His exoneration was high profile, with his story and photo splashed across print and television media. He admits being uncomfortable going out in public for fear that someone who disagreed with his exoneration might accost him.

FEELINGS OF LOSS and grief are engrained in our conversations with exonerees. These feelings do not appear to be attenuated with the passage of time. Possibly these are emotions that could have been dealt with if exonerees had access to mental health services after release, but few do. As a result, they are left to grapple with an emptiness in their lives created by the losses of time, security, relationships, and loved ones. These losses make obvious to exonerees all that is missing in the new lives they try to rebuild.

CHAPTER 6

Rebuilding Relationships

> [My parents], they lost their identity pretty much.
> Everywhere they went they were like the mother or
> the father of an individual so vile and so reprehensible
> that not only had he forfeited his right to live in
> society, he'd forfeited his right to live altogether. Try
> living with that. My parents, you know, they did it for
> nine years.   —Greg Wilhoit

THE IMPACT OF A WRONGFUL conviction extends
beyond the exoneree to include family members and partners (see also
Grounds 2004; Sharp 2005). Studies of families of incarcerated inmates
and trauma survivors similarly reveal that such experiences are disruptive
to the family unit (Austin and Hardyman 2004; Ferraro et al. 1983;
Fullerton and Ursano 1997; Jamieson and Grounds 2005; Murray 2005;
Travis and Waul 2003; Williams et al. 2003). However, this dimension
of the aftermath receives even less attention than the direct impact of the
wrongful conviction on the exoneree. But, of course, family members of
exonerees watched while their loved ones were arrested and charged
with unspeakable crimes. They often sat in the courtroom as witness
after witness portrayed their child or sibling as a monster and heard the
jury and judge condemn them to extermination because they were no
longer worthy of life. Loved ones were then left to build a life around
periodic visits to prison, occasional letters, missed births and birthdays,
and constant worry. Exonerees watched from prison as children were
born and grew up, siblings and parents died, and spouses divorced them.
Then, just as suddenly as they were taken away, our participants, one
day, were released from prison and reinserted back into family dynamics
that had become accustomed to their absence. They struggle to reestablish a place within the family unit. For better or worse, their relationships

with those closest to them are never the same again. Without interviews with family members themselves, we cannot say for sure what their experience of the wrongful conviction was, but we offer some insight through the perspectives of our participants.

WEB OF IMPACT

Participants often noted the impact of their wrongful conviction and incarceration on those closest to them. As Alfred Rivera describes, "I would like others to know about my experience with regard to my family, that they were affected in many ways as far as trying to cope with a loved one being sentenced to death for a false conviction. They cried many tears. Some stayed strong for me and some disappeared because they couldn't cope with the situation." The participants focused primarily on their parents, siblings, and children. About his own parents, Perry Cobb describes how overpowering the stress and worry was:

> If you can imagine your child is in jail somewhere and you're watching the news and you see there's been some type of killing up in that same jail where your child [is]. You know that's gonna keep you on edge until you get your child up out of there. And if you can't get 'em out and they send 'em to [the] penitentiary or to death row, how is that gonna make you feel? Your child is gonna go on death row with all these murderers. . . . You know your child is innocent, but he had to get locked up. Don't you know that's tearing that mama up?

Several exonerees discuss the sacrifices parents made to continue the investigation and pay for attorneys in their cases. Kirk Bloodsworth tearfully recounts how his mother would not buy things for herself and had holes in her clothes so that she could continue to support him. Ray Krone's parents went to forensic conferences to seek out experts in bite-mark evidence to counter the prosecution's claims of a bite-mark match in his case. Alan Gell says this of his mother, "She's struggling like for years. She's focused on trying to . . . get me home. It's like [she] wakes up every day and thinks, 'God, I want my boy back home. I need my son. I love my baby. Just give me my baby back.' She would call my lawyers and write letters and just communicate with other people on the progress of it [his case] and everything." While most of the exonerees focused specifically on their mothers, Kirk Bloodsworth also discussed how difficult the situation was for his father to manage. His father had to cope not only with the wrongful conviction and loss of his son but also with the stress and worry that consumed his wife (Bloodsworth's mother), who eventually died before Bloodsworth's exoneration after a battle with cancer. Bloodsworth noted that his father suffered greatly during those years while trying to manage the stress and sadness.

In several cases, exonerees reflected on the impact of their wrongful conviction on siblings who were left behind. Alan Gell's little sister was nine years old when he went to jail at age twenty. She finished elementary school, middle school, and high school in a small community where everyone knew who she was. Although Gell claims that she did not face much stigmatization because of his conviction, she was sheltered by their parents, who limited her social life during those years. They feared she might get involved with drugs and the "wrong crowd" and be led down a path similar to Gell's. The fear of losing two children was more than they could bear. The impact of Gary Gauger's wrongful conviction on his twin sister, Ginger, was particularly difficult, given that she also lost her parents in the homicide for which Gauger was convicted. Although Gary and Ginger remained close throughout the experience, they became estranged from their brother when he decided that Gauger was guilty. At the time of the crime, Ginger and her husband were ski instructors and living far from the small farmhouse and bike shop in rural Illinois where Gauger was living with his parents. After her parents' deaths and Gauger's incarceration, Ginger and her husband quit their jobs and moved back to manage the farm. Gauger describes his sister's experience as disorienting and traumatic: "All of a sudden, she's in my parents' house and nobody's around, and it's empty, and it's all surreal, and her whole life has been flipped upside down." According to Gauger, Ginger's interpretation was as if "aliens had landed and abducted me and my parents."

Finally, exonerees often discuss the impact of their wrongful convictions on their children who, in many cases, were quite young when the exonerees were initially tried and convicted (see also Vollen and Eggers 2005). Studies examining the impact of a parent's incarceration on children have found that children struggle with many issues, including feelings of shame, rejection, and guilt, stigma, declining school performance, and mental health problems (Blieszner et al. 2007; Dallaire 2007; Fishman 1981; Murray 2005; Shillingford and Edwards 2008; Travis and Waul 2003). In many ways, children of those wrongly convicted are quite similar. In some cases, children struggled with being stigmatized because of the death sentences carried by their parents. Several reveal how their children were bullied and left out by other children. The parents' pain was obvious as they recounted learning about the abuse heaped upon their children because of their own wrongful convictions. Cobb remembers, "I got my baby girl who was going to school and who had friends whose parents didn't want them to play with her because they daddy had been earmarked an armed robber and a murderer. This one [child] hurt my youngest baby. Know that hurts. She crying. Got little scratches on her face. Nothing I could do about that. But I'll never forget that." Delbert Tibbs considers the possible impact his incarceration had on his son whom Tibbs told, at a young age, to "take care of your mom and your sister." Tibbs fears his son felt underappreciated and replaced when Tibbs was exonerated and returned as a hero. His son struggled many years with complex problems after his father's release.

Although most exonerees note the negative impact that their wrongful convictions had on family members, a few also point to positive outcomes. In particular, they note that the trial, conviction, and incarceration constituted a journey they took together with their families and that the shared journey, in the end, brought them closer together. For several exonerees who were not terribly close to family before their wrongful conviction, they learned from the experience who they could truly count on and who truly mattered. Greg Wilhoit explains how being sent to death row brought him closer to his family: "I have a wonderful family. . . . I owe my relationship now with my family for being on death row. I was kind of an absent family member at a lot of functions and stuff. I didn't have any problems with my family. They just weren't much fun is the way I looked at it. . . . But no, that all changed. It made me, well, like they say, 'You don't appreciate what you got until you don't have it anymore.'" After his release, Wilhoit became very close to his parents and his sister, Nancy, and rebuilt relationships with his children. This family support became essential in the last several years as Wilhoit struggled to survive a life-threatening accident and serious illness. Charles Fain also notes that the quality of his relationships with his father and siblings was positively impacted by his time on death row, which provided the impetus his father needed to stop drinking, something that had always impaired their ability to connect. After his release, Fain noticed that he, his father, and his siblings do a better job of keeping up and generally show more affection than in the past.

Negative or positive, the ripple effects of a wrongful conviction extend beyond the life of the exoneree to touch the lives of all those with whom the exoneree has relationships. Although no doubt exonerees need assistance in coping with their emotions, losses, and adjustment, the same can be said for their family members. They need help as individuals but also as a family unit in negotiating the process of rebuilding their relationships with each other.

REESTABLISHING RELATIONSHIPS

A common thread that emerged from their discussions about the impact of their wrongful convictions on family is the challenge of rebuilding those relationships when they come home (Sharp 2005). Delbert Tibbs notes, "All of the brokenness that you might suspect was there." Even though he has been out of prison for over thirty years, he admits that he still is trying to rebuild those broken relationships from so many years ago. The difficulty of that process is shaped by the amount of time the exoneree was away. Rediscovering common ground and reconstructing shared experiences can be jolting and exhausting. Alan Gell explains trying to fill that gap of time with his younger sister:

> My youngest sister, she was nine whenever I went away, and she was at the elementary school here. . . . I remember a lot from nine back, but I don't have no memories of nine forward until I got out. Mom would send me pictures and stuff, but of course she didn't want to take my sister into the prison scene and everything. Going in with her nine and coming out with her seventeen fixing to graduate high school was like, what in the world? We can't talk about the same things we used to talk about. And this is odd to suddenly realize that she was a stranger, and I didn't know who in the hell she was. And we had to build the relationship from scratch.

Another factor that makes reestablishing relationships difficult is the fact that everyone has been traumatized by the experience and is trying to cope in their own way. It may be easy to see that exonerees are struggling to readjust but forget that their family members are as well, and it is often difficult for everyone to work through their own feelings of grief and loss to find each other. As Greg Wilhoit so aptly states about his relationship with his parents after release: "Our anguish was overlapping." While they share the experience of trying to adjust to the new situation, their styles of coping with that adjustment may sometimes clash. For example, Alan Gell and Greg Wilhoit both explain how they often got into disputes with their parents, with whom they were living after release. Their parents wanted them close by and wanted to limit their behavior (out of fear), while Gell and Wilhoit wanted to "stretch their legs" and enjoy their freedom. In both cases, our participants eventually moved out of their parents' home though maintained close emotional relationships with them.

It would be wrong, however, to leave the impression that these relationships are always irrevocably damaged. In many cases, exonerees successfully rebuilt relationships in spite of significant overlapping trauma. Wilhoit's parents remain among his staunchest supporters and have recently played key roles in helping him regain his seriously damaged health. Alan Gell reports a new appreciation for his stepfather with whom he frequently clashed before his conviction. But after seeing his stepfather's unflinching support for his mother and himself during the time of his incarceration, Gell realized that his stepfather was deserving of his respect and admiration. Delbert Tibbs talks about his children, brimming with a father's pride. Though their relationships with family may be damaged when they first return, the relationships are not always beyond repair.

Another theme many exonerees address is the problem of relearning how to socialize with other adults, in particular how to manage intimate relationships, an issue also noted among exonerees getting assistance from LAEP (Vollen and Eggers 2005). Interestingly, our sole woman exoneree, Sabrina Butler, did not discuss this issue, though many of the men did, all of whom are heterosexual. First, they note that relearning the social cues and complexities of appropriate social interaction is difficult when they get out. They found the social dynamics in prison to be much more clear-cut and up-front. Initially, the nuances of social interaction on the outside baffled them: "There's a lot of gray area . . . when you get to acting with adults . . . and people that you know . . . there's a lot of gray area. You gotta get back used to them. See, in there it was . . . a lot of this stuff was straightforward. . . . Out here, it's a lot more complex" (Gary James).

This problem is then compounded in intimate relationships, especially given that cultural norms governing appropriate heterosexual dynamics had shifted dramatically for some exonerees who had been incarcerated for long periods of time. One participant noted that he had missed the entire women's movement! Expectations for men in heterosexual relationships in the 1970s and early 1980s, when several exonerees went into prison, had changed significantly by their release in the early 2000s (Cherlin and Walters 1981; Ehrenreich 1983; Schnittker 2007; Thornton and Young-DeMarco 2001). This shift confounded many of them. They simply did not know how to behave. In some cases, exonerees who were married when they went into prison were divorced soon after release. Several struggled with monogamy, drifting in and out of relationships. One admitted that he had been arrested several times on domestic violence and disorderly conduct charges.

Several exonerees revealed that sexual intimacy was difficult for them. One admitted that he simply could not get sexually aroused. "Contrary to popular belief, not all inmates are sexually ravenous when released; after years of suppressing sexual urges, many exonerees experience substantially decreased sexual drives" (Vollen and Eggers 2005, 42). Kirk Bloodsworth and Shabaka Brown both explained how such intimate contact was uncomfortable early on. They instead preferred their space. Brown says, "I think my most difficult adjustment was sleeping with another person. Lying next to another person. You sleep, and you feel this person shift and you're, 'Where the hell you come from?' You know, because you been in a cell by yourself. You didn't have no human contact there." Bloodsworth agrees: "It takes me a while to warm up to somebody, not because I don't want to have sex but because I'm scared to. . . . I want my little space on this side of the bed." Difficulty rekindling intimate relationships with earlier partners or developing new ones was clearly an area that caused many participants a great deal of frustration.

IT IS MISGUIDED to think that the impact of a wrongful capital conviction is felt only by the exoneree. While the exoneree certainly bears the brunt of the aftermath, the ripple effects of the loss, grief, and stigma are felt by all of those within their immediate circle of support. They too have been traumatized by the wrongful conviction, and when the exoneree returns, the entire family is left, mostly on their own, to try to find their way back to a new normal.

CHAPTER 7

Negotiating Emotional Terrain

A lot of times if I'm speaking . . . I'm asked, "Listen
Shabaka, do you have hatred?" I say, "Yes." "Do you
have bitterness?" I say, "Yes." "Are you frustrated?"
I say, "Yes." "Are you angry?" I say, "Yes. Why
shouldn't I [be]?"   —Shabaka Brown

THE RANGE OF EMOTIONS with which exonerees
struggle after release is broad and deep and in some cases debilitating.
This emotional turmoil interferes with their interpersonal relationships
and employment and contributes to dependencies on drugs and alcohol.
Few received psychological assistance or counseling upon release and
thus face this terrain alone or with the help of family and friends who
stick with them through the struggle (Illinois Criminal Justice
Information Authority 2002). Not surprisingly, our participants describe
multiple emotions consistent with posttraumatic stress disorder (PTSD),
including depression, detachment, disorientation, mistrust, and survivor
guilt. In his psychiatric evaluations of eighteen wrongly convicted
individuals, Adrian Grounds (2004, 168–169) also finds evidence of
PTSD and "enduring personality change" caused by their long-term
catastrophic experience. Robert Simon's (1993) case studies of three
falsely arrested and jailed individuals similarly demonstrate evidence of
PTSD and other short-term dissociative, adjustment, and anxiety disorders (see also Vollen and Eggers 2005). Trauma survivors of all types
note a similar range of emotions and reactions (Brashers et al. 1999;
Brison 2002; Erikson 1976; Lifton 1967; Schneider 1975; Schoenfeld
2005). We focus, here, on what they describe as their most intractable
and enduring emotional battles.

THE DESTRUCTION OF TRUST

More exonerees raised the problem of trust than any other single emotional issue. Other studies of exonerees after release also find distrust is common (Campbell and Denov 2004; Illinois Criminal Justice Information Authority 2002; Vollen and Eggers 2005). Although a few participants related that they gained insight into whom or what to trust as a result of their experience (such as loved ones, their appellate attorney, or the media), the overwhelming majority recounted how their wrongful conviction destroyed their trust in the criminal justice system and people in general. Many admit that this represents a significant shift from before their wrongful conviction, noting that they had strongly believed in "the system" and rule of law. As Dave Keaton says, "I was brought up [believing] the right thing. . . . I believed in the law. I believed that if a man or woman went to jail or to prison, they did what they was charged [with]. Shoot, I [have] changed my whole outlook. It was just destroyed."

The most common target for their mistrust is the government, government officials, the law—"the system." Prior to their wrongful convictions, most held government officials and criminal justice personnel in high regard. At the same time that they admit their distrust, they also admit to the depth of their astonishment and disappointment at how wrong and corrupt the system can be. This astonishment and disappointment is expressed by Scott Taylor: "The thing that really, really, really bothered me . . . [the system officials who prosecuted his case] didn't even come close to telling the truth. [They] didn't even come close to the truth."

This disillusionment is at the heart of Alan Gell's recollection of when his lawyer discovered evidence that would eventually exonerate him. Gell's conviction hinged on the testimony of two fifteen-year-old young women; one was Gell's ex-girlfriend. The two girls testified that they were present when Gell shot Allen Ray Jenkins. The girls had told numerous conflicting versions of events to police and prosecutors. One had been audiotaped talking with her boyfriend about the story she would fabricate to tell police. The tape was never disclosed to Gell's defense attorneys. Prosecutors also failed to disclose police interviews with numerous witnesses who said they had seen Jenkins, alive and well, many days after the day Gell was alleged to have killed him. Four years after his capital conviction and seven since his initial arrest, Gell's appellate attorney revealed that this evidence had been discovered, and she hoped that his conviction now would be overturned:

I just was happy. It's hard to put into words how happy and elated I was. . . . I left that attorney's visit and went back to my block celebrating. I told everybody I'd be home next week 'cause I had evidence that surfaced! It was like a year and a half later that I finally went home. But, I remember that night laying in bed, thinking, "Oh my God. It's finally Christmas. I knew there was something out there that could help me. Damn right. I knew it." And then, in the middle of the happiness, celebrating and throwing my party, I just got slapped real hard [with] reality. Where was it [the evidence]? Where did it go? The state had it in their files? Where the girls said they had to make up a story? Don't that mean that they [the prosecution and police] knew that the story was made up? Don't that mean that they put people on the stand to testify against me knowing they weren't telling the truth? Seventeen people saw [Jenkins] alive. What if they [the state] knew the seventeen? What does that imply? What does that mean? I suddenly had to deal with, why? . . . For years, I believed that the girls had manipulated the system and that the system didn't know no better. They weren't the system's fault. They [the state] just believed them, and the girls misled them. . . . Suddenly, I'm seeing a whole different picture. They [police and prosecutors] knew, and they're conspiring with them [the girls]. . . . I'm not guilty, and they know I'm not. And yet they're still trying to kill me. How crazy does that sound? But, it was true. . . . It wasn't so much raising anger as it was disappointment. I had still believed in the system, even though I was on death row. I still believed in the system. I just felt like the system had been manipulated by the girls. Part of my belief that I'd one day be found innocent and back home where I belonged was just the system was gonna catch the problem. And [now] I had just been told by my lawyer that the system was the problem. So, it really messed me up. . . . I still find it discouraging that I'm the hundred and thirteenth mistake [one hundred and thirteen person exonerated from death row]. It seems like after the second mistake or first mistake, you'd say, "Oh wait. How are we doing this?" And try to prevent it from happening again.

Interestingly, Gell's disillusionment with the system did not result from his initial wrongful conviction. Even after being sent to death row for a crime he did not commit, he still believed in the efficacy of the system and that, in fact, the system would come to his final rescue. His distrust of the system took root only after the failures of the system itself came to his attention during the reinvestigation of the case. A similar realization as to the complicity of the system and state officials in their wrongful convictions characterizes the distrust of several others. After uncovering the details behind the wrongful conviction of Gary James and himself, Tim Howard angrily blurts out, "I'm saying it was conspiracy! It was a plot. These people plotted. This wasn't no mistake." Their distrust and disillusionment is coupled with a new disregard for those in authority whom they see as responsible for their wrongful convictions. Perry Cobb observes, "These are people that you are supposed to have high regard for. . . . People who are in office who have your life in their hands, most of them are more crooked than a tree itself. And it's hard for me to have any respect for any of them."

A second theme of distrust focuses on people in general and relationships with women more particularly. Exonerees are wary of people and cautious of their motives for befriending them. In some cases, details about their cases are well known, including pending compensation or lawsuits, and they fear that people, women in particular, want something from them—fame, money, public attention. Scott Taylor says, "My main thing is trust. . . . Somebody might want to come and be my friend now. For what, now? What's your motive for wanting to be my friend? You think [you're] . . . gonna get paid, because you saw me on TV or it's a big deal?" Gary James notes that he is frequently approached by women at the bar where he works. He is suspicious, acknowledging that "everybody knows I got a lawsuit [pending]." He goes on to explain how he decides whether to start a relationship with a woman: "So how I get into a relationship . . . I might be sending them through some tests. . . . I say, 'Well, if they can get through this, they gonna win,' but ain't none of them got through it."

Alan Gell's distrust of women as prospective romantic partners and subsequent misgivings about relationships constitute a reaction to the role that women played in his wrongful conviction:

> When I first got out, of course, I desired to meet a girl and be with a girl, but I didn't think that I could trust a girl. . . . I thought that I might end up being betrayed or backstabbed or hurt again. So, what I did is I created this image of what a girl was or what a woman was. And it was basically biblical. They're all horrible and terrible persons that cause nothing but grief and pain to men. . . . *I had to consider that, and this is like literal, my last girlfriend almost killed me.* (emphasis added)

Greg Wilhoit admits that his general mistrust of people also is rooted in the realization that his trust had been misplaced so often during his case: "Every lawyer I've had, except Mark Barrett [his appellate attorney], has screwed me. But am I bitter?"

Repeatedly, exonerees raise the issue of trust. They are openly skeptical about the operation of the criminal justice system and are disheartened by the abuses of power that they believe played key roles in their own wrongful convictions. Even these many years later, they were surprised by the gulf between their prior belief in the efficacy and honesty of the system and the failures of that system on display in their cases. This distrust seeps into other aspects of their lives as well, affecting their relationships and level of comfort around others.

Guilt

Second to trust, exonerees struggle with guilt. Survivor guilt is a symptom of PTSD (American Psychiatric Association 2000) and is common among survivors of catastrophic and life-threatening events, ranging from the Holocaust, war, and natural disasters to disease (Ayalon et al. 2007; Brison 2002; Erikson 1976; Herman 1997; Lee Hyer et al. 1990; Lifton 1967, 1970, 1985; Schneider 1975; Wayment et al. 1995). The guilt our participants describe revolves around two primary issues: survivor guilt over those who remain incarcerated and on death row and guilt for behaviors they worry put them at risk for their wrongful conviction. In effect, they feel partly responsible for their plight, despite not having committed capital murder.

Survivor guilt occurs when exonerees question why they were "saved" from execution while others were not (see Lifton 1967). As Gary Gauger queries, "There's a lot of people in jail that don't deserve to be there. You feel guilty about it. You just, 'Why was I spared and they weren't?' . . . It's very hard on you emotionally." While they are relieved to be exonerated, they feel guilt and responsibility for those left behind. For Juan Melendez, this guilt emerged on the very day of his release. Within hours of learning of his release, he had gathered his belongings and left the prison grounds. He describes the emotional process of leaving death row in Florida after almost eighteen years:

> And then they took me upstairs [to my cell], and by that time, the news had spread. Some of them [fellow death row inmates] know it. And then I told them, I say, "I'm fixin' to leave tonight." . . . One of them sent me a cup of coffee. I gave all my stuff away. . . . A friend of mine sent me a cigar, and told me to light it up when I get back home. And they sent me pictures and stuff like that so I take them with me. And then when they came and got me, I was in the next cell to last, and I couldn't say nothing. I just got up and looked at my friend next door to me, then I looked at everyone of them. Some of them was crying. Some of them say to me, "Good luck and take it easy down there." And then all of them start clapping their hands, and then I could hear the clapping on all the floors. And I left. . . . I felt happy but I felt sad because I left them in there. . . . And I still feel sad today about it. [Melendez lets out a frustrating and emotional sigh and gets up to walk around.]

Scott Taylor echoes this experience as he describes looking back at the prison as he drove away on his day of release: "I could look right back to where I was for all those years. And it really made me sad, even though it was a joyful time in my life. And it's still sad to this day that these guys are still in those cages like animals. I don't even like going to the zoo now."

In many ways, they feel a responsibility to those left behind, a responsibility to stay in touch, fight for them, tell their stories. But they find that guilt disrupts their ability to stay in touch with those who remain on death row, even those with whom they had friendships. They do not know what to say, what to discuss, what to reveal in those contacts. They feel guilty for discussing their newly constructed lives on the outside and even more so for complaining about the array of problems they are confronting; after all, those still on death row "aren't outside; they are in there; it don't feel right," as Juan Melendez explains. Gary Gauger says,

> I thought I would write prisoners I knew that were still behind bars, and I cannot bring myself to write them. I cannot bring myself to read their letters. I had a really good friend who's stuck there for life. . . . I can't bring myself to read his letters. I can't write people. . . . I don't know why. I feel very guilty about it. But, I know what they're going through. I know what they're into. And I feel like all I can say is, "Yeah. That's too bad. Sucks, don't it?" I just don't feel I have anything for them. I have nothing to give them. And I know that any kind of letter's gold in prison. I really should give them that. I don't.

Guilt compounds guilt and prevents them from contacting those left behind, which compounds their emotional distress. Delbert Tibbs simply says, "It's very painful just to be in touch with that."

A smaller number of exonerees also feel guilt over what they perceive as their partial responsibility for their wrongful conviction. Although they acknowledge the failures of the system that resulted in their arrest and conviction, they also argue that the fact that they were well known to police in the area made them easy targets for officials looking for someone to arrest. They feel guilt over their past lives, in particular the impact of those histories on their loved ones, and believe that they set themselves up for their wrongful arrest and conviction. Alan Gell is emblematic of this type of guilt:

> My lifestyle at the time before I was arrested, I was doing drugs, dealing drugs, and using. Didn't have a job. I thought that life was one big party. Already had pretty much shamed and disgraced my mom to the point that I wasn't a productive person in what way she probably envisioned me being when I was younger. . . . The police would have never been able to even entertain the idea that I've done

this had I been something other than a drug dealer. Had I been something positive in our society. So, I beat myself up over it. . . . I looked at it as what I had done to my family. . . . It really ate me up.

Possibly, Gell is overestimating the extent to which his prior history played into the willingness of police and prosecutors to "entertain the idea" that he had committed the homicide. A clean record and legitimate employment did not prevent the state from prosecuting Ray Krone, a postal worker and honorably discharged veteran with no criminal record, or Kirk Bloodsworth, a star athlete and honorably discharged marine with no prior record. Regardless, Gell reports struggling significantly with this guilt while he was in prison, knowing that his mother was suffering as the subject of gossip and rumor in his hometown in rural North Carolina.

Thus, guilt, in one form or another, plagues the emotions of exonerees. It interferes with their ability to embrace their freedom and serves as a constant reminder of the painful past they are trying to move beyond. Bound in this way to those in their past, they buckle under the weight of claiming responsibility for their own happiness and those they still feel responsible for.

BOUTS OF ANGER

The anger exonerees feel is easy to access. They openly discuss the anger they experience over a variety of issues—anger over their false convictions, over the time they lost with family and friends, over the conditions they were subjected to while incarcerated, over people who forgot about them when they were incarcerated. However, they also recognize how overwhelming this particular emotion could be if not managed. Shabaka Brown says, "God forbid if a day comes that those emotions so overwhelm me that I can't deal with it. I hope that I will be in a room by myself because I cannot sit here and tell either of you that if such would ever happen that I would be able to deal with the feelings I have." They understand the necessity to control that anger and find a coping mechanism that works for them.

Several exonerees reveal that their anger has been easy to trigger and has overwhelmed them when they could no longer hold it in. Alfred Rivera explains that "my anger was encased from the outset but then it came flowing out, and I couldn't hold it anymore," and Gary James recognizes that at one time "the least little thing would make me angry." Shabaka Brown recounts a time when he and his wife saw the movie *The Hurricane* about Rubin "Hurricane" Carter.[1] A particular scene in the movie reminded Brown of the night on death row when he almost committed suicide. He found himself overcome with anger: "I left my wife sitting in the movie. I just had to get out of there." He took a walk to decompress and gain control of his emotions.

Exonerees identify multiple triggers to their anger. Kirk Bloodsworth's anger appeared when he began discussing his experiences in prison. He became more and more agitated while describing having to eat the same food every day, watch as others were raped, stabbed, and beaten up, and sleep underneath the gas chamber. Alan Gell describes how the anger he fears might take control of him if confronted with the two girls who served as the primary witnesses against him at trial, girls who are now young women living in his community. Scott Taylor's anger is most prominent when discussing the friends and family who deserted him when he needed them most:

> I'm angry. . . . Where were these people when I was pleading these things? Where were you? Where were you? Sixteen years. Where were you? Now everybody wants to be my friend. . . . Those who I want to be around were the people that were there when my back was to the wall. I don't like fair-weather friends. . . . I don't need your support and concern now. I needed it when I was being falsely accused and I was in this hellhole and these people are intending on killing me.

Taylor returns to the subject later on in the interview, clearly still upset: "That's what angers me. These fair-weather friends and it's not what they can do for you; it's what they can get out of you. And it just angers me."

At the same time, they realize the importance of controlling and coping with their anger. One motivating factor behind the need to control the rage is the fear of being overcome by it. Another is the acknowledgment that confrontations risk drawing public and police attention to them. They very much want to stay out of the spotlight to decrease the risk of being caught in the system again. For those who have chosen to advocate for changes to the system by using their cases as exemplars of what can go wrong, they recognize the futility of expressing their anger to those in positions of power. Alan Gell tells us that "screaming and hollering" will not get the outcomes he seeks. Instead, he says, "I got to put a smile on my face, and I got to go in, and I got to be talking reasonably and rationally and hide that anger, keep that anger down and keep it from surfacing, keep something ugly from happening."

An emotion related to anger identified by some exonerees was their focus on revenge. Interestingly, it was only among this small number of exonerees that the anger expressed more generally was directed at officials whom they perceived to be at fault for their convictions. Anger and hostility directed personally at those responsible was not widely expressed, though, as noted earlier, distrust of those parties most certainly was. But a small group did direct their anger at police and prosecutors whom they wanted held accountable for their failures. As Tim Howard says about the assistant district attorney who prosecuted his case: "He's not going to keep stepping on me. And just because I receive some financial funds from this [through a lawsuit pending against the state] doesn't mean I'm going to stop banging him. I'm going to bang him until he can't take it no more, until he realizes that he can't do people like that. Just because you poor and whatever color you are, you just can't treat people any kind of way." Howard concludes with a promise, "They started it. I'll finish it. Okay? Put it that way." Howard's anger is focused specifically on the individuals he holds personally responsible for his twenty-six years in prison, and his anger is directed at exacting revenge for their actions.

The anger expressed by our participants is not surprising. What may be surprising is the target of the anger is more diffused than might be expected and in most cases is not directed specifically at those responsible for their wrongful convictions. While they are angry at those parties, as exonerees have revealed in other settings (e.g., Illinois Criminal Justice Information Authority 2002), their anger is more encompassing and, as a result, overwhelming.

DEPRESSION, DISORIENTATION, AND DETACHMENT

These represent a final group of emotions that emerged as themes. Our participants often describe these emotions as occurring together, which structures our choice to discuss them as a group. All three are co-occurring symptoms of PTSD (American Psychiatric Association 2000) and are symptoms commonly experienced by victims of life-threatening trauma (Erikson 1976; Fullerton and Ursano 1997; Herman 1997; Lifton 1967, 1970). Several exonerees discuss their feelings of emptiness, lack of feeling, detachment, and flatness. Several simply describe themselves as depressed (see also Grounds 2004; Simon 1993). In some cases, these are feelings that overwhelmed them immediately after release, though the emotions attenuated as time went on. Others struggle episodically with sudden onsets of these emotions. In all cases, they attribute these emotional difficulties to their wrongful convictions and incarceration.

Those who say they are depressed struggle to describe their emotional state during those times. Dave Keaton says his depression is a state of "total emptiness" during which "I didn't really sit down. I didn't want to walk. I didn't want to eat. . . . And there was nothing. . . . It was just a bore, a total, total bore. There was nothing, nothing, nothing." Gary Gauger is most vocal about his intermittent struggles with depression. He says,

> [The depression] really screws up my thinking. Just the frustration, the inability to do anything. . . . Good days, bad days, days are days. They're all the same. They're all different. My depression, it comes and goes unexpectedly. Sometimes it'll go for weeks, and I don't even know it until it lifts, and then I go, "Wow! That was a rough one." . . . It's like you've been slogging through the swamp in the fog for three weeks, and all of a sudden, you're up on good ground again. You see where you're going. You have a sense of direction and purpose again.

Both Keaton and Gauger are frustrated that their depression interferes with normal functioning and communication. Keaton says, "I would express myself to some people sometimes but then no one seems to understand me. It feels like I'm above my thoughts, and everything I try to express to people, [they] look at me [and say], 'Man, you crazy.'" One characteristic of the depressive episodes Gauger experiences is a disorientation that leaves him confused and unable to communicate effectively: "[I]t feels like what I would imagine having a stroke [is like]. I don't lose physical mobility, but I get very confused. It's very frustrating. I can't articulate even simple ideas. People ask you simple questions, and I can't answer back. . . . It's like having a stroke."

The depression is episodic and often emerges unexpectedly; its unpredictable nature is disturbing and disruptive. Gary James found himself having an emotional episode on the freeway one afternoon: "I was driving and I was going too fast. I just kinda spun out, and just sat there and started crying. A guy came up to me who was getting on the freeway. . . . He gets out of his car and asks me was I all right. I just backed up, turned around, and went back on the freeway." Gauger also discusses the episodic nature of the depressive episodes, noting that he cannot predict when a discussion of his wrongful conviction will cause him serious distress. Sometimes when he gives a public lecture about his case, he experiences a severe depression for as long as a week afterward; however, other times he appears to manage the situation with few aftereffects. Aside from the depression being difficult for him emotionally, its unpredictable nature is disruptive to his relationship with his wife, whom he describes as "not a crabby person."

As part of their depression, our participants describe feeling numb or emotionally empty. Perry Cobb says, "I didn't have no feelings. I didn't like. I didn't love. I didn't hate. I didn't dislike. I was just, I see you and that was it." Cobb found this detachment to be particularly painful because it prevented loved ones from understanding the depth of his emotional turmoil:

> I was wearing two hundred and forty some pounds [when I was released]. . . . And everyone thought that I was just callous to everything. I was this great big guy. I'd been on death row all these years . . . and it's like I'm not human. I had to set them down and tell them, "I hurt. It matters not how large I am or how rough I might look, I hurt. I am hurting now." . . . And I was in pain. . . . It was like an ongoing injury, like a saw that's constantly going. It never stopped.

This lack of feeling also was a significant barrier to his ability to reconnect with his wife after release. Although they tried many times to reconcile, he admits that "I couldn't be with my wife because I didn't have any feelings." They divorced soon after.

Gauger also experiences this feeling of flatness and emotional detachment and admits to the frustration it causes in his relationship with his wife:

> Rubin Carter's definition of being alive . . . I haven't made it yet. I still really don't feel emotionally a whole lot. I feel frustration and impatience are about the only two emotions I was left with. Once in a while I get a glimpse of feelings. My cat got run over two weeks ago, and I had to deal with a little feeling there. But at least it is a normal feeling. Once it happened, I kind of welcomed the opportunity to actually get in touch with my feelings a little. It becomes very frustrating . . . I have a woman that just dearly loves me, and it's very frustrating to really just not feel anything. It is. It's frustrating to her too. . . . I think my feelings are so painful, I choose not to process them. . . . Once in a while, I'll have a glimpse of a feeling, and I tend to shut them down. I feel if I ever started crying I wouldn't be able to stop.

Here, Gauger reveals the depth of his emotional trauma—the detachment, the feeling of being dead, the fear of being overwhelmed by his emotions. His emotional distress, now seven years after his release from prison, is still so painful that he chooses to avoid the feelings rather than confront them. While this may shield him from the pain in the short term, this strategy may exacerbate the trauma over time (Herman 1997).

All of these emotions experienced by exonerees can, no doubt, be understood in clinical terms as evidence of PTSD or "disaster syndrome" or some type of depressive disorder (Erikson 1976; Fullerton and Ursano 1997), and it is essential that they receive mental health services to assist them in managing these issues. However, beyond the clinical diagnoses, these emotional responses to their wrongful convictions reveal very human reactions to being rejected by society, disconnected from community, and alienated from their families and support networks and even from their own sense of self. When exonerees are reinjected back into the communities from which they had previously been excommunicated, the canyon they experience between self and society can be overwhelming.

It is this gulf and loss of connection that lies at the core of the exoneree experience upon release. Struggles with the challenges of everyday life and barriers to employment, housing, and medical care, losses of family and missed opportunities, ruptured relationships, and emotional disarray—these all reflect the larger experience of being dislodged and displaced, thrown into a state of anomie with little to no assistance with reconstructing or refinding connection and community. At the core of the exoneree experience is their expulsion from their place in this world: Where do they fit in? Where do they now belong? Finding where they now fit is made more difficult because community and official responses to their situation exacerbate the chasm. In most cases, they are left on their own to find ways to reconnect and relocate themselves within their own ideas of self, their relationships, and their communities. Some do better than others in finding their new place. Some say they are satisfied with the place they have now created, while others are still searching. For all, finding their place has been a process with ups and downs, good moments and bad, a process marked by the traumatic experience from which they have just emerged. While their degree of satisfaction fluctuates, they share common struggles along the way.

Looking back over the multidimensional array of issues facing exonerees outlined in part 2, it is easier now to understand why Gary Gauger says that he feels like "a plastic barrier holding back the ocean . . . not much substance and a lot of weight," or as Greg Wilhoit sums it up, less poetically but no less accurately, "[A]ssimilating is a mother fucker!" From the mundane everyday tasks of pumping gas and grocery shopping to the emotionally draining difficulties of managing loss, guilt, and depression, they confront new battles around every turn. Sent into the fray with no preparation and little or no assistance, they struggle to build a new life and find a new home. Although some have more success than others in building that life, the process for all of them is painful and challenging. How do they confront the difficulties they encounter? What strategies do they use to cope with the problems enumerated thus far? Part 3 provides a framework for understanding where they go from here to find their new place in the world.

PART THREE

 Coping with Innocence

THE DAY OUR PARTICIPANTS walked out of prison the challenges described in part 2 were embedded in their daily struggles to rebuild their lives. They all needed to start a new life, to reconnect with partners, children, family, and friends, and to find a place away from the pain and trauma that had consumed them since their wrongful conviction. But with neither help from the state nor official recognition of their innocence, many begin life outside prison bereft of money, a home, employment, and health care and depend on a small group of loved ones who also have been traumatized by their ordeal. How do they begin to rebuild? To avoid psychological breakdown, homelessness, and even reincarceration, they must confront these issues of physical, economic, and emotional survival. What strategies do they use to negotiate the internal and external barriers to reintegration into their families and communities? How do they move forward? How do they cope?

The exonerees' coping begins when they hear that they have been found guilty and sentenced to death, facing execution for a crime they did not commit. They are transported to prison, most of them directly to death row, fearing for their own survival, let alone their freedom. They must cope with living on death row while knowing that they do not belong there. We begin with this piece of their coping process in chapter 8.

In chapter 9, we introduce the coping strategies adopted by exonerees as they negotiate reintegration back into their communities. People wrongly convicted of crimes, in particular of capital crimes, are much like other survivors of life-threatening trauma. Their experience, for example, resembles that of survivors of disasters, survivors of prolonged abuse, or prisoners of war in that exonerees have faced protracted abuse and stigma attacking core beliefs about their self and the world around them. Research into coping mechanisms used by these similarly situated survivors provides insight into coping strategies used by exonerees. These strategies, however, vary among exonerees and over time. Thus, we also outline factors that affect coping and strategy choice.

A significant component to the coping process is the task of reclaiming innocence as core to their identities. Since their wrongful conviction, others—police, prosecutors, the media, even family—have controlled the definition of who they are. The exonerees are defined as murderers, rapists, perpetrators, prisoners, heinous monsters not worthy of life. Even after exoneration and release, they often return to communities where they are not welcome. Community members believe they "got out on a technicality" and call them out in grocery stores, churches, and restaurants. While the exonerees work on finding a job, rebuilding their families, and overcoming their anger and depression, they face attacks on their self and identity and must find ways to combat stigma to reconstruct a new self based on innocence.

The central roles that identity reconstruction and stigma management play in coping are addressed more fully in chapter 10. At the heart of the exonerees' attempts to reintegrate is their need to rebuild identity around their claims of innocence. This often requires battling opposing claims from community members and system officials who insist on their guilt. Coping with innocence transcends their battles to reintegrate and rebuild and cuts to the core of who they are and the new self they want others to know.

CHAPTER 8

Confronting Life on Death Row

> It's a struggle every day, a mind struggle. They got the body, but they don't have the head. I know they're trying to kill me; they're not trying to help me. When you're in a cage, you'd be surprised, if you look and search real deep, you'll find something to do. What saved me was my dreams. A lot of dreams. A lot of times I wanted to commit suicide.　—Juan Melendez

LIVING UNDER A SENTENCE of death is an extremely stressful experience (R. Johnson 1982). According to Robert Johnson (1982, 140), "Death row is a pressure cooker in which feelings of helplessness, vulnerability, and loneliness are widespread." Inmates are powerless to control their environment or pursue their own interests and often feel debilitating loneliness to the point where they cry out in the night or, worse, attempt suicide. Inmates are perpetually vulnerable to the brutality of other inmates who need to be "tough" to survive and to the brutality and capriciousness of the guards (R. Johnson 1998). This creates what Robert Johnson (1998, 104) calls a "crucible of deterioration" that takes many forms—emotional, psychological, social, and physical. Robert Johnson and Hans Toch (1982, 15) refer to prisons as human "storage" for inmates where death row is a "prison within a prison" (Cabana 1996, 120). Austere prison conditions in general reflect an even more austere atmosphere on death row that is a "forlorn place" that "exacts a toll in human destruction" (Cabana 1996, 148).

Death row inmates must adjust to living in close proximity to others who are convicted of often heinous murders and to absorbing the fact that the state intends to kill them. They must manage the realities of other inmates' demise by suicide or execution and protect themselves against the physical and psychological abuse inflicted on them in this foreign environment. It is from this place that our participants promote their claims of innocence through the long dark tunnel of despair in which they are unjustly held captive.

UPON SENTENCE OF DEATH

Our participants began their journey through death row at the point they were wrongly convicted of capital murder charges, a long and difficult ordeal that favors the prosecution: death-qualified juries are partial to conviction and condemnation; media portrayals of the trial favor the prosecution's version of events; defense attorneys often are ill equipped, overburdened, or underprepared for the legal gyrations of a capital trial; and community sentiment toward the accused is hostile (Haney 2005). They describe their experiences with being wrongly convicted as harrowing and traumatic. For Alan Gell, the jury's verdict of guilt was incomprehensible to him. He says, "I remember they just said 'guilty.' I was just waiting for the 'not,' you know? Where's the 'not' part? And I remember hearing my mom hollering, 'I need to see him!' . . . that was the devastating blow. It really tore me apart." When he was later sentenced to death, he was numb: "It don't matter if I've got to spend the rest of my life in prison for something I didn't do. Either way I'm being punished for something I didn't do and I'm gonna die either in prison or by prison for something I didn't do." For others, being sentenced to death was deeply terrifying. Scott Taylor says, "I felt like I couldn't breathe, everything just went silent." And Perry Cobb remembers, "I was shooken inside, that's where I experienced my first fear and it kind of shook me inside." When Greg Wilhoit was sentenced to death, the judge went beyond the required script and outlined in grim detail the methods of execution to be used. Wilhoit recalls the judge saying, "[We'll kill you by] lethal injection, but if that fails, we'll kill you by electrocution. If the power goes out, we'll hang you. If the rope breaks, we'll take you out back and shoot you." Wilhoit "was aghast" by the manner in which the judge issued the death sentence even though he "saw it coming." He continues, "But then he blindsided me by tellin' me all this other shit. And I about shit! It was just me, and the prosecutor, and the judge in this big giant courtroom. . . . I've realized this was the most sobering moment in my life. Nobody's ever been sentenced like that!"

As Robert Johnson (1982, 136) notes, "Condemned prisoners view the custodial regime of death row as a planned assault on their humanity." This dehumanization entails "the loss—in whole or in part, situationally or generally—of one's humanity. A dehumanized person is in some sense dead as a person" (R. Johnson 1998, 204). For our participants, this process of dehumanization begins at the point of their conviction and sentencing and results from being told they are no longer worthy of life by a prosecutor, jury, and judge who believe them capable of inflicting brutal violence on another person. They are no longer considered viable as human beings and are told their existence will be forcefully exterminated by the state. Alan Gell explains this dehumanization process, saying, "Society's got to perceive us as monsters, because to perceive us as a human being, it wouldn't be acceptable to execute us. You got to take the humanity away for the death penalty to be okay."

For Gary Beeman, this dehumanization is symbolized by the judge calling him by the wrong name—Carl—when he sentenced Beeman to death. Beeman says, "He didn't get my name right, so they can't execute me, [so] maybe I never absorbed it." Gary James offers another example of the dehumanization of the condemned that begins at the moment of sentencing. He says,

> I knew it [the death sentence] was coming, everybody around me was emotional. I guess I was too but I didn't show it. About two weeks later, though, the judge called me back, so I'm thinking they found out I didn't do this. 'Cause didn't nobody tell me nothing. I didn't even see no lawyer. They had to take me back when I was there for two hours in front of the judge, and he apologized to me and said that when he sent me to die that he forgot to give me the seven to twenty-five years that they found me guilty for on the robbery. I just looked at him. I mean, he can't give me no more!

Once convicted and sentenced to death, they are transported from the local jail often directly to death row. In many cases, our participants had lived for years in the local jail while awaiting trial. Then, within one day, they are shackled and moved to their new "home" on death row. When inmates begin their adjustment to captivity, they experience entry shock as a "disruptive and disorganizing experience" (Gibbs 1982, 100). Alfred Rivera summarizes this feeling of disorientation when he reflects,

"[I] looked around daily and said to myself, 'I don't belong here' and why am I amongst this guy or that guy, guys who maybe said or pleaded to their guilt and did not have a care in the world about it. I often expressed to my family that it didn't seem real that I was there on death row." Scott Taylor echoes this feeling, wondering, "Is this real? I don't believe this. I had never been locked up like that."

Robert Johnson (1981) reports that, in those early days, prisoners adapt to death row in several ways: with denial, projection of responsibility onto others, and anger and fear. Chronic fear results in both physical and emotional withdrawal. Prisoners physically withdraw to maintain a low profile. Such voluntary social isolation reduces the risk of inflaming anger in others, which reduces their risk of physical violence, but also prevents them from building bonds with others that might be shattered later through execution. Emotional withdrawal, or "emotional death," numbs the prisoner to the onslaught of emotional trauma that rushes in as he or she confronts death row for the first time (R. Johnson 1981, 112).

Our participants relied on these adaptations in the first days and weeks to manage the trauma and fear they experienced. Alan Gell recalls the fear he felt when he was transported to death row: "These are like the worst of the worst and I'm fixing to have Charles Manson and Hannibal Lechter and just, you know, evil, evil monsters surrounding me. And you know, [I'm wondering] am I going to survive that? Never mind what the state's gonna do to me, I mean, what are *they* gonna do to me?" (his emphasis). Ray Krone explains his use of emotional withdrawal in those first days: "You almost become automated then, where you don't have to have emotional responses." Dave Keaton agrees, saying, "I didn't know how to respond to prison life, just to keep to myself, don't say anything to nobody, keep the frown there and walk around stoic. I have to protect my feelings." Greg Wilhoit, who was placed in cell 13 on Oklahoma's death row, explains his reaction of physical withdrawal: "I spent three Friday the 13ths on death row, in cell 13 . . . [and for] the first six months I was there, I didn't go out in the yard, I literally laid in bed the whole time." Wilhoit withdrew by covering his cell bars with newspapers, leaving only a small slit for the food tray and "pretending I was on a desert island somewhere watching my TV and reading my books." Perry Cobb perpetually and vocally proclaimed his innocence, saying, "I told them the rules and regulations didn't apply to me, I said, 'because I'm innocent and you don't have any[thing] here for innocent people.' They really thought I was dingy dingy, you know; 'This man can't have good sense. He talking like he innocent.' What am I supposed to do, get in a shell and not respond?" Interestingly, within Johnson's adaptation framework, wrongly convicted death row prisoners' claims of innocence would be understood as denial and attempts to project responsibility onto others, refusing to take responsibility for their crimes.

DAILY LIFE ON DEATH ROW

Death row has been described as isolating and lonely for inmates (Cabana 1996; R. Johnson 1981, 1982, 1998), who are "usually held in the most secluded quarters of the prison—a condition that . . . invites, indeed almost authorizes, abuse" (R. Johnson 1998, 101). Isolation and abuse are two sides of the same coin. The condemned are isolated from family and friends, society in general, and even other inmates. They refuse to interact or are refused interaction with significant others as a means of self-protection. Robert Johnson (1998, 96) writes, "Each day is a redundant experience of failure and rejection—of being powerless to effect change, cut off from supportive human contact, vulnerable to others in a world where people want you dead." A common enemy is boredom. They must devise strategies for occupying their time, which can range from crossword puzzles and board games to napping and doing calisthenics. But this life of boredom and isolation is often interrupted by periods of violence and abuse (Bowker 1982; Sykes 1958).

Our participants certainly agree that daily life on death row is an isolated existence, free of stimulation and unbearably lonely and routine. "We got to go out to the yard . . . got an hour a day, five days a week" on death row in Oklahoma, Greg Wilhoit remembers, though most of that hour was spent being shackled and unshackled to get to and from the yard. Delbert Tibbs says that "each day is pretty much the same as the next and to the one before" with little variety in activities. Ray Krone offers a bit more detail about daily life and its impact on him:

Most anybody that's done a little bit of time, the isolation time like death row, are gonna have suppression of their emotions. I mean, even anxiety, you don't even know what anxiety is anymore because you've been through so much. Like anxiety is the fact that your mail doesn't come that day, or your food don't come. I mean, even if it's late—late's one thing, but it's like if it don't come at all, that would cause anxiety, 'cause you're expecting it. . . . You get into a routine where the patterns become the pattern and you expect it to stay that way. I mean, like a Monday's the same as a Saturday, weekends didn't even matter.

Alfred Rivera summarizes the effect of the routinization and isolation: "On death row you truly die even before death, mentally. You have nothing to look forward to as far as programs that can benefit [you]. So, how about those like myself. . . . what have I gained? Those who sat waiting, wasting away."

Bubbling underneath the dehumanization and isolation of death row is the ever-present possibility of violence, and this tension periodically erupts into outbreaks of extreme violence and abuse (Bowker 1982; Sykes 1958). Lee Bowker (1982, 63–64) argues that prison life can be characterized as a "controlled war" among inmates as well as between inmates and guards. He attributes this continuous battle in part to inadequate staffing, easy access to lethal weapons among inmates, and a tinderbox of tension as a component of daily life. Exposure to this environment often results in inmates feeling helpless, depressed, and stressed, sometimes responding in self-destructive ways, which can lead to "increased difficulties in adjusting to life after release" (Bowker 1982, 69). In their examination of the life histories of forty-three death row inmates, David Lisak and Sara Beszterczey (2007) contend that much of the violence and abuse associated with life in prison, and on death row in particular, results from the hyper-masculine environment that dominates and guides action. They argue that "incarceration becomes another likely source of intensification of the masculine socialization-abuse interaction. The hyper-masculine and violent environment of the prison allows for few alternatives to the exaggerated display of toughness, and the denial of vulnerability that are the foundations of hyper-masculinity" (Lisak and Beszterczey 2007, 126).

The experiences of our participants confirm that prison life, even on isolated death row cell blocks, is laced with violence and brutality. Kirk

Bloodsworth recalls the feelings of despair living within this tinderbox: "You know you're innocent. You know you didn't kill this little girl. So, you say to yourself, 'Self, why are you letting yourself get depressed?' Because it's so damn depressing in there. Hell, you're peeling paint on the walls, rats running around, people getting stabbed every hour of the day, people screaming 'cause they're getting raped right down the hallway, you know. . . . I mean, it's the most brutal existence you could live in under *any* circumstance, I think" (his emphasis). Bloodsworth goes on to describe several instances of being attacked by other inmates while in prison, including when he was assaulted with a sock full of batteries and stabbed. Ray Krone describes that he felt it was necessary to craft a tough demeanor while in prison in order to fend off potential violence. He did this by defiantly bluffing other inmates to attack him; he says, "They're not gonna play you off like you're a little weakling and you learn. You don't do all this stuff the first day. You learn it as you go to survive in there."

Violence among inmates is not the only form of violence our participants described. Some also were aware of prison guards who used violence arbitrarily to control inmates. Perry Cobb recalls an incident when another inmate was sprayed with Mace by the guards:

> They came to my cell. They sprayed it on me. I hadn't did one thing. But [his] cell is right beside mine. So when they did that, it created a problem because I told [the other inmate] how to deal with Mace . . . and they didn't like that. So, they took us and they put us in South Unit by ourselves; they would send one officer over there [who] had instructions on how to mistreat us. . . . This is how we had to deal on death row in order to survive. They was making up laws every day for us, they wasn't going by the book.

Surviving violence from the guards and other inmates became a source of stress but also an opportunity to prove one's mettle. Kirk Bloodsworth drew on his history of being in the U.S. Marine Corps to defend himself. He says, "I've never been a fighter, but I never back down. . . . I came out of that thing unscathed, and I don't have to go through the details out to you, but you know what I'm talking about. My manhood is intact. And I kept it that way on purpose." Ray Krone experienced significant amounts of violence while incarcerated, and over time he realized that "you evolve your defenses as you go. And the better you get at it, the less excitable you are because you already know how to deal with it." Thus, our participants' experiences with being "warehoused for death" (R. Johnson 1998, 94) required them to remain as solitary as possible, maintain a bravado of toughness, and defend themselves against violence and abuse by others in order to survive.

EXPERIENCING EXECUTIONS

Of course, the daily brutality and violence of prison life must be understood within the broader prism of death by execution. The prospect of death, their own or that of a fellow prisoner, pervades the atmosphere of "the row" and creates a constant overlay of stress and tension. While a prison guard in Florida when John Spinkelink was electrocuted, Donald Cabana (1996, 120) observed three recently condemned inmates react to the execution: "The three of them had become sullen, irritable, and yes, introspective. . . . [T]he reality of it all began to squeeze their emotions like a vise." Robert Johnson (1982, 138–139) reports that "death anxieties are widespread . . . [and] the most powerful source of death anxiety is conduct by guards that draws attention to the prisoner's impending executions." Amanda Gil et al. (2006) describe "secondary trauma" of executions that is borne by people close to the executions: family of the condemned, family of the murder victim, and justice system officials. They do not identify other death row inmates as victims of this secondary trauma. However, we do.

Several exonerees discuss the secondary trauma when they experienced executions on death row. Walter McMillian, prior to being wrongly convicted and condemned, was held for trial on Alabama's death row. He believes the state used his stay on death row as a tool of intimidation to frighten him into a confession. Shortly after he was taken to death row to await his trial, he says, "They executed one guy about four days after they got to keep me down there. That's why they done that, I think, to try to scare me, you know. They put me up high, upstairs, so that I could look right over there, right at the building with the chair in it, where they execute in . . . and I reckon they just done that to try to irritate me, make me give up." Alan Gell explains that execution day is particularly difficult when the person being killed is someone he had gotten to know while on death row. At one point, he befriended another condemned inmate prior to the other inmate's execution:

> He made me promise that when I got out that in some way I would try and spread that message—you know, here's me, here's Alan, drug user and drug dealer, sent to death row for something I didn't do; and here's [other inmate] . . . [whose] poor decision ultimately cost him his life, you know, he was drunk; and every week we would sit around in our cell and talk about what we could do. This is what you gotta do, you gotta go and tell kids this, ya know? He wrote me a letter from the death chamber telling me not to forget what we had talked about and that he'd be looking down on me to make sure I didn't fall back into drugs or anything like that. It was rough to deal with.

Greg Wilhoit echoes this experience, full of emotion when recalling the execution of Chuck Coleman in Oklahoma. The two had developed a close friendship while on death row. Wilhoit tearfully recalls Coleman's execution:

> Chuck's number was up, you know. And he wasn't wild about the idea. [When he was moved to the execution chamber,] we said our goodbyes. I really didn't think it bothered me too much. . . . And it was a big deal because nobody'd been executed in like thirty years. . . . They were covering it on TV and it was one minute after midnight, and they were counting it down like it was New Year's Eve. . . . Eleven minutes after midnight, [they] announced that Charles Troy Coleman had been pronounced dead. And, like I said, I really didn't think it'd bother me. So nobody could have been more surprised than I was when instead of indifference I was overwhelmed with grief.

Juan Melendez, on death row in Florida during a period when executions were quite frequent, remembers the execution of other inmates as the most difficult and emotionally draining of experiences for him: "That was one of the hardest parts of being there, was when they kill somebody. You got to recognize this, you living in a cell, you got a man next door to you for nine years, ten years, you become attached without even knowing it. And, now they come, they snatch him, they kill him. And you think, 'I'll probably be next.' So, that was the part I say was the hardest part for me in there, when they kill someone."

Most terrifying of all, naturally, are the exonerees' experiences with their own execution dates. Sabrina Butler had what she believed was a real execution date. When her sentence of death was pronounced, the judge scheduled her to be electrocuted on July 2, 1990. As a nineteen-year-old, she was the youngest person sentenced to death in Mississippi. As a young woman without formal education, she was unaware that her execution would be stayed pending her required appeals. She believed she was to be killed on July 2, 1990, and anticipated it with extreme fear and dread:

> When that day came, I was the scaredest person in the world. This is a feeling that I wouldn't wish on my worst enemy. I stood there at the little old door . . . and I thought, by me watching TV and stuff, that they was gonna come and get you and you was gonna have this ball and chain on . . . and I was scared to death and the [other condemned woman in the cell next to her] kept telling me "Sabrina, they're not gonna do nothing" and I was standing there crying. I kept telling her, "Yeah, they gonna kill me; they gonna kill me. Somebody call my mama, or something and tell 'em that I love 'em." . . . That is the most humiliating, scary thing that any person could ever go through. I was scared to death because I thought that they was gonna kill me for something that I didn't do, and I couldn't tell nobody to help me. Wasn't nobody there.

Only later did Butler learn that she had received a stay of execution pending her appeals.

Shabaka Brown, however, had a very real execution date and came within fifteen hours of being electrocuted in Florida:

> My execution date was scheduled for September 18 [1983] and interestingly enough my oldest grandson, that was the day he was born. . . . He was my good luck piece. When I think of that time on death watch—my being murdered or not murdered wasn't such a big concern. My big concern was my family. You know, especially my mom, 'cause I wanted them to know that I was alright, that I was

gonna be alright. . . . They took me out of that cell . . . and they took the handcuffs off me, and asked me to raise my hands, and the tape measure went around my chest, and around my waist, and the inseams of my leg. And, then it struck me. Son of a bitch is measuring me for my burial suit, you know? And I struck out. I mean, 'cause I was standing there, and they was doing this so mechanically. . . . It was almost like I was an inanimate object. And for some reason, something just [Brown shouts out in rage and frustration] . . . and I was determined right then and there that if they were going to kill me, they were going to do it with some damn dignity. And I struck out.

The prospect of death (their own and others around them) surrounds condemned inmates and contaminates, dehumanizes, and demoralizes them every day. This begs the question of how they survive with their humanity and sanity intact.

Coping with Survival Inside

Given these harrowing experiences and stressful conditions, our exonerees had to devise mechanisms for coping with their survival—mental, emotional, and physical—while they were incarcerated. Researchers note a number of coping strategies used by prisoners in general, death row inmates more particularly, to combat the stress, violence, and dehumanization they encounter every day. These include using diversions to pass time, escaping from reality (through drugs, dreams, or even suicide), cultivating hope, taking action to seek redress for their cases, and relying on their spiritual faith and social support from family, friends, attorneys, and even other inmates (Budd and Budd 2010; R. Johnson 1981, 1998; Vollen and Eggers 2005; Zamble and Porporino 1988).

A common struggle was killing time. Exonerees were painfully aware that they were "frozen in time" (Zamble and Porporino 1988, 152). Juan Melendez says, "When you're on death row, the world stops. All you've got is the past, all you've got to lean on is from the past, so you just work from the past and you analyze what went wrong . . . and you go to change it. If you can't go in your mind, you'll go crazy 'cause them walls sometimes get too close, you can't even think. That's how

I survived, thinking about how I grew up." Ray Krone says he abandoned wearing a watch while in prison. He had no need to keep track of time, except for working out in the weight room: "Oh, I know what I got a watch for! Actually, 'cause you could time seconds. And we used to work out . . . that's right, you had the little timer things on 'em where you could set a timer, and you'd see how many push-ups you could do, or pull-ups. . . . But, time didn't have a big grip on you."

To combat the mundane and kill time, many of our participants discussed the importance of having a routine for their daily schedules, and they relied on each other to create diversions to pass the time. These routines and diversions included exercise, activities such as board games and television, as well as napping, reading, and writing letters. Kirk Bloodsworth was devoted to watching the television game show *Jeopardy* from its first days on the air. He says, "I've been with Alex Trebek for twenty years 'cause I've watched him since the show started twenty years ago, in prison." He also enjoyed watching cooking shows on television: "I taught myself how to cook on TV shows. Never cooked one dish while I was in jail or nothing, you know. But, I wrote all those recipes down." Gary James became an avid Scrabble player and recalled one of his big regrets in a word choice that lost him a game in a tournament with other inmates. He put down "voice" instead of "vice" and says, "That would have won me the game . . . I put down both my vowels and I shouldn't have done that." (We thought, however, that his choice of word seemed quite understandable and even ironic.) For others, routines they developed included faith-centered activities, such as group Bible studies or Alcoholics Anonymous meetings. The key for many was to break the days into discrete units that could be endured, bit by bit. Gary James says, "I can slow it down to the point where I can have just the fullest day in there . . . [I] broke myself down to do it like that. I had to find a way to make a life in there." Physical exercise was an important part of the routine for many. Ray Krone says, "I stayed active. I did push-ups, things like that; worked myself up to where I was doing one hundred push-ups at one time. . . . You stay busy—there was competitiveness, too . . . so I started working out with the guys."

As with other prisoners (R. Johnson 1981; Zamble and Porporino 1988), our participants sought opportunities to escape their predicament.

Their options for escapist coping included sleeping and dreaming, drug use, and/or suicide. Greg Wilhoit shares that he pretended to be on vacation and slept a great deal through the first six months on death row. Juan Melendez describes how his dreams of home in Puerto Rico saved him. Several of our participants mention having resorted to drugs while on death row, as Delbert Tibbs shares, "or I would have gone stark raving mad." Gary Beeman obtained barbiturates from a prison doctor: "I got Talwin from him right away. It's an opiate synthetic, like morphine, Demerol, up in that class. I had to shoot it a few times, but anyway you snort it or shoot it. I love barbiturates, and he started giving me barbiturates. And then I said I need some Valium for night to get to sleep, and then I said, 'Doc, I'm feeling kinda tired of all this stuff,' so he gave me Dexadrine."

Shabaka Brown contemplated (and some attempted) suicide while in prison, having gotten dangerously close to losing all hope and succumbing to the despair of his ordeal. He courageously shared with us his struggle with being suicidal:

In '79, I attempted suicide. . . . Being in a cage has a way of playing with your psyche. And when you in that little cage, you know, it teaches you a lot about yourself. It lets you know that no matter how big you are or how bad you think you is, there is something that can touch you. There is something that will break you down. When you get lonely and everything starts to pile up, there is something that can make you yell. You can't yell loud because you on death row. You not supposed to be heard by the other inmates. . . . Nine of them committed suicide when I was there. I almost went that route.

Eventually, he found reading Viktor Frankl's memoir *Man's Search for Meaning* (1984) to be a turning point for him:

That man's talking about Nazi Germany. And then I read it again. And then it dawned on me that what he was describing was the same thing that was happening to me. It was just a different period of time. . . . That's probably the one book that really helped me. One of the worst things about it is being there and knowing you ain't done no damn thing to be there for . . . and those little hours of the night, it's dark and it'll make you cry out. And the only thing comes out of you in that cell with your little tears that nobody see. You can't show no sign of weakness. You got to dig. You got to dig, and you got to do it for yourself because there are some sick people trying to kill you. And you can't help them. So I popped out. I didn't commit suicide.

Juan Melendez describes his suicide attempt when he obtained a plastic garbage bag with the assistance of an inmate runner. Before tying the bag around his neck, he decided to lie down in his bunk and think it over, one more time. He fell asleep and dreamed of a beach in Puerto Rico where he grew up. During our interview, we walked on that beach with him. He says,

I dreamed of that beach right there. I was right there swimming, real deep. I wish you could see when the sun comes out, it's so blue, beautiful blue. And I'm just swimming in there. Like a kid. And I'm just smiling and having fun and jumping up and down in the water. And all of a sudden I look back and here come four dolphins, not sharks, dolphins! Two get on this side, two get on the other side. They start jumping and they're playing with me in the water. And I look at the beach and I see my mama waving and smiling at me. Then when I wake up, I know I didn't wanna die then. So, I think the dream was a sign that one day I was gonna get out. I say this was God telling me.

A significant challenge during our participants' time in prison was to maintain hope of exoneration in order to combat despair and fear. Of course, all of the exonerees were afraid the state would execute them before they had the chance to prove their innocence. Holding on to hope was one way to address this conundrum. Their hope ebbed and flowed, over long stretches—even years—of no progress and profound boredom. Juan Melendez aptly describes the struggle to maintain hope with this analogy: "Hope? Hope is like a little kid learning to walk. He falls. He falls. He don't stay on the ground. He cries; he finds ways to get up and walk again. But you just find ways to get up and walk again, just like a little kid." Shabaka Brown developed what he called "the toothpaste tube technique" for maintaining hope:

> You know that we gets up in the morning, we brush our teeth, for those of us who have some, we use this toothpaste tube all the time, and when it gets old and wrinkled, the first thing we do is throw it away because it's empty. However, if you get that same old and wrinkled toothpaste tube that you think is empty, if you squeeze it just right, something will come out if it every time. And that's what I did. I just reached down there, I didn't care if it was just *that* much [indicating a tiny amount]. . . . I don't think about tomorrow or five years down the road, I need to survive today . . . that's all you need, you don't need much just to get through the day.

Many exonerees kept hope alive by searching for any form of redress, giving them hope that what the state declared a permanent and irreversible punishment could be transformed into a temporary situation from which they would emerge vindicated (V. Braithwaite 2004). Edward Zamble and Frank Porporino (1988, 96) refer to this as a "common palliative" coping strategy: "[I]n its promise that the present situation was temporary, [this strategy] helped them to live through what might otherwise have been intolerable." Gary Gauger says he went through a "message in a bottle period" where "I . . . was just writing anybody and everybody I thought could possibly help me. All the newspapers, magazines, TV talk shows, anything . . . law firms. I thought all I gotta do is get in touch with Connie Chung or somebody and I'd be out within two weeks. I was very naïve."

Tim Howard also relied on this strategy in his quest for someone to take his and Gary James's case. As codefendants in Ohio, they were originally sentenced to death, but one year later their sentence was commuted to life without parole when the Ohio death penalty statute was declared unconstitutional. What this meant for Howard and James, however, was that their mandatory appeals at the state and federal levels were abandoned; the state was no longer required to provide them with representation on appeal. Howard sought assistance relentlessly, saying, "I'm the one that wrote the letters and got turned down. . . . I went out on a limb, wrote letters and got turned down, got beat up and everything like that. And so you know, that takes an effect on you over the years. I knew Gary was innocent. I did the best I can for Gary; I never left Gary behind. I never spoke only for me. I always spoke for myself and Mr. James. But, the thing is, I'm the one that's getting the rejected letters." Eventually, Howard found the assistance he sought in Jim Owen and Centurion Ministries, and he and James were exonerated in 2004.

Several exonerees turned to their religious faith to help them cope with the despair of death row. Scott Taylor says, "God would not allow me to get too angry to the point where I would just want to take my own life, or hurt someone else or become violent or become frustrated with the court system, which [was] trying to kill me. . . . I knew that just God was telling me, it's just a matter of time." While in prison, Taylor was asked if he was "plugged in," meaning in a gang. He replied, "No, man, I'm not in a gang. I'm a Christian, and [the guy] said 'So am I' and come to find out half the deck were Christians." Taylor also shares with us how important it was that his attorney was a Christian. The two would pray together, and he had faith in his attorney as well as in God, which helped to bolster his hope for an eventual exoneration. Perry Cobb talks about his belief that, eventually, he would be released: "It had to come from God, I believed that because of the way I was raised."

Social support also was important to their coping. For most, family members were a main source of support during incarceration. Without their mothers, sisters, aunts, fathers, brothers, and children who continued to support them, they would have been emotionally lost. Juan Melendez recalls that "my mama and my five aunts" saved his life by staying in contact and always believing in him: "They'd send me letters from the little children that were born and the cousins and all that, the grandchildren." Shabaka Brown was permitted to have physical contact visits for a while on death row. About that, he says, "you needed that human contact, you needed to feel that warmth, you need balance in your life." Gary Gauger's twin sister maintained her support for him while she also grieved the deaths of their parents: "My sister would come visit me three or four times a year. She'd come every Christmas." And Delbert Tibbs recalls having support from his brother who was a police officer and who was "very much in the forefront of my legal defense team." Sabrina Butler's mother was with her "all the way" through her ordeal. For Kirk Bloodsworth, his mother's support was pivotal in his determination to maintain his fight, making her death, five months before his release, all the more painful.

Support from friends also was important for our participants. Delbert Tibbs quoted a poem to explain what it meant to him: "As a guy said in a poem, 'that I rode that far alive' you know. It was because of that, it was because of their love, and caring, and my girlfriend, my sweetheart with whom I had lived for like two or three years." Tibbs's case became a cause célèbre in the anti–death penalty movement of the late 1970s. Folk musician Pete Seeger wrote a song about Tibbs and performed it during a concert to raise awareness for his plight while he was still on death row in Florida. As a result, even strangers offered support and assistance to Tibbs. He was surprised that "people that didn't even know me [helped], and it cut across the whole race thing which was very good, which is good for my heart . . . it cut across all that crap and people were really quite beautiful. As ugly as human beings are, and we are quite ugly, I've seen big beauty in people."

Interestingly, several exonerees noted that moral support from their attorneys (typically, appellate attorneys) was an essential component of their coping. Alan Gell describes what his attorney's support meant to him: "She said, 'Alan, I believe that you're innocent. I believe in you' and that's all I ever wanted to hear. . . . It was just inspirational. When they came and told me that my first appeal was turned down and that my execution date was gonna be drawing near, I was like 'I knew that. She told me that six months ago, a year and a half ago' and it weren't a letdown. And I started to think of positive things to make me believe in the system." Several exonerees describe their attorneys as being among a very small group of supporters they truly trusted.

Some exonerees reveal how other inmates helped them to maintain hope and were primary support systems for them. Walter McMillian, for instance, describes the other inmates on death row: "I had a lot of support. They were good guys. They were just as good as the lawyers out there; they the ones had my hopes lifted up so good 'cause they told me 'I don't think you're going to die in there. You the one man gonna go home. Man, you ain't got no business being in prison. How in the world they arrest you with no evidence?'" Occasionally, our participants describe supportive relationships with prison guards as well. Alan Gell's guards offered their support by urging, "'Man, I hope when you get home that you sue them for so much money that they have to lay me off 'cause they can't afford to pay me anymore,' yeah, a guard said it, I had a bunch of 'em say it to me."

To survive death row requires extreme mental focus on the goal of prevailing in the legal battle but even more so on managing the psychological and emotional turmoil characteristic of life on death row. To survive mentally and physically and walk out of prison when they have "maintain[ed] a precarious existence in a world circumscribed by death" is a testament to our exonerees' resilience (R. Johnson 1981, 117).

LEAVING DEATH ROW

For our exonerees, leaving death row alive was an unexpectedly bittersweet experience. While they all had dreamed of their day of release, many found it to be a surprising, even disheartening, experience on several fronts. Alan Gell says, "I pictured how wonderful and great it would be when I was released. . . . I just made all kinds of plans on how wonderful it would be." Then, during the final court proceeding, Gell heard the judge say, "Mr. Gell, you are free to go," and he recalls, "I had been wanting to hear them words forever and ever and ever. But, it dawned on me when he said that I was free to go, that there was something missing, and he didn't ask where I was going. He didn't ask did I have anywhere to go. He didn't tell me he was sorry."

Two aspects of their release most often caught them by surprise: the brevity of the time frame for preparing for it and the sadness they felt upon leaving their friends behind who were still incarcerated. Juan Melendez had about an hour from hearing the news of his release to walking out of prison. Sabrina Butler's release followed her second trial, at which she was acquitted. She was taken back to the county jail where she had been held for the second trial, was allowed to collect her personal belongings, and was escorted out the door, with nowhere to go and no one to assist her in reclaiming a life. Charles Fain had only a few hours' notice of his release from death row, where he had lived for the past eighteen years. Gary James learned of his imminent release the night before on the eleven o'clock news. Needless to say, it is difficult to plan for one's future with only a few hours' notice.

Leaving behind the friends they had made while incarcerated was difficult for some. Gary Gauger continues to feel some "survivor guilt" and cannot maintain contact with the men he had befriended in prison. Juan Melendez, after having the warden inform him of his release, was escorted back to his death row cell to collect his belongings and was cheered by hundreds of other inmates as he left death row for the last time: "I gave all my stuff away. . . . I just got up and looked at my friend next door to me, then I looked at every one of them. Some of them was crying. Some of them say to me, 'Good luck and take it easy down there.' And then all of them start clapping their hands, and then I could hear the clapping on all the floors. And I left. . . . I felt happy but I felt sad because I left them in there." At this point, Melendez became agitated and had to get up and pace around the room while he processed the difficult emotions this memory illuminated.

Views on the Death Penalty

"Expertise" comes in many forms, although our academic worlds tend to view scholars as the experts in various fields. It also is true that our exonerees' harrowing experiences of wrongful capital convictions, incarceration, and survival create an expertise with a different set of credentials. Having stared down the barrel of the gun, as it were, and survived, their views on the death penalty as a social policy issue are well informed and compelling. Seventeen of our eighteen exonerees have come to oppose the death penalty. One person supports the death penalty and sees it as appropriate in a limited number of cases, though he did not elaborate on that view. For the majority, their reasons for opposing the death penalty include seeing executions as arbitrary and anti-Christian and the probability of innocent people being wrongly convicted and executed.

Echoing concerns from many scholars that the death penalty is arbitrary and capricious (Jacobs et al. 2007; Petrie and Coverdill 2010; Radelet 1981, 1989; Radelet and Pierce 1991), Alfred Rivera observes that "death sentences are illegally handed down in order to present a false picture of closure, and should be abolished in this country altogether because of disparities that exist in the prosecution of criminal defendants of a certain race or class." Gary Beeman describes those subject to the death penalty as mostly "the poor and defenseless, the castaways" whereas Greg Wilhoit believes it is randomly applied: "I don't think they flip a coin but who knows?"

Greg Wilhoit's views on the death penalty are grounded in his Christian faith and his very personal experience with the execution of his friend Chuck Coleman. Until the execution of Coleman, Wilhoit supported capital punishment, and he regrets that Coleman went to his execution believing that he supported it: "I didn't change my mind about the death penalty because of my situation. I changed my mind . . . I'm sorry [crying and sobbing], I changed my mind because my friend got executed. I'm sorry. And also, I'm not really opposed to the death penalty because I was almost a victim of it. It's because of my religion. The cornerstone of Christianity is forgiveness. It bothers me to this day that he went to his death thinking that I thought he deserved it." Perry Cobb shares Wilhoit's religious conviction that the death penalty is contrary to Christianity. He recalls a conversation with a woman in his church who supported the death penalty in a particular case and says, "When Jesus said, 'Those among you who are without sin cast the first stone,' that's supposed to be there for everything. How can she be a Christian and say they should kill him?"

Not surprisingly, our exonerees are deeply concerned about errors and wrongful convictions as a reality within the modern death penalty system. Juan Melendez was released from prison and vowed that his two goals for the rest of his life were to "take care of my mama and abolish the death penalty." He is convinced the death penalty system "cannot be reformed because the justice system is always going to be subject to human error. It's that simple; some innocent people are going to be messed up. We're not perfect." Kirk Bloodsworth is convinced that innocent people have been put to death in the United States, though official recognition of an erroneous execution has not yet occurred. He says, "[I]t's really foolhardy to sit here and say that [no innocents have been executed]. Any kind of rational, logical person [who can] sit here and say that there's never been an innocent man executed is downright bull crap. Downright bull, I mean just the odds." Having come closest to his own execution among our participants, Shabaka Brown recognizes the "normal human emotion" for those whose loved ones have been murdered to seek the death penalty—"to deny it would be denying your humanness"—but "we pause, and say that we do not need a penalty on our books with such finality where we know we're gonna make a mistake. Take it off. That's all I'm saying."

Alan Gell believes that we have a justice system to avoid vigilante justice so that "cooler heads will prevail." He elaborates, "[T]he [system is like the] bizarre side of a bad parent, one that smokes and drinks telling your kids don't smoke and drink. How can you tell your kids don't smoke when you got one in your mouth? Do as I say and not as I do? That's our government. I don't believe in the death penalty." Brown sums it up concisely: "Complete abolition is what I'm for. My position is that I'm not for capital punishment or against capital punishment. I'm against killing. Whether that killing is done by an individual or a state or a government dropping bombs, that's what I'm against. To me, life is sacred. All lives. So I don't get caught up in fancy words. Murder is murder, whether you say it's the law or not, it's murder."

A Note on Family Members

Death row inmates endure captivity directly and literally. Their family members experience their own personal version of captivity (Beck et al. 2007; King 2005; Sharp 2005; Vandiver 1989; Vandiver and Berardo 2000). While the main focus of our research explores the personal experiences of death row exonerees, we would be remiss not to acknowledge the impact on their family members. During several interviews with participants, we met their loved ones—mothers, sisters, girlfriends, fathers. Our participants frequently mention the importance of family members who supported them through this catastrophe. While it is beyond the scope of this book to describe and analyze these family members' experiences with the death sentences of their loved ones, we encourage more systematic research on the impact of wrongful death sentences on family members.

"Death is unarguably different from all other criminal punishments and . . . has an unmistakably different effect on persons who debate, advocate, oppose and litigate capital punishment" (Haney 2005, 243). Our participants experience death row confinement as profoundly dehumanizing and torturous (see also R. Johnson 1998). Their survival is not a consequence of the criminal justice system working; rather, their survival is a testament to their resilience, their determination to keep their cases alive when all mandatory reviews were exhausted, their stubbornness in refusing to concede defeat although some nearly gave up through suicide. Because they are irrefutable proof that wrongful capital convictions occur, their views on the death penalty inform the broader public debate on capital punishment as a policy question in the United States. Their survival is consequential; their voices are significant.

Sadly, once they leave the confines of prison and death row, their battle is not yet over. Emerging from the "deep freeze" of prison, their return to society is a jarring and alienating experience (Zamble and Porporino 1988, 152). They must dig still deeper to confront the challenges that await them.

CHAPTER 9

Coping with Life after Death Row

It's easy for people to say what I should and what I shouldn't do. . . . And I don't want nobody . . . experiencing what we experienced. It's easy to say what we should do, but it's not easy to do. We've been taken care of all of our lives [during twenty-six years of incarceration]. We've had no responsibilities. No pay, no bills. We [did not have] to worry about living out here in society. And then we out here trying to adjust. Well, [people] trying to say, "Get over it, get over it!" I still go through a lot of stuff here. Right? I'm shocked; it's hard to get over. You just can't get over it.   —Tim Howard

HOW DO YOU GET OVER being taken from your home, convicted of something you did not do, told you were going to die for it, isolated on death row, incarcerated for many years, and then released back into society just as suddenly as you were first taken, with little assistance, no explanation, and no apology? Or do you get over it? How do you make sense of that experience for yourself and your family? How do you find your place back in your home and community? How do you overcome the many barriers set in your way? These are all questions that confront exonerees when they return home. In negotiating their dislocation and the economic and emotional terrain of life after death row, they begin a process of recovery that, for many, will be a roller coaster ride of ups and downs, successes and failures. Some will find this process more problematic and fraught with setbacks than others, but all will find it difficult.

Exonerees as Trauma Survivors

This process of recovery is not unlike that negotiated by survivors of other types of catastrophic, life-threatening events that uproot people from their lives and communities and jeopardize core beliefs about the self. Exonerees walk a road similar to survivors of disasters and atrocities—floods, earthquakes, war, the Holocaust—and life-threatening disease and illness—AIDS and cancer. Interestingly, disaster survivors and exonerees alike recognize their similarities of experience, perhaps more so than us experts and definitely more than criminal justice professionals responsible for the exonerees' situation. One survivor of the Buffalo Creek mining accident and flood that wiped out entire communities in the Appalachians of West Virginia wrote, "I feel as I'm sure a prisoner must feel who has been sentenced to prison for a crime he didn't commit" (Erikson 1976, 13)—dislocated, uprooted from place and community, isolated, detached. Likewise, exoneree Alfred Rivera recognizes his situation in that of returning war veterans: "When one comes home from war, he is afforded the opportunity to be dealt with by those who can help diagnose the symptoms [of the] aftereffects of the trauma one has recently returned from. We know of posttraumatic stress disorder. Could it be that one who is caged up and told that he will be injected with a formula which will in turn end his or her life, then [is] released from such conditions, [may] suffer PTSD also?" Trauma is the common element that exonerees share with other types of survivors.

Judith Herman (1997, 33) defines traumatic events as different from "commonplace misfortunes" in that they "involve threats to life or bodily integrity, or a close personal encounter with violence and death" and "overwhelm the ordinary human adaptations to life." Stanley Cohen and Laurie Taylor (1972, 42) distinguish the "mundane" disturbances of life from traumatic ones in that "the problem is so extreme, so dreadful that one's physical existence, one's sense of self or one's whole view of the world is at risk." Most certainly, being wrongly convicted of heinous crimes and condemned to death constitutes a trauma of this magnitude (Grounds 2004; Simon 1993; Weigand 2009). All of our exonerees know the experience of being fully and completely rejected by society, to the extent of being told they are no longer worthy of life. While awaiting their own execution, they are surrounded by the despair of others, some of whom take their own lives or are taken for execution:

> Life on death row is stressful, as one should imagine. Dealing with the possibility of being executed is a heavy burden that causes psychological trauma and emotional damage. I remember one guy on death row [who] jumped over a rail about two stories up, trying to cause his death. I remember a guy who did not want to continue litigation of his appeals because he was tired of continually having to live in the condition of a sitting duck. . . . It's hard on death row knowing that the day your appeals are exhausted you're doomed to execution. It's hard on death row becoming intimate friends with a guy and then seeing him be led out to await his death. . . . It's hard to look at a guy and see how he may be executed for something he may not have done. There's nothing easy psychologically [or] mentally about death row. It's pure pain and suffering. (Alfred Rivera)

A trauma of this magnitude overwhelms the capacities for coping and adaptation used to manage more "commonplace misfortunes" and "mundane" disturbances: "I couldn't work. I just could not function at all. Could not. Almost incapacitated" (Kirk Bloodsworth).

Catastrophic trauma has many forms. It can be of human design, such as being a prisoner of war, Holocaust survivor, or victim of prolonged abuse or sexual assault. It can be a consequence of nature, such as surviving a flood or earthquake. Herman (1997) notes that the language we use to denote each type differs, referring to catastrophes of nature as "disasters" and catastrophes of human creation as "atrocities." However, in each case, survivors share the experience of being "rendered helpless by overwhelming force" (Herman 1997, 33). Another distinction in form though not effect is between catastrophic trauma that occurs in a single, sudden event and trauma that is prolonged and repetitive. The first can be thought of as a "discrete" disaster, such as an earthquake or nuclear explosion; such events "have something approaching an endpoint: The effects reverberate over years or even decades, but the catastrophe itself is over" (Lifton 2001, 213). The second is more of a "sustained catastrophe" during which the danger and threats to life and self extend over a period of time when the catastrophe itself continues day after day, year after year with no discernable end (Lifton 2001, 213). The Holocaust experience is an example of such a sustained catastrophe, as is that of an abuse victim who is isolated and repeatedly victimized over time (Herman 1997; Lifton 1970; Schoenfeld 2005). We argue that the incarceration of an innocent person on death row constitutes just such a sustained catastrophe, a catastrophe of human design, an atrocity (Westervelt and Cook 2008, 2010).

No matter the form, however, the effects remain quite similar:

> Sometimes the blow is sudden and physical: a motor car accident, being caught in a flood or hurricane. Sometimes it is long lasting: suffering a prolonged illness, fighting through a war, being evacuated to a strange area, or being cut off from loved ones. Such experiences have disturbing consequences: we talk of people "going gray overnight," "being scarred for life," "becoming stunted" or "crippled" or even "never being the same again." These experiences are literally or metaphorically shattering: they break the web of meaning we have built up around ourselves and at the same time show how fragile this web is. (Cohen and Taylor 1972, 42–43)

The significance of recognizing the "commonality of affliction" between exonerees and survivors of other types of discrete and sustained catastrophes is the value of recognizing the common elements to their victimizations and common challenges for their coping and recovery (Herman 1997).

The literature on the impact of catastrophic trauma for survivors is voluminous and beyond the scope of this discussion. Our focus is to identify commonalities between the aftereffects of catastrophic trauma and those experienced by exonerees and common strategies they use to negotiate these aftereffects. As noted throughout part 2, most of the struggles exonerees face are experienced by survivors of discrete and sustained catastrophes more generally. Aftereffects commonly noted in the trauma literature that parallel those experienced by exonerees include disconnection from and dislocation within the posttrauma world in which survivors find themselves (Brison 2002; Erikson 1976; Frankl 1984; Henry 2004; Herman 1997; Lifton 1967; Schoenfeld 2005), grief and mourning over losses and disruptions (Brashers et al. 1999; Erikson 1976; Herman 1997; Williams et al. 2003), damage to familial relationships and friendship networks (Fullerton and Ursano 1997; Williams et al. 2003), and feelings of survivor guilt, distrust, revenge, and anger (Brashers et al. 1999; Brison 2002; Erikson 1976; Herman 1997; Lifton 1967; Schneider 1975; Schoenfeld 2005; Williams et al. 2003).

To the extent that the experience of long-term incarceration and captivity causes trauma on the scale of a sustained catastrophe (Cohen and Taylor 1972; Herman 1997; Jamieson and Grounds 2005), it should not be surprising then that exonerees are equally, if not more so, traumatized than other prisoners. As noted in chapter 2, exonerees share many postrelease experiences common to parolees. Being wrongly incarcerated does not make them immune to the negative aftereffects of incarceration; it is possible, in fact, that the injustice associated with their experience of incarceration heightens, rather than dampens, the damage they incur (Campbell and Denov 2004). Both groups confront problems finding housing and employment and suffer from health problems exacerbated (if not caused) by their incarceration and lack of health care. They grapple with grief over losses of time, loved ones, and relationships and face psychological and emotional aftereffects from their incarceration. Long-term incarceration is in itself a prolonged and traumatic disruption in the life course, and the trauma literature has been used to understand life after release: "[S]tudies of victims of disaster [are] relevant [to the study of the effects of long-term incarceration] because such studies are similarly concerned with the consequences of sudden and overwhelming dislocations that affect the individual's total life" (Jamieson and Grounds 2005, 58; see also Cohen and Taylor 1972). Given these similarities between the postrelease experiences of exonerees and those of other similarly situated survivors of all types, the trauma and coping literature provides an appropriate analytical lens to examine life after death row for exonerees.

COPING WITH THE AFTERMATH OF SUSTAINED CATASTROPHES

"Coping" is a central concept in a variety of disciplinary literatures, including those related to resiliency, grief and loss, counseling, trauma and stress management, stigma management, and disaster relief. These literatures share a fundamental concern with how people cope with trauma, yet they differ in the aspects of trauma on which they focus: the grief and loss so often felt by trauma survivors, the stigma sometimes attached to trauma victims, the resources that should be provided by disaster relief workers to assist survivors with coping. Needless to say, providing a review of this literature of any depth or breadth would be expansive and, we think, beyond the needs of our discussion here.[1] Our intent, instead, is to extract and adapt concepts from these literatures to help analyze how our participants manage the disconnection and dislocation they encounter after release.

We, in fact, even hesitate to use the word *coping* to describe the strategies used by exonerees. The most widely referenced definition of coping comes from the pioneering work of Richard Lazarus and Susan Folkman (1984, 141), who define coping as "constantly changing cognitive and behavioral efforts to manage specific external and/or internal demands that are appraised as taxing or exceeding the resources of a person." As coping is a central concept in psychological assessments and inventories, most heavily quantitative, we hesitate when referring to "coping" strategies of exonerees, given our research is neither psychological in approach nor quantitative in design. Because "coping" taps into this aspect of the literature, we want to be clear in our use of terminology.

That said, we analyze eighteen powerful firsthand accounts of how exonerees manage the aftermath of the sustained catastrophe of their wrongful capital convictions. If interpreted within a broader framework, the Lazarus and Folkman definition focuses on "how the individual interprets his or her situation and how he or she behaves in response to a particular stressor" (Ibañez et al. 2004, 69). When used in this light, the definition clearly applies to the postrelease experiences of exonerees. No doubt as the chapters in part 2 reveal, exonerees interpret their postrelease situations as stressful, and as this chapter explains, they use a variety of techniques when managing the stress of aftermath. Thus, from this broader perspective, it seems appropriate to discuss the ways we find exonerees "coping" with their lives after release. Another way of thinking about these coping strategies are as "management" techniques—how exonerees think about their lives and the ways they behave after release that assist them in managing the aftermath of their wrongful convictions. We use both of these terms—coping strategies and management techniques—interchangeably throughout the discussion that follows.

Trauma survivors use many techniques to manage the effects of trauma when they resume their lives. We have chosen to group these individual techniques together as indicative of two broader styles of or approaches to coping. Thus, we focus on these two broader approaches to coping and a number of more specific techniques that rely on each approach. The approaches are determined by the degree to which survivors confront and integrate the traumatic experience into their reconstructed lives. We call these two primary approaches or styles of coping the *incorporation approach* and *avoidance approach*.

The incorporation approach to coping focuses on survivors' efforts to master their circumstances after the trauma and create or move toward constructive outcomes for themselves and others. This approach has been identified as empowerment oriented, promotion focused, and/or proactive (Oyserman and Swim 2001; Shih 2004; Siegel et al. 1998). While it goes too far to say that survivors embrace the trauma and difficulties caused by it, this approach does assume an inclination to examine and search for resolutions to problems caused by the trauma. Thus, coping strategies grouped under this approach reflect attempts to integrate or incorporate, to some degree, the traumatic experience into the new life being constructed in the midst of the aftermath. We call these "strategies of incorporation."

The survivor literature identifies coping strategies that characterize this incorporation approach. For example, telling the story of the trauma, privately and publicly to supportive audiences, is important to managing the aftereffects of traumatic events (Brison 2002; Herman 1997; Kaniasty and Norris 1999; Williams et al. 2003). Telling the "trauma story" helps the survivor reconstruct the meaning of the traumatic event so that it can be "integrated into the survivor's life story" (Herman 1997, 175). It also connects survivors to supportive others and diminishes the isolation and dislocation they experience.

A second management strategy that relies on an incorporation approach is to create or attach meaning to the traumatic event (Bonanno 2004; C. Davis 2001; Frankl 1984; Henry 2004; Neimeyer 2001). For some, it is important to make sense out of their trauma and why they were victimized. The capacity to make sense of the trauma and attach meaning to it occurs only if survivors have some acceptance of the experience and are no longer denying or avoiding their new posttrauma reality (C. Davis 2001). Creating meaning allows survivors to recontextualize the trauma so they recognize it as significant in their life journey. In some cases, this "making of meaning" occurs within a spiritual or religious framework in which survivors attribute their suffering to "God's plan" or some larger spiritual purpose. Although survivors initially experienced the trauma as arbitrary, inexplicable, and unjust, they have reframed the experience and now see the trauma as part of a larger spiritual journey that will bring them to a deeper understanding of God, some other existential force, and their own spiritual selves (C. Davis 2001; Richards 2001; Richardson 2002).

For some survivors, this private making of meaning is transformed into a public cause or "survivor mission" (Henry 2004; Herman 1997). As Judith Herman (1997, 207) explains, "Most survivors seek the resolution of their traumatic experience within the confines of their personal lives. But a significant minority, as a result of the trauma, feel called upon to engage in the wider world. These survivors recognize a political or religious dimension to their misfortune and discover that they can transform the meaning of their personal tragedy by making it the basis for social action. While there is no way to compensate for an atrocity, there is a way to transcend it, by making it a gift to others." Their personal trauma becomes a platform for educating others and advocating for social change (Siegel et al. 1998).

This coping strategy involves revelations or disclosures of their personal tragedy and telling of their trauma story and provides the personal benefit or sense of empowerment gained by using their situation to speak to larger political or social issues. Thus, they derive meaning from making sense of their experience for themselves and from offering their narrative to assist others in making meaning of their experiences. This engagement with the wider world also connects them to other survivors, supporters, and advocates for change, reducing their experience of disconnection and disruption. The personal indeed becomes political (Mills 1959).

A final strategy of incorporation is the value survivors often gain from connecting to and sharing with other similarly situated survivors (Fearday and Cape 2004; Herman 1997). Such connections provide survivors opportunities to tell their trauma stories and to be heard by those who most fully understand their experience. Such moments of sharing and understanding are empowering and freeing as survivors' fears of being misunderstood, diminished, or devalued are minimized, if not totally relieved: "Trauma isolates; the group [of similarly situated survivors] recreates a sense of belonging. Trauma shames and stigmatizes; the group bears witness and affirms. Trauma degrades the victim; the group exalts. . . . Trauma dehumanizes the victim; the group restores . . . humanity. . . . The restoration of social bonds begins with the discovery that one is not alone" (Herman 1997, 214, 215). Establishing connections to other survivors provides a way to acknowledge the depth of their losses, grief, isolation, and fear. As is true of all of the strategies of incorporation, this technique paves the way for recognition and integration of the trauma into one's understanding of self and purpose while creating attachment and involvement of the survivor in the lives of others and the broader community.

The other primary style of coping on which we focus is the avoidance approach. Although strategies of incorporation tend to involve confronting the aftereffects of trauma and creating constructive outcomes for survivors, strategies that rely on the avoidance approach are more defensive, aimed at reducing or avoiding negative consequences of the trauma. This may mean avoiding situations that remind the survivor of the trauma or that elicit stressful emotional reactions (Endler and Parker 1999). This approach has been referred to as prevention-focused, reactive, and defensive coping (Oyserman and Swim 2001; Shih 2004; Siegel et al. 1998). Because the primary focus here is on avoiding, rather than confronting, the aftereffects of the traumatic experience, we call the management techniques that rely on this approach "strategies of avoidance." These strategies include withdrawal and numbing.

Withdrawal entails a reluctance to be in situations that invoke the traumatic event, situations that raise strong emotions that can be overwhelming (Bonanno 2004; Herman 1997; Phillips and Lindsay 2010). For some survivors, reliving the trauma, with its emotional and psychological baggage, provides opportunities for mastery and integration. But for others, reliving the trauma is something to "dread and fear" because such moments "carry with [them] the emotional intensity of the original event" (Herman 1997, 42). To avoid such situations, they may withdraw from relationships and community. The possibility of being reminded of the trauma is enhanced in cases where the survivor is well known for that status and identified as such by others. Thus, survivors may choose, in particular, to withdraw or distance themselves from connections to other survivors (Herman 1997; Shih 2004; Siegel et al. 1998). Such distancing reduces the emotional distress caused by the sharing and retelling of trauma stories common to survivor groups but also reduces the degree that others associate the survivor with the status of "survivor." To the extent that others do not identify the survivor as such, they are able to further avoid situations in which someone in their community may ask them to recall or account for their survivor experience in some way. Withdrawal, then, provides a mechanism to avoid potentially stressful situations.

Another strategy of avoidance is to cope by numbing one's self to the traumatic aftereffects of the experience through the use of alcohol and drugs (Erikson 1976; Herman 1997; Phillips and Lindsay 2010; Zamble and Porporino 1988). Numbing provides a way to dissociate from the distress, suppress or "wall off" intrusive thoughts about the event, and dampen the survivor guilt many feel (Erikson 1976; Herman 1997). Numbing, however, further isolates survivors and increases, rather than decreases, feelings of disconnection as it often negatively affects relationships. It also interferes with survivors' "anticipation and planning for the future" (Herman 1997, 46). In some cases, numbing coupled with other strategies of avoidance impair the ability of survivors even to envision a future (Herman 1997). They narrow the survivors' focus and patterns of living to the present and decrease their ability to see beyond their immediate sphere of experiences. Perpetually in the moment and with their cognitive and emotional processes muted, they cannot imagine a life different from the present or see beyond a few days or weeks.

These two broad approaches to coping—the incorporation and avoidance approaches—and the various management techniques within each approach are the foundation for our understanding of how exonerees manage life after death row. These approaches are most certainly used by our participants to manage the disruption they experience upon release from prison. But before moving to this discussion, we offer two additional points. First, it would be easy to assume that one approach is "positive" while the other is "negative" or one "adaptive" and the other "maladaptive." For example, given our cultural tendency to view alcohol and drug abuse as problematic behavior deserving of intervention and remedy, some might automatically assume that numbing is a maladaptive or ineffective coping strategy. However, Richard

Lazarus (1999) warns against such assumptions. The usefulness of coping approaches depends on the contexts in which they are used, and thus each one may be both adaptive and maladaptive, effective and ineffective, depending on the circumstances at hand. George Bonanno (2004, 26) agrees. He finds, for example, that repressive coping that relies on emotional dissociation to avoid stressful thoughts and emotions is generally viewed as maladaptive, yet he argues that studies reveal that this strategy "appear[s] to foster adaptation to extreme adversity." Thus, we caution against thinking about the management techniques used by exonerees as either good or bad, helpful or unhelpful, useful or not useful. We try to avoid these types of judgments in our discussion and recommend the reader do the same.

Second, we think of coping as a process rather than a stagnant state (E. Miller 2003; Richardson 2002). Survivors use numerous coping strategies from both approaches at any given time and "try on" new ones when others become less helpful or more problematic: "Coping is a dynamic process. One's choice of coping alternatives may change with changes in awareness or interpretation of the problem. If one strategy is ineffective in reducing distress, the individual may search the solution schema for alternative strategies" (Yates et al. 1999, 156). We find this to be particularly true for our participants. In our interviews, the participants revealed strategies they currently were using, but also discussed how coping had changed over time. In some cases, the strategies they discuss are primarily from one of the approaches, either incorporation or avoidance. Ray Krone, for example, relies primarily on strategies of incorporation. He enjoys both connecting to other exonerees and engaging in his survivor mission. In fact, in his work with the organization Witness to Innocence, which he helped to establish, he combines both of these strategies into one as the focus of the organization is to change policies related to life after exoneration and bring together death row exonerees to assist them in their postrelease adjustment.[2] For others, the strategies exonerees use come from both approaches and are used at varying times depending upon the circumstance or even simultaneously. For example, Gary Gauger uses withdrawal, a strategy of avoidance, in his everyday life and admits that being around people makes him uncomfortable: "I used to like to go out and get involved in things, and talk with people. Now, I just don't wanna leave the house." However, he also derives satisfaction from telling his story at speaking engagements, a strategy of incorporation. Although these often take an emotional toll on him, he finds that telling his story is meaningful and gives him a sense of purpose.

Exonerees also disclose that their coping strategies have changed over time as they have discarded techniques and adopted new ones. Gary Beeman discusses how his primary coping strategies shifted from the avoidance approach, numbing in particular, to incorporation approach, such as telling his story and connecting to other exonerees: "The first several years after I was [out] I was okay. . . . And then the drinking got worse . . . and all the stuff that is caused by drinking took over. . . . When they got me to Chicago [for the first Northwestern School of Law conference for exonerees], that's when I thought maybe I should do what I wanted a long time ago. Maybe I should get involved with this." Soon after, Beeman began talking more about his experiences in public forums and advocacy events. Perry Cobb describes a similar shift from avoidance to incorporation strategies: "[At first] I was just trying to be quiet and stay away from everything. But, I wind up doing it [speaking in public] and going places."

These experiences confirm that coping is a dynamic process. Their coping continually shifts and emerges as they resolve difficulties associated with their wrongful capital convictions but continue to encounter new ones. Emblematic of the dynamic nature of their coping process is the realization by Kirk Bloodsworth who, five years after his exoneration, decided that his initial strategies of avoidance were no longer working for him and that it was time to try something new. He summed up this shift by declaring, "I'm not running [from it] no more. I'm running to it now." What he ran to were strategies of incorporation that included telling his trauma story, connecting to other exonerees, and embarking on a survivor mission. Given that coping, then, is a process, the experiences described by individual exonerees below illustrate a variety of coping strategies. This just reflects the ever-changing nature of the coping process.

COPING WITH LIFE AFTER DEATH ROW

Immediately upon release, exonerees confront many practical, financial, and emotional difficulties. Of the eighteen participants in our study, no one said that their road after release was easy, although they did vary in how difficult they saw the journey they faced. For example, Walter McMillian and Charles Fain generally felt accepted by their communities, while Sabrina Butler and Kirk Bloodsworth felt outcast, stigmatized, and isolated. The degree to which exonerees experienced their wrongful capital conviction as disruptive to their lives, of course, varied, as is true of the experience of all trauma survivors (Bonanno 2004). Yet within that variation is some consistency in the coping strategies they used in their postrelease adjustment. Like the strategies other trauma survivors use, these coping strategies generally revolve around the approaches of incorporation and avoidance. As Shabaka Brown says of life after exoneration: "Let me put it like this here. If you are offered a challenge, you have two choices, either to accept or to reject." As the experiences of our participants reveal, this is a choice they face repeatedly from the moment they step outside the prison gates. Sometimes they choose acceptance, sometimes rejection. Their choice often shifts over time and by circumstance. They use whichever and whatever they can to try to put their lives back together.

Strategies of Incorporation

The strategies of incorporation—telling their trauma story, making meaning, connecting to other survivors—are often cited by our exonerees as techniques they adopt when rebuilding after exoneration and release. Several implicitly recognize the value of the incorporation approach to their coping and note that they prefer that approach to avoidance of the situation. Their perspective is that they must accept their situation, recognize it for what it is, and find ways to move forward from it without dwelling on the past. As Perry Cobb notes, "I have to deal with the reality of life and not turn my head or bury my head in the sand like a ostrich. I got to face these things." Juan Melendez is very clear on the importance of moving forward toward creating a better life rather than looking backward to his past: "You've got to accept it. . . . See that's the way you got to look at it. It's not a loss. It's lost if you let it [be lost]. . . . If we learn to let things go, you move forward. But if you still prey on the past and the bad things that happened in the past, you're gonna be miserable. You not going nowhere. And you're wasting energy. . . . What's done is done. What I'm gonna do now, that's what counts." Ray Krone sees it as no longer allowing those from the past who caused his wrongful conviction to shape his life: "I don't want to allow them people that caused me to be in there to have any more grip on my life *at all*. They have no more control over me now. They're done. They had their shot at me. They had their ten years' worth. They're done! I ain't allowing them anymore power in my life!" (his emphasis).

Kirk Bloodsworth is the most explicit in his discussion of adopting an incorporation approach. He reveals how attending the National Conference on Wrongful Conviction and the Death Penalty, the first conference for exonerees, at the Northwestern Center on Wrongful Convictions in 1998 changed his perspective. It was the first time that exonerees had been brought together to meet and share their experiences with each other and the public. Until that point, Bloodsworth had primarily relied on avoidance approach techniques to cope—numbing and withdrawal. However, at Northwestern, he met other exonerees, realized he was not alone, and told his story in public for the first time. He found that experience empowering and transformative and decided that crucial to his new approach was accepting that he was a survivor and using that status to his advantage: "I'm an exonerated man accused of killing a little girl 'til I die. It's simple. But, I don't wanna look at the horror no more." He understood for the first time that acceptance of his new situation and status does not require him to live in the past—"the horror"—but instead provides a way to move forward into new opportunities, opportunities that have taken him to the halls of Congress to advocate for criminal justice reform, opportunities that have connected him to other exonerees, politicians, criminal justice professionals, students, and audiences around the world. For Bloodsworth, acceptance and incorporation became the keys to repairing and re-creating his connection to people and community.

Half of the exonerees explain that talking about their experience is helpful to them, that they do not mind sharing their story with others. As Alfred Rivera says, "I do not mind sharing my experience, talking of it, or giving my picture of it. [Being] asked to indulge in conversation about my views or thoughts and emotions does not bother me." Walter McMillian agrees, "I'm just as happy to talk about it as you probably. . . . I talk about it all the time to people. . . . White or black. Don't make no difference. I just tell them straight up." Thus, for some, telling their trauma story is not a wrenching process but an opportunity they embrace. Those in our study have often been asked to talk about their experiences to students, advocacy groups, and public forums. They discuss the value they gain from telling their story to others. For many, telling their story is emotionally healing and therapeutic. Kirk Bloodsworth and Scott Taylor say just that: "[It] is catharsis for me. This is why I do it. This is something I learned a long time ago, never keep it in because you're doing yourself a grave disservice if you do because you gotta get it out; whether you just talk to yourself in the mirror, get it out! Write a journal. Put it on tape. Whatever. Get it out of your system" (Bloodsworth); "[It] was actually therapy for me, because I wanted everybody to know this is what happened to me" (Taylor).

Others note the feelings of validation and support they get by telling their stories and how positive such opportunities are for them. As Greg Wilhoit explains, "When I give one of my little talks, for me anyway, it validates my whole experience, personally. And it's really helped me out . . . getting a lot of positive feedback." He also discusses the positive feelings he gets from knowing that his story might help others in some way: "I get such quality feedback from people, and it's a little bit of a buzz when people acknowledge that perhaps you are doing something that would help somebody." Perry Cobb agrees, "Sometimes it's . . . a relief to educate people as to what's going on with the system. Yeah. I [get] quite a bit out of it that way." This belief that they are helping others and educating the public about the inner workings and flaws in the criminal justice system leads to a sense of pride and accomplishment. For these exonerees, telling their stories to supportive audiences provides a way to turn their negative trauma experience into something more positive and meaningful for their own lives and the lives of others. The feedback they receive and feelings of accomplishment that result buoy their self-esteem and feelings of self-worth.

Three of those we interviewed—Gary Gauger, Delbert Tibbs, and Dave Keaton—were included in the play *The Exonerated* (2004). All three discussed how meaningful their participation in the play was because it provided a venue for their stories to be told to audiences they never imagined reaching. Gary Gauger sums it up best: "[*The Exonerated*] is reaching a different audience. See we always preach to the choir or to people like the prosecutor that's just so against you. But to have it just reaching people that it wouldn't have otherwise reached, that really don't have a clue . . . that is great!"

Telling their trauma stories also decreases their isolation and provides a way to connect with others in their community. Several exonerees expressed amazement and gratitude at the people they have met and worked with as a result of their willingness to talk about their experiences. Alfred Rivera, for example, recognizes that he was able to secure some assistance from the community by telling his story: "I was able to express my feelings, sometimes emotional, to those who were interested in the plight of those on death row and those who are vindicated from false arrests and convictions. Some people I met were willing to extend their friendship and network ability to ensure that I could achieve basic necessities." Greg Wilhoit frequently talks about his friendship while on death row with Ron Williamson, whose story was told in John Grisham's *The Innocent Man* (2006). Wilhoit was released first and was instrumental in asking his own appellate lawyer, Mark Barrett, to assist Williamson in securing his release. Wilhoit often participates with an advocacy group based in California called Death Penalty Focus, and he interacts with many of the television and movie stars who serve on its board: "I've met such wonderful people. I've never met anybody who was an asshole. Everybody's just completely compassionate, tolerant. It's just amazing. Plus, I get to do some interesting stuff. I hang out with the movie stars and this sort of thing."[3]

Perry Cobb has a slightly different perspective on the value of telling his story to making connections to others. He focuses more on the importance of talking about his experience when developing new relationships, in particular with women. He says, "If you have not told your complete story and/or dealt with your complete self with [your partner] and something happens, how can they help you? How can they fully love you if they don't fully know you?" Cobb sees honesty and revelation as essential to creating a strong relationship and connection with a woman. Whether on this more personal level or within the wider community, telling their story draws them out and places them in situations where they receive positive, affirmative support. It is a technique that allows them to turn a negative into a positive that is meaningful for themselves and others.

No doubt, telling their trauma story is one way that exonerees find meaning in their wrongful capital conviction. They use their story to educate and help others, which in turn provides them with validation and confidence. The ability to make the traumatic event meaningful for their own understanding of their lives is another coping strategy within the incorporation approach. To come to some type of belief about why the event happened to them combats the emotional dissonance created by thinking that life is just an accumulation of random, disconnected events and that they just happened to be the unlucky one. Finding meaning in their trauma gives order and consequence to something that might otherwise create feelings of powerlessness. About half of the exonerees said that they had come to believe that their wrongful capital conviction happened to them for a reason.

Both Delbert Tibbs and Alan Gell said that they had gone through this experience so that they could then reveal the inequalities and flaws of the system through public speaking. Gell says, "Everything that happened, happened so I could live on to tell it and share it with our lawmakers who possibly [could] bring about some justice reform." Tibbs's focus is more exclusively on the abolition of the death penalty, demonstrated when he says quite powerfully, "I believe that [the Great Spirit] took me to death row so that I could be a witness and a voice against it." Perry Cobb shares this certainty in the belief that his wrongful conviction happened for a reason: "I believe in my heart that everything has a reason. Everything happens for a reason. I don't believe in accidents and coincidences." However, he goes on to reveal that, while he does not believe in random chance, he is not yet sure exactly what the greater purpose for his wrongful conviction is.

Several exonerees believe that their wrongful capital conviction happened to make them reevaluate their life path. Until the point of conviction, they were engaged in harmful activities, and their wrongful conviction gave them a new perspective. As Sabrina Butler says, "It's a harsh way to get somebody to wake up . . . but I really feel like [God] sent me through that because I used to like to go to clubs all the time. I used to like to party. . . . I feel like he saw that I was going the wrong way. And he knows how hardheaded I am. . . . So, I feel, it was a harsh way for me to learn." Charles Fain also attributes his conviction to God's intervention to get him back on the right path. When asked what he now thought about a witness, and former acquaintance, who testified against him at trial, Fain responds, "He hurt himself. He didn't hurt me in the long term," to which one of us replied, "He put you on death row." Fain continues, "Yep, but best thing that happened to me. I look at it that he was just helping God out. God was using him. . . . 'Cause it changed the way I think. And when I think about breaking the law and hurting other people's rights . . . somebody was [now] trampling on my rights. So I learned what it was like to have somebody do something to you." Juan Melendez comes right out and attributes his wrongful conviction to saving his life: "I'd probably be dead [if this had not happened to me]. I would have been killed. My life was crazy. I was doing crazy stuff, so in a strange way, this saved my life."

Walter McMillian has a different variation on this theme of how the wrongful conviction changed his life path, though like the others he still sees it in a relatively positive light:

> It was just like a rest period, you might say, because I had worked so long. I started working when I was twelve years old, right here on this land. I just worked . . . all work, all work, work, work, work, work, in the woods picking cotton. That's how I worked all my life. I just said, "Well, this might be just a rest period." I just needed to rest because if I hadn't gotten locked up, I still would've been working in the woods like I was. And I'm so glad. I hate I got locked up and went to prison, but I'm glad somehow I come out of them woods.

For these exonerees, they have attributed their wrongful convictions and stints on death row with being a turning point in their lives. But it may be surprising to some that they see this, in many ways, as a positive turning point, a break from the past and opportunity to create a new present and future. This does not mean that they report no problems with postrelease adjustment, but it does mean that they have found a way to make sense out of the experience that allows them the possibility to move forward.

From these quotations, it is obvious that the exonerees who construct meaning from their experience often do so within a religious or spiritual framework. They see their journey as part of God's plan for them as being used by a greater power for a greater purpose. Delbert

Tibbs believes that a higher power is using him as a mouthpiece to agitate for change and eradicate the death penalty. Tibbs refers to this higher power as the "Great Spirit" and "That Being." He says, "That Being said, 'You fool, I see you just ain't gonna preach the way your mama and everybody else . . . wants you to do, so I'm gonna make you another kind of preacher. I'm gonna make you a teacher preacher, and give you something to teach about. And that is That.'" In his twenties, Tibbs had attended seminary to study religion and enter the ministry but had left seminary early because of a need to see the world and broaden his perspective. It was during his travels around the United States, while in Florida, that his wrongful conviction occurred. Thus, he sees his wrongful conviction as the Great Spirit's way of bringing him back to his original calling, just through a different door.

Charles Fain also uses spirituality, which he found on death row, as a primary coping strategy to give meaning to his experience. On his fifth day in prison, Fain was visited by a Gideon who talked with him about the forgiving and saving power of belief in Jesus Christ. While he admits to being closed to thinking about such issues before his wrongful conviction, on this particular occasion he was open to it, and he converted. Frequently throughout the interview, Fain discussed the role that his faith played in helping him survive death row and manage life afterward. We, in fact, met for his interview at his church, the place he said he would be most comfortable. Fain explained that describing his journey to and from death row to various audiences, while emphasizing the power of his faith in confronting the atrocity of it, illuminates how God uses him to bring others into the faith as well. Furthermore, he tells the story of a friend who visited the prison where Fain had been on death row for eighteen years in order to share Fain's story with the inmates: "He went out there and told my story from the third person, and two guys came to Jesus. I didn't have to do a thing." Thus, Fain attributes meaning to his experience through his belief in God and God's plan for his life.

Many exonerees have used spiritual or religious resources to help them cope postrelease, even if not directly by giving purpose or meaning to their experience. Both Charles Fain and Scott Taylor often reference the role their ministers play in their lives, providing advice, guidance, and support. Several exonerees credit God or a higher power with giving them strength to endure the struggles of life after exoneration. Both Greg Wilhoit and Gary Beeman say they are able to keep going through "the grace of God." Delbert Tibbs again references the Great Spirit, saying, "I'm a believer. The Great Spirit sustained me. It really did and does." Juan Melendez attributes his ability to continue his intense schedule of advocacy work to the strength he gets from God: "I know it's a job that I got to do. And I know he gives me the strength." Dave Keaton sums up the way that his spirituality allows him to accept his situation and move forward by saying, "I would just meditate on some of those things and it would help me to just lift myself up a little bit to just accept the fact that, okay, whatever it is, whatever it is, is going to happen."

Others use their spiritual meaning system to provide some peace in the midst of their tumult after release. They use their spirituality to calm their present and cope with memories from the past. Their spirituality provides them with a way to accept what has happened to them without dwelling on the pain and suffering caused to them. As Alfred Rivera says, "Resources that were a plus after my ordeal were mainly spiritual because I totally realized that spiritual peace is what allowed me to deal with most of the torment I had encountered. I kept up the practice of prayer and spiritual recitation and found peace in it." Both Charles Fain and Greg Wilhoit rely on their religious beliefs to help them forgive those in the past who were instrumental in producing their wrongful convictions. As mentioned earlier, Fain believes that the former acquaintance who testified against him hurt himself more than Fain and in fact did Fain a favor by helping to put him on death row. When asked what he would do if he ran into the prosecutor in his case in the grocery store, Wilhoit replies, "I'd forgiven him a long time ago. I'm all about forgiveness, and tolerance, and all that kind of crap . . . well, not crap. . . . I've been a Christian most of my life. I was brought up in the church, Methodist church. I signed on with Jesus years ago, and I'm not one to change horses midstream, and it really helped me out." While these fall short of saying that they were sent to death row for a particular purpose designed by God or a higher power, they do indicate that spiritual and religious frameworks help them leave the past in the past and move forward without hatred and bitterness.

By constructing meaning, about one-third of our participants transformed their personal journey into a survivor mission to promote social change. They have converted the personal meaning they created into a driving purpose for their lives in their new posttrauma, postexoneration reality. These exonerees say, "I was sent to death row for a reason and it changed my life," and add, "The reason is to change policy, change the criminal justice system, increase awareness, use my story to create a better world." In the first case, the meaning constructed around the experience is about the place of that experience within their own personal journey—to give them peace or a new start, to help them forgive and put the past behind them. In the second case, the meaning constructed around the experience is about using their voice to speak to others, to reach out, to make their experiences consequential for social change. The first is directed inward; the second is directed outward. It is possible that the first must precede the second; they must find meaning for themselves before they can use it for political and social change. Regardless, several exonerees use this coping strategy to make their trauma meaningful to the wider community and reestablish themselves as people of value with something to contribute.

Ray Krone discusses the meaning that his advocacy work gives to his experience and the sense of purpose it creates for him. Krone speaks around the country about issues related to wrongful convictions and was instrumental in establishing Witness to Innocence, which provides assistance to death row exonerees by helping them develop speaking skills and land paid speaking engagements. About his advocacy work, Krone says, "I feel more involved in my life. Even though it is your life and you think you're the only one involved . . . I feel like it's more, that it is . . . a purpose. That I am working as a solid entity rather than as just something that can go in any direction. I feel like I'm more like a rolling mat . . . like I got momentum behind me now, rather than just idling or floating." Kirk Bloodsworth echoes this feeling of purpose and direction. He explains why it is important for him to recognize the trauma created by his wrongful conviction but not let that trauma restrain him from action. Instead, it drives him to create change and make his experience consequential to criminal justice and death penalty reform:

> After twenty years, I'm still devastated by this damn thing that happened to me; *however*, I want to use it to my advantage. And that's the best way I can really say to not dwell on the fact that I was in

prison for eight years, eleven months, and nineteen days, and two years on death row, but after I did, I started a wellspring of effort to stop executions in the United States. And to change some laws about innocent people. And to make people stand up and take notice. And *that* is what is important. (his emphasis)

Bloodsworth went on to work for the Justice Project as an advocate for criminal justice reform and to lobby Congress to pass the Innocence Protection Act (IPA) of 2004.[4] When passed, the IPA included funding for DNA testing for incarcerated inmates with claims of innocence under the Kirk Bloodsworth Post-Conviction DNA Testing Grant Program. In 2008, Bloodsworth served on the Maryland Commission on Capital Punishment, charged with examining the operation of the death penalty in Maryland and making recommendations for reform or abolition to the governor.

Several other exonerees express how important it is for their advocacy and sharing of their story to make a difference for political and social change. For example, Alan Gell says that he recognized how critical this was early on: "I got out and two things happened. One is I realized I couldn't ignore what had happened to me. One is I realized that part of making everything that happened to me have meaning and purpose is me going out spreading the word and making a difference with things." Gell realized that he must confront his past, rather than avoid it, and that the key to giving that past meaning is to use it for a larger purpose. Scott Taylor says that he uses the media to advance his cause in much the same way the media were used against him to convince the public of his guilt: "Just like they used the media to convict me, I'm using the media to convict them now. I'm using the media to affect people's conscience about the death penalty." Gary Gauger adds that his mission to agitate for change is driven by his own desire to effect change and his feeling of responsibility to other wrongly convicted individuals who remain in the system or are too damaged to advocate themselves:

If not me, who? A lot of these guys can't do it. And I can understand why. I was only in prison for three and a half years. Some of these guys were in there for fifteen, seventeen years. And I see how profoundly it affects me. I can only imagine it's compounded ten times for these guys. . . . I know how hard it is. I do it because I feel I can. And it needs to be done. And I caught a lot of breaks that a lot of other people didn't catch. I had a place to come back to. I had the support team from the get-go. . . . So I had hope. These other guys—three, four, five, eight years into their sentence—their hope is gonna just run out. . . . I didn't have to endure all that, so I think it's a good thing for me to go out and try to prevent this. . . . I think it's important that we're educating [people] and it is making a difference.

Juan Melendez repeatedly reveals the depth of his commitment to this survivor mission and discusses how he believes he has no option but to pursue abolition. His advocacy work is something that he *must* do; it is not a choice but a calling. As noted previously, his two goals in life are "to take care of my mama and abolish the death penalty." His passion and purpose are evident when he says, "In order to beat the death penalty, I got to fight, I know this. I don't [always] fight the same way all the time. I might slow down a little bit. I might be more aggressive sometime. . . . But I always *will fight*. As long as I can breathe, I will fight" (his emphasis).

By telling their stories and finding meaning and purpose in their mission, exonerees who embrace the survivor mission blend several strategies from the incorporation approach. They reveal to the world their fears and pain and are greeted with support and affirmation. In doing so, they confront, rather than avoid, the aftereffects of the trauma in their lives. They turn their trauma into a source of personal revelation and public engagement and give meaning to the experience for themselves and the broader community. Exonerees who use this strategy get involved. They reach beyond themselves and their past. They connect to a wider community of people and to a purpose larger than themselves, harnessing energy for further action:

We can make a difference. I never thought the individual could really make a difference. The forces just seemed to be so unified and strong against you, and yet to watch these changes that have come about in the last ten years and watch the people that did it and see how they did it. And the way you do it is, first of all, you have to believe in something that's better, and already exists. And then to promote it, and to demonstrate it, and to continually demonstrate it until it becomes a reality. And that's great that we can do that. We can make a difference. (Gary Gauger)

The final strategy of incorporation used by exonerees is their connection to other survivors, in this case other exonerees. It is in the company of other trauma survivors that survivors find comfort, acceptance, and understanding, all with very little input or effort on their part. These connections reduce their isolation and detachment from those around them and help them realize they are not alone in their struggles. Several exonerees first realized the value of these connections when they attended the conferences for exonerees held by the Northwestern Center on Wrongful Convictions in 1998 and 2002.[5] For many, this was the first time they had talked with another exoneree, and they found the experience both comforting and energizing. Since then, our participants have often seen each other at conferences or advocacy events, and they draw solace from these encounters. A few quotes reveal the value of these connections:

[Being around other exonerees] builds that bond because you can understand that you are not the only other person this has happened to. (Dave Keaton)

It's like we're friends. We share a common experience, and we always seem to be glad to see each other. It's like we can kind of understand where the other guy's coming from. (Gary Gauger)

It was really, really great to be surrounded by people that have the same things in common as me. And it was like weren't nobody looking at me as a poor guy or this and that. We could tell prison stories and just totally relate to each other. (Alan Gell)

In talking about his trip to the first Northwestern conference in 1998, Gary Beeman reveals that he was nervous and hesitant: "In twenty-six, twenty-seven years, [it was] the first time ever I would have a chance to talk to somebody else who had been through this. I thought I have no idea where this is going emotionally. It could be explosive."

This emotional toll concerned Beeman since he was newly clean and sober after twenty years of struggling with drugs and alcohol after exoneration. However, he soon learned what a supportive environment he was in: "They constantly checked with me and made sure I was okay. . . . I realized if I go to the bar, if I wanted a drink, I knew some people [were] going to come up and say 'What are you doing, Gary?'" Beeman and Charles Fain both noted that connecting to other exonerees not only helps them feel as if they are not alone but also puts their own wrongful conviction into perspective. Beeman says, "I'm listening to these guys talk and Juan [Melendez] with eighteen years, and Kerry [Max Cook] with twenty-two, and another guy with eight, and I'm thinking I'm just a baby. My little experience was nothing what these guys went through." Fain sums it up by saying that he realized that "I've had it pretty good compared to them since I got out."

Kirk Bloodsworth found understanding and acceptance around the other exonerees at the first Northwestern conference, and he found his mission. It was after speaking there that he realized he had a story to tell and that he was pretty good at telling it. He decided to take a new direction: "I went to Northwestern and that really cemented me into a place. And I said, 'I think I've found what I need to do.' . . . I'm not running [from it] no more. I'm running to it now." Shabaka Brown describes the value he finds in the company of other exonerees: "The *greatest* thing that ever happened to me was in 1998, that first conference in Chicago, because here I was amongst people that I could just open my mouth and didn't have to explain what I was saying. That was such a hell of a feeling. . . . If y'all was there and felt *the impact, the bonding, the love.* . . . Oh my goodness! Ain't no type of therapy could do nothing [like that]" (his emphasis).

Telling their trauma story, finding meaning in their wrongful conviction, embarking on a survivor mission, connecting with other exonerees—all of these strategies of incorporation help them cope with their trauma, by helping them look past the traumatic experience and toward new opportunities to connect with others and their communities. Using these strategies, our participants situate their past as a meaningful part of their broader life journey rather than focus on their past as an insurmountable obstacle. Thus, they are able to get relief from the disruption and detachment caused by their wrongful convictions.

Strategies of Avoidance

In some cases, strategies of avoidance also provide relief for exonerees and are mechanisms by which they can (at least temporarily) escape the painful emotions and community rejection haunting them. Through withdrawal and numbing, they avoid situations that may expose intrusive emotions and reminders of the past. When discussing his incorporation-oriented coping techniques, Ray Krone considers how common avoidance strategies are among many of the exonerees he knows: "I know that some of these guys are more in avoidance. . . . They really have not adjusted . . . or come to grips with what happened and accepting that it has happened. . . . They are hiding from something. They do have something that they are repressing." Exonerees relying on the avoidance approach withdraw from, rather than confront, situations that emphasize their wrongful capital convictions.

Several exonerees describe their use of the avoidance approach by saying that they "ran from" their past for a long time. Kirk Bloodsworth's turning point was clear: "I'm not running [from it]. . . . I'm running to it. . . ." Gary Beeman similarly says when explaining his shift from avoidance to incorporation strategies after fifteen or twenty years, "I was running from something for a long time." Gary Gauger discusses his tendency to "run from" and avoid situations that cause him to relive the pain of his wrongful conviction. He stopped seeing a psychologist because the painful emotions his sessions evoked were too much, and instead he buries himself in farming to avoid feeling this pain:

> I just haven't taken the time to deal with it . . . actually that's my justification. I think mostly I just know that it's so incredibly painful I choose not to deal with it. I bury myself in my work, and I've become more intellectual rather than emotional. . . . I like [farming] because you have to focus or you will get hurt. So, I don't have to think. And it's hard physically, so it's something demanding for my body to do. So, it just physically occupies my attention. And I like that. Then I don't have to think about things. If I start thinking about things, I start going nuts. I find myself, when I'm riding on the tractor, screaming at the top of my lungs because then nobody can hear me. It's kind of a cathartic release.

Gauger repeats often how "I don't like to think." When discussing how difficult speaking engagements can be for him, he says, "It used to be really hard when I had a speaking engagement coming up. I'd be worthless a couple of days before and a few days after. And I developed a defense mechanism of literally not thinking about it, and then just doing it." For Gauger, "not thinking" allows him to go through the motions of telling his story without having to confront the emotional anguish retelling can cause. It is Gauger's way of "running from" or dampening the hurtful consequences of his past.

One strategy exonerees use to avoid potentially uncomfortable situations is to withdraw from interactions with others. Several exonerees prefer to stay at home and do not like to be out and about town. Their circle of friends is small. In some sense, they are loners. As Scott Taylor says, "I don't really hang with anybody other than immediate family. Otherwise, I don't have friends." And Perry Cobb says, "I don't go out a lot. I don't do a lot of things. . . . I did all the partying I was gonna do [growing up]. I went here. I went there. I don't do that anymore." Gauger elaborates, preferring to be on his own, screaming out his frustrations from atop his tractor in the middle of an empty field: "I hate to even have the phone ring. I don't like to talk to people on the phone. So, what's the point? I can't write letters. I can't talk on the phone. I don't like to visit. I don't like to go anywhere. I don't like to leave the house. What's the point? . . . Don't wanna bust out of my comfort zone." Their isolation prevents them from being in uncomfortable situations where they might be identified or called to reveal, or even defend, their exoneree status. Gauger recalled when his wife came home from a shopping trip where she was identified by a community member as Gauger's wife. The stranger told her he thought Gauger was guilty. Such occasions emphasize for Gauger the value of withdrawal to avoid such painful encounters.

For some, withdrawal involves retreating from the situation altogether. Several exonerees discussed relocating from their communities, where they were well known for their status as death row exonerees. Scott Taylor, whose gubernatorial pardon made him a celebrity of sorts after his release, moved away soon after his release, although he returned to be with his mother during a protracted illness. When we interviewed him, he was talking about changing his name and again moving away as soon as her health stabilized. When asked if he wished he could leave and regain some anonymity, he responded emphatically, "I do. Yep. I do." Since then, he has relocated and lives in a different region of the country. Both Greg Wilhoit and Perry Cobb also chose to relocate. After living briefly in Oklahoma and Illinois, respectively, each decided that their past was too continuously intrusive into their present, and they moved. About his move to Sacramento, Wilhoit says, "One thing I love about living out here is no matter where I go, I never run into anybody I know. I can be myself." After several uncomfortable run-ins with police and family members of the victims in his case, Cobb decided it was safer and less problematic for him simply to relocate. He moved to another state to be closer to children and grandchildren. Thus, for some, withdrawal results in a complete retreat in an attempt to increase their anonymity. By moving, they find comfort in knowing that few people will recognize them and associate them with their exoneree status. Thus, they can decide when to disclose this aspect of who they are, which gives them control over the contexts in which they reveal and grapple with their past.

Numbing is another strategy of avoidance often used by our participants. About half of our exonerees admit to significant alcohol and/or drug use during the years since their exoneration. As Judith Herman (1997) explains, numbing provides a way for survivors to "wall off" intrusive emotions and thoughts and avoid having to confront painful memories. In some ways, numbing is another form of retreat. Several exonerees are quite open about their use of alcohol and/or drugs to cope with their emotional turmoil after exoneration. Dave Keaton gets straight to the point: "I was drinking [to] cope." Gary Beeman, who had a substantial alcohol problem for almost twenty years after his release, admits that he was somewhat surprised by the impact that his capital conviction had on him, an impact he tried to manage with alcohol and drug use: "I didn't really think [death row] would have an impact on me. It was just another place in the joint. I had already done time. It wasn't fun, but it was just a tougher place, and [I] didn't really [think it would] have that much of an impact on me, so I thought. But then as I look back, for the next more than two decades, I threw my life away with drugs and alcohol. So, it had some kind of impact." Delbert Tibbs sums it up when he says, "I suspect that's many of us, the drug and alcohol abuse. I certainly had my battle with that. I suspect that's many of us."

Several now see their drug and alcohol use as a strategy to forget their past, to avoid or "wall off" the past from their present. Dave Keaton says as much: "I would drink. . . . I [would] drink to get drunk to forget." For Kirk Bloodsworth, drinking had a silencing effect on the voices of his past that invaded his thoughts and emotions when he was sober:

> The only thing I wanted to do [in the years after he was first released], and I hate to admit to a misdemeanor, but is get high and drink, and I mean get butthole drunk. You know, just fall down and sloppy because I wanted to forget. . . . I wanted to feel nothing. . . . When me and him [Jack Daniels] got together, he never hollered at me. He never said I was a killer. He was always there for me. "Come and wake me up Kirk. You ready? Come and get me. Pour me in a glass. I'm right here for ya." He was killing me too at the same time.

For others, alcohol and drugs were a way to manage or dampen their rage and bitterness over their wrongful conviction. They recognized and feared that their rage could be all-consuming if it were fully expressed and destructive to themselves and possibly to others. Numbing is a technique they used to get control of that explosive possibility: "The rage is there. And I think sometimes, in fact I'm pretty sure, that when I use drugs . . . and stuff like that, I think that's what it is because those are ways that we dissipate that. Not in a socially acceptable way, but more socially acceptable than me taking a magnum and running up and down the street shooting people" (Delbert Tibbs). Although Tibbs recognizes that some may think of his use of numbing as problematic, he instead argues that it is preferable to even less desirable coping strategies, such as the use of violence.

The coping literature notes that use of avoidance strategies often results in survivors being unable to envision themselves in the future (Herman 1997). Muting their emotional responses, avoidance of the past, and withdrawal keep them in the present, thus preventing them from making plans, seeking new opportunities, or setting goals for the future. In a way, this keeps survivors from moving forward since they are not able to conceive of a future worth moving into. It is important to note that only a minority of our exonerees struggle to envision the future. The majority are able to set goals for themselves, including starting a family, building a comfortable life, traveling, and creating change in the criminal justice system. In each of these cases, exonerees see themselves as active participants in their lives in the future, as working to create or build something new.

But it is the case that a few indicate that they do not think about the future or are not able to conceive of the future, and that they only live in the present. As Tim Howard says, "I really don't think about the future that much. I'm more or less a day-to-day person." But, many among this group of exonerees do not rely most heavily on strategies of avoidance, which is counter-intuitive based on the literature. Instead, they attribute their inability to envision the future to the "prison effect." While incarcerated, especially on death row, exonerees needed to live in the present because the future was uncertain and, in many ways, unknowable, but mostly, the future was not of their making. As Gary Gauger explains, "I can't really see more than two weeks in advance. I've lost the ability to really comprehend that. I think I got that [in prison] because commissary comes every two weeks. And that was a finite thing where I could make a plan, write things on paper, and if you were lucky and you weren't on lockdown, two weeks later you'd get something for your commissary." Prison puts the imprisoned in survival mode, surviving the circumstances of their confinement from one day to the next: "I don't think about the future. To me, the future is now. . . . That's the only way I could live [on death row]. I lived in a small cage for many years, where my whole concentration [had to be] right there for today. To survive today. Forget about tomorrow. I don't know about tomorrow. I just have enough energy, enough strength, to survive today and do what I have to do. And I still do that" (Shabaka Brown). Any plans they may make are certain to be broken, and the simple fact of their wrongful conviction and incarceration exemplifies the degree to which the future is beyond their control. As Ray Krone explains, making a plan brings with it the expectation that things will work out as planned. But, in prison, that principle does not hold:

> I don't know what the future holds. I can only do what I think is right now, and you never had too many long-term goals in prison.

When I was working at the post office, I had to plan my retirement, how old I was going to be. I was already looking to buy property in northern Arizona. I was thinking [ahead] and planning at thirty-five. I had a little bit of a career mapped out. Well, of course, then this crap with prison comes up, and it's like, "Well, everything is out the window now." And then you quit planning anything because you can't plan nothing in the justice system. You don't know when anything is going to happen. And now I'm still not into that mode of planning too far ahead. I just don't worry about it. It's a stressful thing because when you plan stuff, you plan stuff with the intention of it working out the way you want it to work out.

In these cases, they struggle to place themselves in the future but not in order to avoid the consequences of their painful pasts. Instead, they see their inability to envision the future as an atrophy from their past rather than as a strategy to cope with it.

The memories of the injustices done to them and the feelings of pain, rage, and bitterness such memories generate are too overwhelming to confront and accept, and as a result, exonerees sometimes turn to strategies of avoidance to mute the experience in their minds and emotions. Some recognize that these strategies could be destructive both physically and psychologically, such as when Kirk Bloodsworth says that his alcohol abuse was "killing me," and Gary Beeman realizes that "I threw my life away with drugs and alcohol." However, exonerees do not always see these strategies in a negative light but instead claim they are, in some instances, more positive choices than others, as when Delbert Tibbs sees alcohol and drug use as preferable to violence. Ultimately, they use strategies of both incorporation and avoidance as techniques to manage the difficult journey that awaits them upon release, trying them on and taking them off as circumstances warrant. In the moment of use, they find value in both approaches.

FACTORS THAT INFLUENCE COPING

Little is known about what shapes coping strategies survivors adopt. Coping is so dynamic that assessing factors that influence each approach and each shift is difficult, to say the least. And, in fact, based on our interviews, we cannot predict what factors may influence an exoneree to choose an incorporation or avoidance strategy at any given time. However, we asked our participants to think about what was most helpful in their postrelease adjustment and what was most problematic. The factors they identified as most helpful, interestingly, shared a common characteristic: they are factors that increased the connectedness exonerees felt with others and their communities. On the other hand, the factors they identified as most problematic shared the characteristic of increasing the disconnection and detachment they experienced after release. Thus, our participants conceptualize the value of the resources available to them after their release in terms of how much they increased or decreased the degree of disruption they were experiencing.

A few factors are identified in the literature as either facilitating or impeding survivors' recovery from trauma, though this literature is not well developed. The two most common factors noted as facilitating recovery are connection to and support from family and friends (Herman 1997; Kaniasty and Norris 1999; Seccombe 2002; Tak and McCubbin 2002; Williams et al. 2003) and community acknowledgment of the trauma experienced by survivors (Herman 1997; Kaniasty and Norris 1999; Seccombe 2002; Shih 2004). The most common factor noted to impede recovery is a hostile, negative response from the community toward the survivors' experience (Herman 1997). We find evidence of these at work in the responses of our exonerees to our inquiry about "what helped the most" and "what made it worse."

Factors That Facilitate Adjustment

The most notable factor that exonerees point to as helping in their postrelease adjustment is connections to and support from family and friends, and, in some cases, lawyers, a pattern of support that continues from their time on death row. Over two-thirds of exonerees mentioned some form of social support as influential in their ability to rebuild after release. Shabaka Brown observes that social support was a factor that had a positive effect for many exonerees: "I'm one of the few that made it. But I believe a lot of fellows don't have what I have, and what I always had [which is] a support network. And I think that was very important." Scott Taylor explains how social support from family and friends has been essential by giving him someone to rely on for help and advice: "Most helpful I think is the continued support. My family. My pastor.

[People at my] job. . . . That's more helpful than anything. If I had a problem, I always have someone I can talk to. Go over and I'm always welcomed." Unwavering acceptance is what Taylor has found most valuable.

While several exonerees mention friends who have been important to them, in most cases, exonerees point to support from family as the most important. As Ray Krone states simply, "I've always had a good supportive family. Always had people that believed in me." Even in cases when one member of the family has not been supportive, such as with Kirk Bloodsworth or Gary Gauger, they note the majority of the family has rallied around them to provide for their material and emotional needs after release. Bloodsworth says that "all of my family [was there when I got out]. We're a real tight group, the Bloodsworths. . . . And I try to keep those people around because they're the ones that are worth something. They're just like precious jewels." Gauger's tone changes to pure gratitude when he discusses the sacrifices made by his twin sister and her husband who kept the family farm afloat while he was incarcerated and had a place for him to stay when he was released.

When discussing family support, most exonerees identify one or two people who were influential, whether parents, siblings, children, or partners. Alan Gell and Ray Krone focus on the support of their parents who believed in their innocence from the outset and pursued evidence and every avenue of redress while they were in prison. Gell and Krone discuss the support of their stepfathers as being particularly meaningful. They are impressed by these men who supported their mothers during a family crisis and who worked tirelessly for their exonerations and release. Krone says, "[My stepdad] married my mom after I was already in prison. I mean imagine coming into a family with something like that. He was there. He is one hundred percent behind me." Both Tim Howard and Gary James, codefendants, credit their sisters as their biggest supporters throughout their journey. James says, "[My sister] was there for me from the beginning to the end. . . . It helped me. Without her, I don't know." In addition to his sister, Gauger points to the importance of his wife as having a calming influence on him. When asked what helps him most, he responds simply, "Sue and coffee."

The value of this support is in the connections they foster for exonerees, connections that help to reduce their isolation and feelings of detachment. These relationships increase their level of investment in others and expose them to feelings of love and acceptance that were taken from them in so many ways as a result of their wrongful convictions. Perry Cobb credits time with his grandchildren with helping his heart to reopen to these positive emotions: "[From my grandchildren and the other children in the neighborhood,] I rediscovered love and emotions. . . . This is an introspective rainbow to me. . . . I have gained a lot from being [with them]. And I am coming more close to being a human being all over again because I've been treated that way [by them]. It was the babies who opened the doors for that." He describes an afternoon when his grandchildren were visiting, and he went to take out the garbage: "I'm on my way to the garbage can, and from the oldest to the baby, I'm like a duck. Every last one, they in a line right behind they granddaddy. . . . So when I experienced this, my heart just fell open. . . . I was crying. . . . The love was new and fresh and authentic, and my heart just fell open to it. It was beautiful. It made me become alive again." Ray Krone describes in an emotional moment the commitment he feels toward his family and friends for their unwavering support for him throughout the ordeal:

> I've been very blessed, very fortunate. I don't wanna let my friends down. I can't pay them back moneywise. The only thing I can hopefully do is make them proud and let them know that I am who I am because they helped save my life. . . . I'm going to make them proud for the rest of my life. They struggled and stressed for those ten years while I was in prison, worrying about me, wondering what they could do, while they're still living their own lives, taking care of their own families, wondering what they can do to help Ray. It's like, that's something. That's gonna be my mission, my goal.

Several exonerees included in this group of supporters the lawyers who had worked on their appeals and exonerations. They became valuable resources for exonerees even after release. Shabaka Brown talks about how he lived with his appellate attorney, Michael Mello, after his release. Tim Howard invited his appellate attorney, Jim Owen, over to meet us when we interviewed him. He explains that Owen has been keeping pressure on him to find a job and get some stability while also pursuing a wrongful incarceration lawsuit on his behalf. Alan Gell is grateful to his attorneys, Mary Pollard and Jim Cooney, for helping him find speaking engagements after his release. He says they keep a check on him as well: "I get emails from them quite often. Most of the time, they tell me that they're proud of me, and proud to see how I'm doing." Given the failure of the criminal justice system to provide adequate assistance to exonerees after release, their appellate attorneys often are key to their chances of effectively rebuilding a life after exoneration.

The second most frequently cited factor to aid reintegration, from their perspectives, was the degree of acceptance they felt from the communities to which they returned. While some exonerees faced open hostility and threats, others were fully welcomed back to the community and note that acceptance is meaningful to them. In some cases, recalling that feeling of understanding and acknowledgment brings them to tears. As Juan Melendez explains, how well exonerees do when they get out is related to how well they are received by their community:

> [My adjustment] has got to do a lot with the way I was received. Even if I wanted to cry, the way I was received, it made me think otherwise. It was helpful. A lot of help. It's hard for a person to get out of jail and everyone may have forgot about him. . . . And I'm quite sure that a lot of people that got out they think that he did the crime. See what I'm saying, I'm quite sure of that. . . . [But my community,] they never forgot. And these are the things that help you in that situation, that help you overcome all the pain and all the suffering, all the things that you can lean on.

Walter McMillian agrees and makes clear a point that is more implied by Melendez. For McMillian, community acceptance means *belief* in his innocence, belief that he is not capable of the heinous crime for which he was convicted and incarcerated: "That helps a lot, to know people still on your side. I ain't had a soul, nobody, I mean black or white, even spoke to me no kind of way [saying I was still guilty] because everybody knows, *everybody* knows I didn't do it" (his emphasis).

Several exonerees reveal that acceptance and belief from family members of the victims in their cases were particularly important to them. After years of believing that the victim survivors hated them and wanted their deaths, they are relieved that the family members wish them no harm and understand that the exoneree also was a victim in the case. Alan Gell met the victim's son during a hearing to investigate the alleged prosecutorial misconduct that led to his conviction (see Neff 2004). He says,

> He apologized for hating me all them years and told me that he was sorry I went through all the things that I did because of them mother fuckers, talking about the police and prosecutors. And he just seemed real bitter and hateful toward them. . . . It felt real good because I was, all that time, [thinking] the victim's family [was] hating me and wanting me dead. I wanted somehow to let them know that I didn't do it and they got the wrong person and that you might want to pursue it because they got me and not the right person. That means you're not getting justice.

The exonerees who have had positive exchanges with victim survivors are at once grateful for the opportunity to have talked with them and also feel sorry for them because they have been so mistreated by the criminal justice system: "The victims, that's a touchy situation too because they usually are inflamed by the prosecutor. The prosecutor wants to keep that anger, that passionate hatred going because every time he had to play it back . . . he wants them angry. He wants to show that so he can get the result that he's pushing for, whether it's the death penalty or blocking parole or whatever. . . . Yet, he's telling them this is closure, this is healing" (Ray Krone). In the end, exonerees who have had positive contact with victim survivors find commonality in their shared experience of being "victims" of a flawed system and those working in it.

Whether it is support from friends and family or acceptance from the wider community, exonerees find the most solace and assistance in connections they make to others, in whatever resources and opportunities close the gap between themselves and those they encounter after release. When facing a journey marked by disruption and isolation, it is those factors that create commitment and investment in others that are valuable to them. Not surprisingly, the factors they discuss as being most problematic are those that maintain distance and lock in their isolation and detachment.

Factors That Impede Adjustment

In fact, exonerees did not discuss many factors that they saw as impeding their adjustment after release. Although they were quick to describe the many obstacles they did face, they were not able to articulate what made their ability to overcome those obstacles more difficult. The two factors mentioned were the roles of the media and of the prosecutor in inflaming the public against them by insinuating their guilt, even after exoneration. These factors decrease community acceptance and belief in their innocence, which in turn increase their isolation and the level of hostility they face from the community. An example of the role the media can play in shaping public sentiment can be found in a chapter about Sabrina Butler that appeared in a book about women on death row.[6] The chapter was not based on an interview with Butler, and no attempt was made to evaluate her side of the story. According to Butler, the chapter was based primarily on the version of events told by one of the lead detectives in her case, someone Butler argues is greatly responsible for her wrongful conviction. The chapter paints her as an abusive, mentally challenged welfare mother who beat her child to death. She believes that this portrait of her has further inflamed public sentiment against her in her small town in Mississippi:

> [The book paints me] as this heinous murderer that stomped my baby. In the book, it says I took [my oldest child] and threw him out a moving pickup truck. I mean he must be plastic or something for all this to be going on with him! That hurt me. When I got that book, my mama sent it to me, and I cried like a baby. I mean, they have just destroyed my life! . . . And it makes me mad because I got children, and my kids hear this. "Okay. Well, you know your mama ain't no good. Your mama killed your brother." That's why I went and got my tubes tied because I was scared to have another baby here in Columbus, Mississippi.

The prosecutor compounds the misrepresentation by continuing to refer to Butler's case whenever other cases of felonious child abuse are prosecuted in the area, thus implying her guilt by association. She believes these factors contribute to her continued isolation within her community, including her inability to find a job and find a church home that will accept her.

Scott Taylor discusses his dismay in the way his case was portrayed on *The Oprah Winfrey Show*. He was frustrated that she chose to show a video clip of one of the victim survivors in his case who said she still believed in Taylor's guilt, even after his very public gubernatorial pardon. Taylor believes that Winfrey used the segment on his case to second-guess the governor's decision to pardon him and thus cast doubt on his true innocence. In this particular case, the most powerful representative of the criminal justice system in his case, the governor of the state, had publicly declared Taylor's innocence, a rare event. But this public declaration and the acceptance and belief Taylor hoped to gain from it were undercut by a media portrayal that was less supportive.

On many occasions, our participants discussed their frustrations over the public declarations of prosecutors and other criminal justice representatives about their exonerations (Westervelt and Cook 2008, 2010). Rather than admitting error, the more common response of system officials is to continue to insist on exonerees' guilt, even in the face of revelations of evidence supporting their innocence. One example of such insistence is found in the case of Kirk Bloodsworth. When the representative from the state's attorney's office announced publicly that, after almost ten years of incarceration, DNA testing had revealed no trace of Bloodsworth at the crime scene, she chose to equivocate as to his actual innocence, saying, "Based on the evidence, our office did the right thing in prosecuting him. . . . I believe he is not guilty. . . . I'm not prepared to say he's innocent" (Junkin 2004, 261). Not long after her statement and his release, Bloodsworth found a note on his truck that said simply "child killer." Aside from the extreme frustration and bitterness that exonerees uniformly express over the failure of anyone in the system to apologize to them for their wrongful conviction, they believe this failure of prosecutors and police to own up to their mistakes in public forums plants only uncertainty in the minds of the public and confirms some people's beliefs that exonerees are not truly innocent but have merely gotten out on a technicality. This heightens, rather than diminishes, hostilities against them and certainly decreases the likelihood of their being widely accepted within the community.

As EXONEREES FACE the struggles that confront them upon release and choose strategies to manage these struggles, they do note factors that both help and hinder that process. In either case, they focus on the extent to which these factors influence their connections to others and community. As they rebuild their lives after the sustained catastrophe of a wrongful capital conviction, they try on several coping strategies to manage the disruption they have experienced. Some of the strategies they try on help them confront the atrocities of their past and create new opportunities to connect with others and the wider community. Some of the strategies, on the other hand, provide relief and respite from the barrage of overwhelming thoughts and emotions that flood their daily lives. They may try several strategies on at once or discard old ones before trying new ones. But, either way, they keep searching, searching for acceptance and understanding and a place to call home.

CHAPTER 10

Reclaiming Innocence

It's just different. I don't know. My thinking is
different. I feel different. I really can't say. I'm just a
different person. I felt I might have been killed that
night too [when my parents were killed], and I've
started a new life. It's just, it's different. It's
completely different. I can't even describe it. It's like
stepping into another universe.   —Gary Gauger

THEIR WRONGFUL CAPITAL conviction and incarcera-
tion not only disrupt exonerees' relationships with others and connections to community but also their sense of self, their identity, and very
personal understandings of who they now are as free people. In addition
to being abruptly released, they return to communities that may or may
not accept their return. Upon release, they discover that others continue
to believe in their guilt, that their exoneration and release are inadequate
to proclaim their status as innocent people. Some must fight to assert
their innocence and reconstruct their reputations as people worthy of
trust. Stuck between the falsely applied "murderer" master status and
the person they are and want others to see them as, they struggle to
reconstruct their identity and reclaim their innocence.

TRAUMA, STIGMA, AND
ASSAULTS ON THE SELF

Trauma disrupts the sense of self. For some, traumatic experiences
attack the very core of survivors' beliefs about self and the world around
them. Trauma shatters preconceived understandings of their worth and
value; it discounts the control and agency that survivors felt they had
over their lives prior to the traumatic experience. As Judith Herman
(1997, 51) explains, "Traumatic events call into question basic human

relationships. They breach the attachments of family, friendship, love, and community. They shatter the construction of the self that is formed and sustained in relation to others. They undermine the belief systems that give meaning to human experience" (see also Brison 2002). In part, this attack on the self emerges from the realization that their "voice" was discredited or silenced during the traumatic event, rendering their perspective, desires, and needs mute. Herman (1997, 53) writes, "At the moment of trauma, almost by definition, the individual's point of view counts for nothing."

Many survivors feel a sense of disorientation or displacement, lost in the new posttrauma reality they confront. Herman (1997, 196) likens this to being an immigrant in one's own life in which survivors speak of "losing and regaining the world" in a moment. They are displaced from their former selves and their place in the world but have not yet established their new selves and where they belong in relation to others, community, and the world at large. Kai Erikson (1976, 212) describes disorientation among survivors of the Buffalo Creek flood. They repeatedly report feeling "strange" and "out of place." He concludes, "People all over the hollow live with a lasting sense of being out of place, uprooted, torn loose from their moorings, and this feeling has long outlasted the initial trauma of the disaster itself." The traumatic event is a marker delineating the point where the old self lost relevance and cast the survivor into a new reality in which he or she wrestles to define who the new self will be.

Many argue that incarceration is traumatic and attacks the self, producing similar disorienting effects for prisoners. Gresham Sykes's (1958) classic study of the "pains of imprisonment" reveals that total control undermines inmates' understandings of self, autonomy, masculinity, and self-worth (see also Cohen and Taylor 1972). True, a spate of prison studies in the latter decades of the twentieth century argued that prison time was akin to a period of "deep freeze" of earlier behavioral patterns that are not seriously impacted, for better or worse, by the conditions of imprisonment (Zamble and Porporino 1988). However, more recent studies have found severe and long-lasting psychological effects resulting from incarceration (Haney 2003a, 2003b; Jamieson and Grounds 2005; Kupers 2008). Ideas first introduced by Sykes regarding the impact of incarceration on understanding self and self-worth are now being revisited. As John Irwin and Barbara Owen (2005, 98) explain, "Long imprisonment assaults and disorganizes the personality in . . . insidious and subtle ways, including loss of agency, assaults on the self and damage to sexual orientation." Though studies of ex-prisoners' adjustment postrelease are few and far between, evidence suggests that, like other trauma survivors, ex-inmates experience periods of disorientation and displacement when they return to their communities (Jamieson and Grounds 2005; Phillips and Lindsay 2010).

Exonerees then endure a double dose of attacks on the self. As individuals incarcerated often for quite long periods of time, they experience the devaluation and disorientation common to those released from prison. However, the assault on identity is compounded by the wrongful conviction experience itself. Exonerees explain the extreme frustration that comes from having friends and family, the community, and the criminal justice system believe they are capable of committing the heinous crimes of which they were convicted: "Anybody knew me growing up and seen me in all different types of situations [know that] I couldn't hurt no child. Cryin' nelly. I *could not believe* . . . and could never understand why people just accepted it like it was [true]. I could never understand that" (Kirk Bloodsworth, his emphasis). Many are shocked and angered that their reputation has been so irrevocably damaged. Sabrina Butler emotionally describes the pain she feels from being treated like someone who would kill her child, even now almost ten years after release: "I'm this person . . . this heinous murderer that stomped my baby. . . . That hurt me. . . . They have just destroyed my life! . . . And I'm very angry because I can't get back what they took from me!" Exonerees feel as if the core of their identity is under assault and has been taken from them against their will. They want people to know that they are innocent, that they are not the type of people who would commit the crimes for which they are accused. Alan Gell keenly expresses this pain and frustration over losing control of his identity as an innocent person when describing the moment he was found guilty of homicide. He explains how his lawyers wanted to focus on the sentencing phase to avoid the death penalty, while Gell told them they had missed the point: "It don't matter if I've got to spend the rest of my life in prison for something I didn't do or if I get the death penalty and they kill me for something I didn't do. Either way, I'm being punished for something I didn't do. . . . I just refused to help and assist the lawyers with the sentencing part because it didn't matter. . . . The most important part ain't life or death. The most important part is guilt or innocence!"

The Liminal Period of Reconstructing Identity

Exonerees experience the wrongful conviction as a long process during which their voices have been silenced and ignored (see also Weigand 2009). Their identity was discredited by a criminal justice system that portrayed them as monsters capable of the most disturbing cruelty. They felt utterly disregarded. Their voices silenced and identities destroyed, they were then expelled from humanity: they would be exterminated because they were deemed so despicable. But, of course, they were not that person, that self the system sought to destroy. Several exonerees try to describe that moment when they are told that the false identity created by the system is to be killed, but it is a moment they find difficult to put into words. Perry Cobb comes closest to explaining the extreme attack on the self he felt upon hearing that he would be executed:

> It's a little hard to describe . . . in words how you really feel. . . . I guess it's like a mother giving birth and the child dies at birth. I don't know. But I do know that it's a pain that no artist can draw if a person's able to give it to him in words. I don't believe that they can put it on a canvas. You talking about self. . . . It was not [just] a loss. I thought about my . . . mother, dad and grandparents, sisters, and especially children. You'll never be able to see them do anything. It's like a dry, rotten weed in the wind. It's gone. It's adjusting and you'll never see them again. It's really hard to give you that. I can't give it to you. That moment was my whole life. That was my life.

To be killed because society holds one's self and personhood in such low regard is the ultimate act of devaluation and destruction.

Like other trauma survivors, this attack on the self results in uncertainty and disorientation after release. Many recognize that they have been changed and that they are no longer the people they once were. However, they are not yet able to say who they are now. As Erikson described above, they feel uprooted and out of place. Perry Cobb, for example, says, "It seems like they gave me another life when they did this to me." He goes on to talk about how singing in public, a central part of his identity before his conviction, now makes him uncomfortable: "I can sing, but I can't perform. That bothers me. That really bothers me because it's a part of me that's absent. If I get that back, then the whole Perry Cobb would be here." Clearly, he feels as if a part of himself has been destroyed, and it bothers him that he is not yet able to reclaim his whole self. Scott Taylor similarly discusses that he feels as if he is a different person now, a person he is trying better to understand: "When I first got out, I didn't know who I was. And to this day I know I've changed. . . . The obstacle [has] really just [been] fitting back in society, trying to get to know myself, my own identity as a free man." Gary Gauger most clearly articulates this feeling of disorientation and uncertainty about his new self when he says, "My life is no longer my own. I really feel sometimes I was actually murdered the same day my parents were, and this is like an alternative life I'm living because the difference is just so abrupt and different."

The disruption of self experienced by trauma survivors and exonerees leads to uncertainty where they are caught between their former beliefs about who they are and their unknown new identity: they are no longer who they were but are not sure who they are going to be. They are caught "between two identity constructions" (Beech 2011, 286). Victor Turner (1969, 95) describes this as a state of liminality when one's identity is "neither here nor there" and is "betwixt and between the positions assigned and arrayed by law, custom, convention, and ceremonial." He continues to argue that liminality is when a person's identity is invisible and not fully acknowledged by others (Turner 1967, 1969). Thus, liminality is a state of uncertainty in which one's identity is unresolved or undefined. For exonerees, this liminal state results in a private and public search for self. Privately, exonerees search for the new relationships and meanings of self that form the core of their new identity, an identity firmly grounded in their innocence. Publicly, they encounter this liminality when they believe they have demonstrated their innocence in court, yet others publicly maintain their guilt. It is the period after release when they believe their identity of innocence and their needs are invisible to the world around them. This gap between their private understanding of self and the public beliefs about them creates a cognitive dissonance that they seek to resolve. How do I convince others of my innocence? Do I try to convince others of my innocence? Do I confront or avoid situations in which my private definitions of self may come into question? How do I make my public self better align with my private self?

False Stigma and Identity Construction

Their public liminality is exacerbated, for some, by the stigma they carry after release, a false yet powerful stigma that shapes public understandings of who they are. For them, the role of stigma in identity construction is central to their reconstructions of self. Erving Goffman (1963, 3, 4) defines stigma as "an attribute that is deeply discrediting" and includes among the types of stigma "blemishes of individual character perceived as weak will, domineering or unnatural passions, treacherous and rigid beliefs, and dishonesty, these being inferred from a known record of, for example, mental disorder, imprisonment, addiction." Goffman (1963, 5) argues that stigma sets the stigmatized apart because of their "undesired differentness." These perceptions of differentness and imperfection form the basis for treating individuals as inferior, problematic, and threatening to the "normals." In essence, the stigma based on their difference "renders them illegitimate" (G. Elliott et al. 1982, 280–281; see also Link and Phelan 2001).

As Goffman and others argue, the status of "ex-con" or "ex-convict" is a type of stigma, or "ill-fame," that is highly discrediting and difficult to discard (Goffman 1963, 70; see also Clear et al. 2001; G. Elliott et al. 1982; D. Harding 2003; Hirschfield and Piquero 2010; Winnick and Bodkin 2007). The "ex-con" status is, in effect, a master status that overpowers all others an individual may want to put forward (Hughes 1945). As such, the stigma of being an ex-prisoner has implications for how others view and treat him or her and "structures the former prisoner's reentry into society" (D. Harding 2003, 572; Link and Phelan 2001). People's interactions with ex-prisoners are negotiated through the prism of the stigma they carry, causing people to treat them with disdain and suspicion. As a result of their discrediting stigma, ex-inmates are perceived as dishonest, immoral, and, in some cases, even less than human. This then affects their ability to get and maintain employment, find housing, and fully reintegrate back into society (Chiricos et al. 2007;

Clear et al. 2001; D. Harding 2003; Shivy et al. 2007; Winnick and Bodkin 2007).

Stigma, of course, is not an attribute inherent in an individual, but is, instead, a characteristic credited to him or her by others: stigma is not "something *in* the person stigmatized, rather a designation that others attach *to* that individual" (R. Parker and Aggleton 2003, 15, emphasis in original; see also Link and Phelan 2001). Stigma, then, is an attribute of one's identity that may or may not match up with one's own personal definition of self. The distinction here can be made between an individual's "virtual social identity" and his or her "actual social identity" (see Goffman 1963; D. Harding 2003; Tewksbury and McGaughey 1997). Virtual social identity refers to those "qualities attributed to [stigmatized people] and the meanings attributed to those qualities," whereas actual social identity is defined as "how they identify themselves" (Tewksbury and McGaughey 1997, 54). The difference between one's virtual and actual identity is the gap between how others view and define an individual and how that individual views and defines himself or herself. It is in this gap, this liminal state, between one's own perceptions of self and others' perceptions of self that exonerees find themselves situated.

Many exonerees profoundly feel the disconnect between these two forms of identity construction. They know that the one certain feature of their actual social identity is their innocence; however, they are made painfully aware that their virtual social identity remains that of ex-offender. Their disorientation and frustration is compounded in that the stigma they carry is false—they are *not* an ex-offender, an ex-con. In other words, even the rightly convicted may experience identity confusion as a result of their status as ex-con. Although they recognize the stigma attached to their virtual social identity is based on their status as an ex-offender, they still may want to distance themselves from that stigma as they try to reshape their lives after release and avoid the pitfalls of recidivism. Although they are an ex-offender, they may want to reconstruct their actual social identity around a different view of self. But, the public liminality experienced by the wrongly convicted is even more complex because their stigma is not one attached to a status they legitimately own. They are not offenders, not perpetrators, thus the stigma attached to them based on those virtual social identities is false and incorrectly applied (see Shih 2004). Howard Becker (1963, 20) calls this status that of a "falsely accused" deviant where "the person is seen by others as having committed an improper action, although in fact he has not done so." Exonerees are not the virtual social identity many in their communities attach to them. As a result, their identity frustration is caused not only by the stigma they confront because of their virtual social identity but even more so by the attribution of the virtual social identity itself. They battle the social and economic consequences of carrying the stigma of ex-con and then must manage the hostility and anger over being wrongly labeled from the start.

Thus, exonerees face a dilemma. They reject the virtual social identity the community often wants to apply. They want to be quite clear; they are *not* the social outcasts and monsters they were constructed into by the criminal justice system. They are not different, not discredited, not disreputable. They want to distance themselves from the identity into which they have been forced by virtue of their wrongful conviction and find a way to reclaim their status as a reputable, innocent person— a "normal" (Goffman 1963). They want their actual social identity grounded in innocence to become the identity that others know them by as well. They want to close the gap between how others see them and how they see themselves. They want to regain power over their definition of self.

Variation in Stigmatization

It is important to note that exonerees vary in the degree to which they are subject to community-imposed stigma, since not all exonerees feel stigmatized to the same degree. Several exonerees discuss how they felt welcomed and accepted by their communities. Half of our participants felt a degree of acceptance within their home communities. One-third described situations in which they believed their ex-offender status influenced their treatment by others. The remaining exonerees did not discuss the issue of stigma as being significant to their postrelease experience. Among those exonerees who felt accepted by their communities, identity issues remained a central concern. In these cases, the wrongful conviction and incarceration experience were enough in themselves to create uncertainty over postrelease identity, and they engage in various strategies to reclaim their innocence (discussed later). However, among those who discussed feeling stigmatized, the uncertainty over self seems to be particularly acute as the stigma creates a palpable disjuncture between their actual and virtual social identities. Before moving to the discussion of identity negotiation strategies, we analyze variation in felt stigma and the case characteristics that we believe contribute to this variation.

In nine cases, exonerees felt accepted in their communities. They could not recount instances in which they were shunned in public or someone publicly accused them of being guilty or duping the legal system. For example, when asked if anyone in his small community had ever said anything negative to him after his release, Alan Gell responds, "Most of the people in the community and neighborhood say that they feel remorse or regret or you see sadness in their eyes. I've never had anybody accuse me of still being guilty." In several cases, exonerees felt warmly received by community members who offered assistance or support or even an apology. As Gary James says about his interactions with the public after his release, "They used to come up to me on the street. They would apologize and hug me. . . . A lot of them would give me money." His codefendant Tim Howard describes an exchange he had with a woman at the local grocery store: "She looked at me and grabbed her mouth. She said, 'Oh my God!' And grabbed her mouth and said, 'Are you Mr. Howard?' I said, 'Yes.' She said, 'Oh, me and my mama was just talking and praying about you. It's so good [to see you].'" Scott Taylor describes similar exchanges in his neighborhood with community members who greeted him openly and said they had been praying for him.

The experiences of two exonerees—Juan Melendez and Walter McMillian—exemplify the acceptance some felt from the community. Juan Melendez was incarcerated in Florida and returned soon after his release to his hometown in Puerto Rico, where his mother still lived. He describes how six to seven hundred people from his hometown came by bus to greet him at the airport in San Juan the day of his return. The mayor of his town and a boyhood friend met him as he came off the plane and offered him jobs on the spot. He says of this welcome, "When I came here [to Puerto Rico], I am a hero. I go everywhere. I didn't even know what respect was until I got out. People treat me with respect. . . . When I get this big welcome and then I make the front page [of the newspaper] . . . I go everywhere and somebody can know me on the island." We can attest to Melendez's notability. We spent two days with him in Puerto Rico and walked with him to a local restaurant. Walking with Melendez was the closest we had ever come to being with a celebrity. Everyone greeted him on the street with a friendly smile and "Hola, Johnny." Older ladies waved out of upper-story windows, and shopkeepers shook his hand as we passed. To say Melendez was warmly received is an understatement. Melendez credits this community acceptance with helping him to avoid some of the emotional and economic struggles he sees as common among his fellow exonerees: "With them, I don't think it was like that. . . . I can see the difference."

Walter McMillian had a similar experience returning to his hometown of Monroeville, Alabama, which also was the location of the crime. McMillian grew up in this small southern town most famous as Harper Lee's hometown and the setting for her classic novel *To Kill a Mockingbird* (1999). He spent his childhood working long hours in the woods, picking cotton and cutting trees for the pulp mill, and had a reputation for being honest and hardworking. By his own admission, he had gotten into a few scrapes in his day but nothing serious. He had not spent time in prison prior to his wrongful conviction and did not have a felony record. After exoneration and release, McMillian says he returned to a town that supported him and treated him with dignity: "I think I get the whole community for support because everybody treat me just like they did before I ever got locked up, or better. Some of them treat me better. . . . So I am blessed." McMillian describes how people helped him get back on his feet and provided assistance getting his business established. He recounts an instance when men working for the county helped him clear and gravel his driveway free of charge, and he explains with a smile that he is greeted warmly by officials at the courthouse whenever he goes there to do business. Like Melendez, he understands how helpful this acceptance has been to him in the years since his release: "That helps a lot to know people still on your side. Stuff like that [he gets emotional] . . . I ain't had a soul, I ain't had a soul, nobody, I mean, black or white, even spoke to me no kind of way like that because everybody know, *everybody* know I didn't do it" (his emphasis). Thus, stigma was not a universal concern of exonerees. Some felt accepted, which made a difference to them. Although their acceptance did not alleviate all of their struggles with adjustment, it did give them some emotional relief. For them, the added burden of false stigma did not contribute to the struggles they already faced.

Not all exonerees were as lucky. One-third of our participants noted feeling stigmatized by a public who believed them to be guilty of the crimes for which they had been incarcerated. In three of these cases, the stigmatization was severe and deeply felt. These exonerees shared incidents where they had been called out in public by community members who openly (and loudly) accused them of heinous crimes or times when people commented to them personally that they believed the exoneree was actually guilty. Gary Gauger recalls a disturbing incident when his wife was confronted by a community member at a local market who began talking to her about Gauger's case when he realized who she was. At one point, the man simply says to her, "Oh, he's guilty," which so upset her that she came home crying. In some cases, even friends and family continued to question their innocence and treated them differently based on these suspicions. Several exonerees note that they no longer have contact with siblings who still believe they are guilty. Dave Keaton says that an aunt who wrote to him regularly asked, "Are you sure you didn't do this?"

Again, the experiences of two exonerees—Sabrina Butler and Kirk Bloodsworth—are worth highlighting. Sabrina Butler returned to her hometown in Mississippi after being acquitted at retrial of the beating death of her infant son Walter Dean. Butler's case had been extensively covered by local media, including photographs of Butler and her dead son and inflammatory statements by the local prosecutor, who portrayed her as an unfit mother. She believes that this notoriety prevented her from being accepted by her community and from the public acknowledging the injustice of her original wrongful conviction. She says, "It's hard because when I first got out, I was trying to find a job. Nobody would give me a chance . . . [or] hire me because they *knew* who I was" (her emphasis). She goes on to say,

> My church . . . they was gonna accept me and everything. And I joined the church. Tried to get in the choir, and all that. Next thing you know, here comes some guy talking about. . . . "Well, I think you need to come to the church and get up before the church and explain to the church why you went to jail." So I stopped going to

that church. . . . My sister-in-law was like, "Well, I can count the people on my hand in the church that don't like you." You know what I'm saying! I mean, God dog![1]

She believes the false stigma is responsible for her husband's being fired from his job as a correctional officer and for the difficulty she had regaining custody of her older child who was taken from her when she was convicted. She says that when she and her husband had a child after her release, the child was subjected to intrusive examinations by physicians at the health department, in spite of positive reports from their family physician: "When he was born . . . his routine visits to the health department, they used to take his clothes off to look for scars and see if I'm abusing him. It's terrible here. I swear it is." She explains that as a result of this rejection she is isolated and rarely ventures out: "It's emotionally depressing to me because, like I said, I really don't have any friends. I choose not to have any friends because once they find out who I am they're like, 'You know, that's the girl they said that killed her baby.' Even though I won the case, and proved my innocence, that doesn't mean nothing here." Since her release, she has wanted to leave Columbus to assume a more anonymous life elsewhere, but they are unable to do so because of severe financial constraints on her employability and problems her husband faces maintaining a stable job. In addition, her mother, her sole support system while in prison, lives in Columbus and cannot leave. In Butler's case, stigma has severely affected her life chances postrelease and hinders her emotional and financial stability. In short, she feels rejected by society but wants desperately for her innocence to be recognized and valued.

Kirk Bloodsworth faced a similar situation when he returned to the small crabbing town on the eastern shore of Maryland where he grew up. One might think that being the first DNA exoneree from death row would ensure acceptance and recognition by the community, given the level of certainty that DNA exonerations are often accorded. However, being the *first* DNA exoneree actually proved to be problematic as the public in 1993 was not yet familiar with this new technology. As a result, Bloodsworth returned to a community still highly suspicious of his involvement in the brutal death of a nine-year-old girl, often claiming that he had simply gotten out "on a technicality." Bloodsworth describes numerous incidents in which he was publicly confronted with accusations of his guilt. One occurred at a local grocery store soon after his release:

> I was a pariah to the community and to everybody around. . . . I was standing in a supermarket, right up [the road]. I hadn't been in a grocery store in nine years. . . . A lady and her little girl . . . I could feel her staring at me. So I just scratched my head, and I said, "Shoot. I'm all right. I'll just do my thing. I won't pay any attention to it." And I started walking that way. I should've went the other way. . . . She grabbed her child up and said, "Don't go near him. He's a child killer." And she took her, left her stuff! Left everything in her cart, and ran out the store. Told the manager, "You got a child killer coming in here," and all this mess. And he never said nothing to me. And he said to her something to the effect of, "Ma'am, he has been adjudicated and he's out. He's a free man. Now he can do what he wants. I can't run him outta here." I walked out by myself. I never went back there for two years just because of that. . . . So that was like one of a hundred different incidents that happened to me since I've been home. People writing "child killer" in the dirt on my truck and "murderer" and "rapist" and just God awful crap.

During this time, Bloodsworth had difficulty finding and keeping a job. For a period of time, he was homeless and living out of his car. He often went door-to-door asking people if they needed work done around the house. At one such stop, the homeowner opened the door to him, saw who he was, and yelled into the air before slamming the door in his face, "Child killer in the neighborhood! Child killer in the neighborhood!" Bloodsworth retreated to the water and returned to the trade of fishing and crabbing that he had learned growing up. While this occupation ensured a degree of isolation for him away from the glaring eyes of the public, it was not terribly lucrative, and the costs of maintaining the boat and equipment often were out of reach. As with Butler, stigma affected his ability to improve his situation and undermined his emotional well-being. In such cases, exonerees are caught between their own insistence on innocence as core to their notions of self and the public's equally entrenched insistence on their guilt.

Factors Affecting Stigmatization

Exonerees' experiences with stigma vary, ranging from the hero's welcome that greeted Juan Melendez to the public humiliation that confronted Kirk Bloodsworth. What accounts for this variation in the application of stigma? Based on our findings, we identify several influential factors worth further investigation: the time period in which the exoneree is released, the public behaviors and pronouncements about the case by system officials, the discovery of the identity of the actual perpetrator, and the role of the media.

Of those exonerees who felt accepted by the community, seven were exonerated after 2000. One was exonerated in 1999. The remaining exoneree, Walter McMillian, was exonerated in 1993. Of the one-third of exonerees who noted struggling with stigmatization, all were exonerated prior to 2000. Thus, it appears that the time period in which the participant was exonerated and released back into the community might influence community acceptance and stigmatization. During the 1980s and 1990s, academic and public discussions of wrongful convictions and innocence were muted at best, if not absent altogether. The public was not yet aware of the various systemic problems that can lead to wrongful convictions or the relative frequency with which such problems occur. Actual exonerations of individuals based on claims of innocence were few and far between and seen as isolated, disconnected events. However, by the turn of the twenty-first century, an innocence framework was being developed and popularized that provided a new lens through which cases of innocence could be interpreted (for an in-depth discussion of the gradual shift in academic and public awareness of the wrongful conviction issue, see Leo 2005; see also Dardis et al. 2008; Garrett 2008; Leo and Gould 2009). Eight of the nine participants who said they did not struggle significantly with stigma were exonerated around the time that this new innocence framework was becoming more available. All of those who struggled with stigma most intensely were exonerated prior to the development of that framework.

Of course, 2000 is not the magical year in which all of our cultural beliefs about the efficacy and accuracy of the criminal justice system changed overnight. However, a few significant events occurred around that time that contributed to the development of this new innocence framework. Until 1996, we knew of only twenty-eight wrongful conviction cases in which DNA had been used to establish innocence (U.S. Department of Justice 1996). However, that number increased dramatically to eighty-two exonerations by the end of 2000, primarily because of the work of Barry Scheck and Peter Neufeld at the Innocence Project at Cardozo Law School in New York City (www.innocence project.org). The characteristics and causes of these cases were detailed in their book *Actual Innocence: Five Days to Execution, and Other Dispatches from the Wrongly Convicted* (with Jim Dwyer), also published in 2000, a book sold widely to the general public. The pace of DNA exonerations continued throughout the first decade of the twenty-first century (Leo 2005; www.innocenceproject.org). The sheer bulk of exonerations was reported by mainstream media as innocence cases were detailed frequently by news magazine shows, talk shows, and local and national newspapers (Dardis et al. 2008; Warden 2003; www.deathpenaltyinfo.org). It is difficult to underestimate the public impact of the proliferation of and public attention to these cases over the past decade. DNA exonerations highlighted as never before the certainty that many convictions in our system are of factually innocent individuals (Leo 2005). These cases were no longer few and far between and no longer carried the residue of guilt so common to exonerations before the DNA era. As Richard Leo (2005, 205–206) says, "As a result of DNA, it has now become widely accepted in the space of just a few years that wrongful convictions occur with regular and troubling frequency in the American criminal justice system."

Additional events contributed to the shift to a more recognized innocence framework. In January 2000, Illinois Governor George Ryan (Republican) imposed a statewide moratorium on the death penalty because more factually innocent individuals had been released from death row in that state than individuals had been executed since the reinstatement of the death penalty in 1973 (Leo 2005). In 2002, North Carolina became the first state to implement an Innocence Commission (the North Carolina Actual Innocence Commission), with the aim of investigating system-level policies that could reduce the incidence of wrongful convictions (Mumma 2004). In response to calls by Scheck and Neufeld in the early part of the decade, innocence projects tasked with the hard work of reinvestigating possible cases of wrongful convictions proliferated across the United States (Scheck and Neufeld 2001;

www.innocenceproject.org). And by 2001, a Harris Poll indicated that 94 percent of Americans believed that innocent people do get executed, marking a significant shift in public opinion about such a possibility (Leo 2005).

Thus, the participants in our study who were released after 2000 possibly found themselves in communities with much different beliefs about the truth of their innocence than the participants released in the 1980s and 1990s. During earlier times, suspicion about their factual innocence was more common as the innocence framework had not yet been developed. The public was not yet aware of the frequency with which factually innocent people really do get convicted of crimes they did not commit or the various ways in which such mistakes are made. Exonerees released after 2000 benefited from a more informed public better prepared to accept their claims of innocence and less likely to view them as ex-offenders.

Another factor that appears to influence the degree of stigmatization felt by exonerees is official proclamations made about their cases by system officials (i.e., police, prosecutors, governors). Exonerees who experienced the most severe stigmatization were more likely to have had officials publicly maintain their guilt, even after release. Those who felt accepted were more often offered a public apology or recognition by officials that confirmed their innocence. For example, in the two cases of severely felt stigma of Kirk Bloodsworth and Sabrina Butler, public officials refused to attest to their innocence. When the representative from the state's attorney's office revealed in a press conference that Bloodsworth's DNA did not match any of the evidence found at the crime scene, she still equivocated as to his factual innocence, saying, "Based on the evidence, our office did the right thing in prosecuting him. . . . I believe he is not guilty. . . . I'm not prepared to say he's innocent" (Junkin 2004, 261). Bloodsworth believes that it is because of the state's unwillingness to admit their mistake publicly that he was judged so harshly by his community. Butler argues the same. She says that after her release in 1995, the prosecutor in her case would use her name as an exemplar in other cases of felonious child abuse discussed in the media, thus persistently keeping her name publicly associated with severe child abuse.

On the other hand, exonerees who felt more accepted were less likely to experience such persistent public accusations by officials. One,

Scott Taylor, received a gubernatorial pardon announced at a public and highly anticipated speech given by the governor. In reference to Taylor's case during his speech, the governor said, "[Scott Taylor] was convicted on the basis of flawed evidence. He was convicted because the jury did not have the benefit of all existing evidence which would have served to exonerate him."[2] About four cases receiving pardons from the governor that day, including Taylor's, the governor goes on to say,

> The system has failed all four men. It has failed the people of this state. . . . Here we have four more men who were wrongfully convicted and sentenced to die by the state for crimes the courts should have seen they did not commit. . . . They are perfect examples of what is so terribly broken about our system. . . . Today I am pardoning them of the crimes for which they were wrongfully prosecuted and sentenced to die. I have reviewed these cases and I believe a manifest injustice has occurred. I have reviewed these cases and I believe these men are innocent.

Taylor indicates that he has never had anyone publicly accuse him of being guilty and, instead, regularly receives supportive comments from total strangers who recognize him on the street.

For several other exonerees, prosecutors or other state officials indicated support for the exonerees' innocence in public statements to the media on the day of their release. The day after Ray Krone's release (April 29, 2002), an article by Laura Laughlin, titled "Apology Accepted: Arizona Clears an Innocent Man of Murder. A Prosecutor Apologizes for the Error," appeared in the *York Daily Record*, Krone's hometown newspaper. At a press conference on the day Charles Fain was released, the prosecutor in the county in which the crime occurred said, "Justice requires the action we have taken today. It also requires that we do everything we can to solve this case. The killer has not yet been apprehended" (Bonner 2001). These public announcements were important for shaping public sentiment toward them once they returned to their communities.

In one unusual case, that of Walter McMillian, it is not only what public officials say but also what they do that matters to him. McMillian notes many instances when he has visited the courthouse on matters related to his business and been greeted openly with smiles and handshakes. He reiterates over and over again that he knows that the officials in the criminal justice system and those in his community believe he is not guilty: "They know they done something wrong. . . . So that's why they had to come forward to make some kind of justice for what they had done. . . . I go up to the courthouse and they shake my hand and speak to me just like I own a piece of gold or something. I'm telling you. Even the judge, he come out shaking my hand. . . . All of them know me, been knowing me all my life. They speak just as good, laugh and talk and crack jokes." In this case, the openly receptive behavior of the court officials paves the way for general community acceptance, leaving McMillian convinced no one holds a grudge against him. As it turns out, quite ironically, one powerful determinant of an exoneree's acceptance by his or her community often rests with the very officials responsible for his or her initial exclusion from that community.

Another significant factor influencing the application of stigma depends on the discovery of the identity of the actual perpetrator. This identification is very important to public sentiment as it creates certainty of the exonerees' factual innocence that often is missing, especially in non-DNA cases (remembering that currently only 17 of the 138 death row exonerations rely on DNA; www.deathpenaltyinfo.org). Identifying the actual perpetrator provides a targeted, specific outlet for continued public outrage over the crime that often remains after an exoneration. It points public sentiment elsewhere, away from the exoneree. In half of our participants' cases, the identity of the actual offender eventually was discovered.[3] The most powerful example of the role that this can play in the stigmatization of exonerees can be seen in the case of Kirk Bloodsworth. As described previously, Bloodsworth carried the severe burden of stigma after his return to his hometown. He struggled with the impact of this stigma for ten years after his release in 1993, until the prosecutor in his case submitted DNA from his case into the national DNA data bank and got a hit. On September 5, 2003, Kimberly Shay Ruffner was announced as the actual perpetrator in the murder of Dawn Hamilton; this was pivotal in Bloodsworth's life. He describes the impact of that discovery as follows: "Up until September 5th, up until the very week, I used to get phone calls, 'You oughta shoot yourself. Do yourself a favor. You think you're so big.' I used to get these phone calls all the time. And then after September 5th, the phone stopped. I haven't gotten one since. And people that were doing these things wave at me and speak to me." The cloud of suspicion was immediately removed and the stigma lifted once the actual perpetrator became known.

Finally, our impression is that the media can shape public perception of the validity of the exoneration and thus the willingness of the community to accept the exoneree when he or she returns. However, a more systematic analysis of the media coverage of each exoneration in our study is in order to say for sure. It is the case that several of our participants who struggled less profoundly with stigma received extensive coverage of their cases that revealed the police and prosecutor errors that ultimately led to their convictions. Alan Gell's case received a four-part investigative analysis by Joseph Neff in the Raleigh *News & Observer* in December 2002 (Neff 2002a, 2002b, 2002c, 2002d). The cases of codefendants Tim Howard and Gary James received similar investigative coverage by Alan Johnson in the *Columbus Dispatch* over a two-year period leading up to their exonerations in 2003 (A. Johnson 2002a, 2002b, 2003a, 2003b, 2003c). Walter McMillian's case was featured on the news magazine *60 Minutes* in 1992, drawing intense public scrutiny to his case. In each case, the media revealed the errors and missteps made by criminal justice officials and openly questioned the validity of the convictions. Thus, it is possible that such investigations laid the foundation for decreased stigmatization once the participants were released. This might particularly be the case for Walter McMillian who was released (in 1993) prior to the development of the innocence framework discussed earlier, which was in place during the exonerations of Gell, Howard, and James. That said, Bloodsworth and Gauger, both of whom noted relatively severe struggles with stigma, also had some positive news coverage upon release, though not to the extent or in as much depth as the others. So, again, our impression here of the possible influence of the media on the impact of stigma on exonerees is speculative.[4]

These four factors—the time period of release, public statements by case officials, the identity of the actual perpetrator, and media coverage—can influence the degree of stigma felt by exonerees after their release. No doubt, these factors conflate, creating a milieu where the public is more or less receptive to exonerees when they return to their communities, a reception that bears significantly on their opportunities and emotional supports during their difficult transition.

NEGOTIATING THE INNOCENT SELF

In the same way that our participants must find coping strategies to manage the difficult process of reintegration (as outlined in chapter 9), they must find ways to negotiate the liminal state of identity construction they experience after release. They again use approaches of incorporation and avoidance to navigate this process. Those most deeply affected by false stigma experience this liminality most profoundly as they frequently confront negative public perceptions of who they really are. Traumatized by the wrongful conviction process and incarceration, and in some cases by the false stigmatization they battle, exonerees reenter the free world asking, "Who am I?" For most, a readily available answer is "I am innocent!" But, for exonerees, that is easier said than done or, more accurately, easier said than believed. They search for the best way to build a new identity around their innocence and project that innocence to the world around them.

Exonerees use strategies of incorporation and avoidance to reclaim their identities as innocent people and distance themselves from the false stigma "unjustly forced on them" during reintegration (Shih 2004, 181; for similar strategies used by other stigmatized groups, see D. Harding 2003; Leary and Schreindorfer 1998; Oyserman and Swim 2001; Siegel et al. 1998; Weitz 1990). These strategies help them establish themselves as people of worth and value, no longer identified by their "undesired differentness" (Goffman 1963, 5). One strategy they use is to fully embrace the identity of "exoneree" (Shih 2004, 181), to incorporate it into their new definition of self. This strategy of incorporation typically involves what Erving Goffman (1963, 24–25, 100) calls "disclosure," or revelation of their wrongful conviction experience to anyone who will listen. For exonerees, this might mean a willingness to talk to others about their experiences, to openly reveal to others who they are. By disclosing, exonerees are able to publicly disavow the virtual social identity of ex-con that others may attribute to them. They gain some control over their definition of self as truly innocent, respectable people.

The strategies of avoidance they use are less revealing of their exoneree status. In Goffman's (1963, 73) terms, some exonerees rely on "passing" where they choose to withdraw from situations to avoid potential confrontations over their false stigma. Or at most they choose to selectively disclose information about their wrongful conviction, only after those with whom they interact have had an opportunity to get to know their "true" self, absent any knowledge of their past. These strategies of avoidance insulate the exoneree from those who may choose to apply the false stigma and create opportunities for their primary interactions to revolve around their actual social identity, rather than their misapplied virtual one.

At the core of each of these strategies are exonerees' attempts to reclaim their identity or reconstruct a new one based on their status as an innocent person. Exonerees who choose disclosure find ways to embrace their exoneree status publicly and make known to others that they "own" their innocence. They publicly project their innocence through advocacy or other forms of disclosure, putting their identity as an innocent person up-front in their discussions of who they are. For some, like Juan Melendez and Kirk Bloodsworth, a large part of their new identity is built around their need to use their innocence to affect public sentiment and policy regarding innocence and death penalty issues. Bloodsworth's melding together of identity and innocence is even institutionalized in the Innocence Protection Act passed in 2004 in that the Kirk Bloodsworth Post-Conviction DNA Testing Grant Program bears his name. Juan Melendez's advocacy for abolition of capital punishment revolves around his identity as an innocent death row survivor, which has taken him around the country and overseas. This identity as advocate is core to his understanding of self: "As long as I can breathe, I will fight." For Dave Keaton, his form of advocacy is less personal but no less public. His story is included in Blank and Jensen's play *The Exonerated* (2004). Although Keaton is removed from the day-to-day business of the play itself, he saw it as a form of advocacy that provided him with satisfaction and a public forum through which to assert his innocence: "*The Exonerated*? Yeah, I enjoyed that. It gave me some relief. It was letting people know that I [wasn't] involved with (that crime). It's spreading the news that innocent people have been convicted and here's the story of six of them."

Aside from public advocacy, several exonerees make clear that they put their innocence up-front even in their daily interactions with people. They explain that, especially when they first got out of prison, they felt a need to convince others of their innocence, to ensure that others understand who they really are. In individual interactions, they sought to close the gap between public perception of their false stigma and their own view of self. Scott Taylor says that his greatest fear was that he would be "executed without the truth being told about my innocence" and that this drives him to convince others of his innocence: "When I go out, I want[ed] people to believe me. Let them know I didn't do it. I'm free and I still plead, 'I didn't do it.' I don't necessarily have to say that anymore, but I still feel like I have to convince people that I didn't do it. [I feel like] before people hear me, I'm being judged. When they mention my case, are they saying, 'Man, maybe he did do it?' . . . I find myself really trying to convince people, still." Dave Keaton also says that when he first was released, "I used to try to convince them."

During our interview with Walter McMillian, we could see this incorporation strategy of disclosure in use throughout our conversation. He repeatedly emphasized his innocence and asserted that it simply was not possible for anyone to believe he could have committed such a crime. For example, early in the interview, he says, "*Everybody* know I didn't do it. I mean it just ain't some 'You mighta coulda did it.' It's impossible for me to done it, you know" (his emphasis). A few minutes later, he again offers, "I ain't seen nobody yet act no kinda way like they mad at me or got nothing against me about saying how they believe I had something to do with the child getting killed . . . black or white. I mean, I talk with all kinda white people, all kinda black people. And *everybody* know it. They know the truth" (his emphasis). And about thirty minutes later, he again insists, "Like I say, everybody's treating me just as good, or better. So I am blessed. See, if it had've been possible that I did it, that would make a difference too, you see. But everybody know it *impossible*" (his emphasis). His reiteration of innocence makes obvious his need to clarify to us that everyone is assured of his identity as an innocent person as if we needed also to be convinced. Adamant assertion of his innocent self was on full display.

While full disclosure was a strategy of incorporation used to manage their new self based on innocence, alternative strategies of avoidance involve distancing their self from public claims of innocence by withdrawing from public discourse around the issue or only selectively disclosing their wrongful conviction experience. Use of these strategies may seem contradictory at first. How can they create an identity based on innocence by distancing themselves from public disclosure of their experience and claims of innocence? But, at their core, these techniques are aimed at creating a self that is as much like a "normal" as possible (Goffman 1963). By retreating from public revelation, they remove opportunities in which their "differentness" becomes the lens through which others interact with them. They, instead, blend in, as if their status as an innocent, reputable person was simply never in question. Gary James describes this strategy when answering a question about whether he ever wishes to be anonymous in his community. He replies, "[Being recognized] don't happen that much no more. But at one point, it was happening a lot. And, yeah, I didn't want people to know. Or if they did know, just keep it to yourself. . . . Say you meet me, and you know this about me. You gonna talk to me like I'm the guy who did twenty-six years. . . . It seems as though they, not talking down, but . . . making me different. You know, set me apart." For James, disclosure of his innocent identity ensured that people treated him differently, whereas he prefers to be treated as if his innocence was never in question and never needed to be reasserted. He makes innocence core to his assertion of self by passing as a normal.

Others have some discomfort with using public disclosure as their primary strategy for negotiating identity. For example, when asked if he ever gets tired of people introducing him as *the* Delbert Tibbs, based on the public recognition his case received in the 1970s and his more recent fame as a participant in *The Exonerated* (2004), he replies, "I have a friend . . . he used to say, 'This is Delbert Tibbs. You know, he was on death row.' I say, 'Man, don't do that,' you know. I say, 'If they know, that's cool. If they don't know, that's cool.' We're all on death row, you know. It's a different death row, but we're all on death row. So no, I don't allow it." Tibbs makes it clear that he does not want to be separated out for his differentness and instead takes the opportunity to assert his commonality with others. Tibbs, of course, also has been an active abolitionist off and on since his exoneration in 1982, which puts his innocence status front and center in his public negotiation of self. But, he reveals here that he prefers to selectively disclose this part of his identity and finds solace as much in what he shares with humanity as in what sets him apart.

Scott Taylor exemplifies this strategy of distancing one's self from public iterations of innocence as a way to create a new self based on innocence. As is obvious from our use of a pseudonym for him, he prefers to remain anonymous. While he does not mind discussing the challenges he has faced after his release, he does not want to be identified by those public claims. In a conversation with him as recently as April 2011, he reveals that he has moved away from the location of his wrongful conviction and has started a new life in his new home. When asked if he would like to talk to one of our classes about his experience, he declines, saying that he prefers to "not look back." He wants to move on and establish a normal life in which those with whom he regularly interacts do not know of his past. This puts innocence quite completely at the core of his identity by almost erasing any evidence that it was ever in question. People in his new life interact with him appropriately as a reputable, honest person simply because they have no reason to do otherwise.

These strategies of incorporation and avoidance help exonerees construct new identities, new views of self, out of the rubble of the self so disrupted by their wrongful convictions. Exonerees emerge from prison shaken and uncertain as to whom they are going to be as a newly free person. Often, they cannot resume being who they were before their wrongful conviction occurred. The jobs they had and relationships they maintained that anchored their sense of self before their wrongful conviction are no longer available to them, having dissolved or been fundamentally altered. Yet which new job or new relationship or new activity that gives meaning to who they are as a person of worth and value is not always obvious when they reenter society. They find themselves stuck between the past and the future, the old and the new, and are left with a lack of clarity as to where they fit in the new scheme of things. One certainty, however, is that they are innocent. They are not the murderers, rapists, monsters, or threats to society that they were labeled. They are not the pariah whose life is so worthless that it should be extinguished. They search for ways to reclaim innocence as the core of their new self and develop strategies for reconnecting to their community through this prism of innocence.

COPING WITH INNOCENCE begins the day they are wrongly convicted and sent to death row. They confront the lonely, isolating environment of prison and must find ways to survive while battling the legal system to regain their reputation and freedom. They emerge profoundly altered people into a foreign world, uprooted and dislodged from all they knew before. Their relationships, communities, and beliefs about who they are and where they fit must be rebuilt. Sometimes, they choose to confront the challenge head-on by claiming their innocence publicly and using it as the lens through which they reconnect with those around them. Other times they choose to withdraw from the public gaze and find a path to a new life that is not centered on their wrongful conviction. No matter the paths they choose, they search for ways to reconnect with others, resituate themselves in the world around them, and rebuild their beliefs about who they are as people of value. They negotiate their new lives with the help of family and friends and sometimes advocates, attorneys, and others in their communities. But they rarely begin this journey with the assistance of anyone responsible for their wrongful conviction or any official acknowledgment of their trauma. Having been designated for execution by the state, they do not understand why they are left on their own after having suffered such an injustice. They move forward into their new lives in spite of the system, not with the help of it.

PART FOUR

Doing Justice

WHEN WE CONCEIVED OF this project in 2001, little attention had been given to life after exoneration, and few resources were available to assist exonerees in rebuilding their lives. Only fifteen states, the District of Columbia, and the federal government had established compensation statutes, and those had very limited provisions.[1] Award amounts were simply token gestures, not intended to provide substantive relief, and statutes provided no services, such as assistance with housing, employment, or medical care.[2] At that time, no nonprofit organizations existed to help exonerees after release, and they were excluded from services provided to parolees.[3] By the time of our first interview, with Charles Fain in 2003, little had changed. Sixteen states had compensation statutes and one state had amended their earlier version.[4] The first organization dedicated to assisting exonerees with their reintegration was established in 2003 when the Life After Exoneration Program opened in Berkeley, California.

The paltry aid available to exonerees is captured in their remarks about their postrelease needs and the inadequate assistance they received. Our eighteen participants were released prior to 2004, and twelve were released in or before 2001, when very little was in place to address their needs. Their experiences reveal a deep and abiding frustration, and even hostility, regarding what they perceive as their invisibility to a system that has so damaged their lives. They are angry over the state's refusal to help them or recognize that they are in need of help. Ultimately, our participants are angry about the state's intransigence to acknowledging them as people who have been wronged and refusal to take responsibility for their wrongful convictions. Thus, our participants feel forgotten and abandoned by a government that they believe destroyed their lives, not once but twice: first by wrongly convicting and sentencing them to death for crimes they did not commit, and second by failing to "own" the injustice or provide appropriate remedies.

Since our first interview in 2003, the issue of aftermath has received more attention. To date (2011), twenty-seven states have passed compensation statutes, ten of which include social service assistance.[5] Ten organizations in the United States assist exonerees after their release from prison.[6] While this certainly is progress, almost half of states still provide no statutory assistance at all, and most states have no organization in place to assist with reintegration. However, we believe that this increased attention has resulted in an interesting shift in public perception. Ten years ago, few were even aware of the struggles faced by exonerees; now most think that all exonerees receive large compensation packages upon release, which is not true.[7] Of our eighteen participants, only two received compensation via statutory provisions. The other six received financial relief only after protracted and costly legal battles with the state, and on average they did not receive any financial award for four years after release. Ten received nothing at all (see table 3.1 in chapter 3). Thus, it appears that total inattention has been replaced by the myth of immediate, substantive financial relief. Both misperceptions are problematic: they render invisible the complex, multidimensional needs exonerees face that remain unmet.

Chapter 11 begins with an overview of assistance currently available to exonerees and discussion of how this has shifted over time. But the chapter focuses primarily on exonerees' reflections on what they got from the state upon release as opposed to what they needed from the state to help them rebuild their lives. In it, their frustration over being abandoned is obvious. Chapter 12 provides our vision for what appropriate relief and redress could look like, drawing primarily from exonerees' views, limited discussions and models provided in the literature, and our own personal experience with exonerees.

As Judith Herman (1997, 70) notes about trauma survivors, "Once it is publicly recognized that a person has been harmed, the community must take action to assign responsibility for the harm and to repair the injury. These two responses—recognition and restitution—are necessary to rebuild the survivor's sense of order and justice." If these are the two responses essential for recovery and reintegration, we still have a long way to go.

CHAPTER 11

Searching for Reintegration and Restoration

The . . . effects involved with being sentenced to death are huge, and one must be given . . . [resources] to suppress the harmful effects of being smashed and broken, and returning to a society that expects so much. . . . It would not cost the state a prodigious amount of money in order to set a project of that sort up. —Alfred Rivera

VERY LITTLE BY WAY of assistance awaits exonerees upon release. What is available varies widely by state and location, may carry so many limitations and exceptions as to render assistance meaningless, and is most likely provided by a local nonprofit agency and not the state. Yet it is the state that is responsible for the situation in which exonerees find themselves (Westervelt and Cook 2010), and exonerees argue that it is the state that should be responsible for assisting them in their transition back into society. But the assistance exonerees seek from the state goes beyond financial relief and social service provision to the core of restoring their identity and community. Exonerees certainly want financial and practical assistance negotiating the burdens of reintegration; even more, they want recognition of the wrong done to them and acknowledgment of their status as an innocent person. They want their wrongful conviction made visible for all to see and their reputation restored (see also Campbell and Denov 2004; Lawrence 2009; Vollen and Eggers 2005; Weigand 2009). Exonerees see the state's resistance to providing true reparation as another layer of trauma, another roadblock to their full acceptance and reintegration.

AVAILABLE RESOURCES

Most discussions of assistance for exonerees begin with financial compensation. And, of course, appropriate compensation is both significant and necessary to their reintegration and recovery. Exonerees have been removed from society for years, sometimes decades, with no opportunities to make a living, build a future, contribute to a retirement fund, provide for a child's college education, or support a family. It will take significant financial resources to get them back on their feet. However, we must understand that meaningful assistance for exonerees cannot be reduced to financial compensation alone. Much of the emotional, psychological, and relationship turmoil they face cannot be repaired simply by giving them money.

In our capitalist society, we tend to believe that most injuries can be healed by money. But this simply is not the case. As Heather Weigand (2009, 431) explains, "Overcoming the tragedy of wrongful conviction cannot be treated with money. While appropriate compensation is an entitlement the exonerated have yet to fully experience in many states, and money is an important part of the puzzle in comprehensive treatment and restoring the exonerated to 'wholeness,' the damage can never be undone." While organizations working with exonerees recognize the multidimensional nature of their needs, and thus multidimensional resources necessary for successful reintegration (Illinois Criminal Justice Information Authority 2002; Innocence Project 2009; Vollen and Eggers 2005; Weigand 2009), the states have yet to fully (or even partially) embrace this facet of reparation. But given the dominance of compensation to the overall discussion of assistance for the wrongly convicted, we begin there.

Compensation for exonerees can be provided via a number of mechanisms—private bills, litigation, and compensation statutes (for a more detailed examination of each of these mechanisms, see Bernhard 2004; Innocence Project 2009; Lonergan 2008). In states without compensation statutes or where a lawsuit is not a viable option, an exoneree can pursue a private bill with a state legislator. To secure compensation for the exoneree, the legislator must introduce a bill on the exoneree's behalf to argue for compensation in his or her case alone. Aside from making the compensation process completely individualized and overly politicized, this mechanism places the burden, yet again, on the shoulders of exonerees to argue for their right to receive aid, ensures wide variability in compensation awards, and depends greatly on the effectiveness or even popularity of the legislator sponsoring the bill (Innocence Project 2009; Norris 2011). According to the Innocence Project (2009), only 9 percent of their clients have been successful at receiving remedy using this mechanism.

In some cases, exonerees can pursue litigation to secure compensation; however, such litigation is available only to exonerees who can prove their wrongful conviction resulted from intentional misconduct by state officials, namely police officers and/or prosecutors (Innocence Project 2009; Kahn 2010). Given that these state officials have absolute (prosecutors and judges) and qualified (police) immunity from prosecutions and lawsuits, the burden of proof is often too high to overcome, making this option unrealistic for most exonerees (Bernhard 2004).[1] While exonerees can potentially receive higher award amounts through this process, as compared to what they may receive from a compensation statute, the process is time-consuming and costly, which leaves them without assistance of any kind in the immediate aftermath of release (Norris 2011). According to the Innocence Project (2009), 28 percent of their clients received compensation through this mechanism, and they waited, on average, four years to collect their award (see also Norris 2011).[2] Among our eighteen participants, six successfully negotiated this process to win compensation and also waited, on average, four years to receive their award (see table 3.1 in chapter 3).

Given the difficulties in pursuing compensation through private bills and litigation, most advocates and scholars working on this issue agree that compensation via statutory provision holds the most promise for providing consistent, substantive, and timely compensation to the wrongly convicted (Bernhard 1999, 2004, 2009; Innocence Project 2009; Kahn 2010). Compensation statutes also provide a mechanism for including social, educational, and psychological services that the other two options do not. Both the American Bar Association and the Innocence Project advocate for the adoption of compensation statutes by states across the nation (Norris 2011), and the Innocence Project provides a model statute that can be adopted by states looking to establish new provisions or amend old ones (see Innocence Project 2009 for a full description of the comprehensive provisions of this model).[3]

The Innocence Project (2009) reports that among DNA exonerees, 33 percent have received compensation through this process. Among our participants, only two—Kirk Bloodsworth and Perry Cobb—received compensation through this mechanism. (See Bernhard 2009 and the Innocence Project website for a listing of compensation statutes and provisions by state.)

While compensation statutes might offer the best hope for meaningful assistance to exonerees, they also have limitations (Bernhard 2004, 2009; Kahn 2010; Lonergan 2008; Norris 2011), including "strict eligibility requirements (e.g., requiring exonerees to obtain a full pardon), high standards of proof, limited awards, numerous disqualifiers, and short time limits" (Norris 2011). The state-by-state variation and often political nature of these statutes creates inconsistency among awards. Thus, exonerees with similar case histories often receive vastly different levels of assistance depending upon where and when they were exonerated. For example, exonerees in Texas are eligible for $80,000 of compensation per year with an additional $25,000 available for each year spent on parole or as a registered sex offender. The statute does not limit compensation to those wrongly convicted of certain types of crimes (e.g., only felonies) and does not require a gubernatorial pardon. In Virginia, exonerees can receive yearly monetary compensation equal to 90 percent of the state's per capita personal income (which in 2009 was $43,874) up to a maximum of twenty years. Compensation is available only to those convicted of a felony. The state of Wisconsin provides only $5,000 per year of wrongful incarceration to a maximum of $25,000, while New Hampshire provides a total of $20,000 no matter the length of the wrongful incarceration (Norris 2011).

Even in those states with arguably higher quality statutes in place, exonerees are not assured of compensation. The provision of compensation can become a political football and subject to the ideological views of the current political administration or budgetary constraints. For example, Scott Pierpoint in North Carolina was released in July 2010 after over seventeen years in prison wrongly convicted of raping a child. Soon after his release, Pierpoint applied for a "pardon for innocence," a provisional requirement in North Carolina to receive compensation. In March 2011, his application was denied by the governor's office without explanation. Pierpoint, thus, is not eligible to receive the $750,000 in compensation provided by North Carolina's compensation statute. Pierpoint and others suspect that the application was denied as a cost-cutting measure at a time when North Carolina struggles to close a $2.4 billion budget gap (Boyle 2011).

Of course, it is important to remember, as Robert Norris (2011) aptly points out, even the states with minimal provisions fare better than the twenty-three states that currently have no provisions, where exonerees are left to their own resources and support networks. In addition, exonerees released prior to the passage of a statute in their state often are left out of compensation and services. In 1932, at the time of Borchard's first study of wrongful conviction, only three states had compensation statutes in place for wrongly convicted or incarcerated individuals (Innocence Project 2009). By 2001, fifteen states (plus the federal government and District of Columbia) had provisions, and since then twelve more states have established statutory compensation provisions (Bernhard 2004, 2009; Innocence Project 2009; Norris 2011). While some states allow exonerees released prior to the establishment of a statute to apply under current guidelines within a set statute of limitations, others do not. Given the amount of time that may have passed since their release and eligibility for compensation, the burden of reproducing the data and documents required for application may be out of reach for many. As always, cost is a hurdle to overcome. Thus, while compensation statutes, if instituted universally and applied uniformly, could provide significant relief to exonerees, they, as yet, do not.

One benefit of compensation statutes, as opposed to use of private bills or litigation, is that social service assistance can be included in the provisions made available to exonerees. The Innocence Project (2009, 21) model statute includes provisions for "immediate services including housing, transportation, education, workforce development, physical and mental health care through the state employee's health care system and other transitional services." However, currently only ten states include social service provisions within their compensation statutes, and these services vary widely (Innocence Project 2009). For example, Texas provides vocational training, tuition, and fees at a state university or college, counseling for one year, assistance obtaining other social services and medical care, and help with child support payments. Virginia does not provide medical or counseling services but does offer reimbursement

for career or technical training up to $10,000. Neither Wisconsin nor
New Hampshire provides additional social services or assistance (Norris
2011; www.innocenceproject.org).

It also is worth noting that exonerees are not eligible for the basic
services provided to parolees. Though states have been cutting severely
into the transitional services provided to parolees in recent years,
many provide limited assistance with transitional housing, employment
services and job skill training, and rehabilitation (Petersilia 2003).
However, exonerees cannot access these services (Innocence Project
2009; Weigand 2009). Even though exonerees and parolees face many of
the same struggles with employment, resocialization, psychological and
emotional strain, and stigma, exonerees "typically [leave] prison with
less help—prerelease counseling, job training, substance-abuse treatment, housing assistance and other services—than some states offer to
paroled prisoners" (Radnofsky, cited in Weigand 2009, 429). Even if
offered, some exonerees are wary of using these services, which reinforce
the "ex-offender" stigma and impose burdensome restrictions on their
activities.

In states where no additional services are provided, exonerees may
rely on a scattered handful of nonprofit organizations for assistance.
However, as is the case with compensation statutes, location is everything. Of the ten exoneree-assistance organizations known to us, three
are located in California and one in each of Illinois, Louisiana, Michigan,
North Carolina, Texas, and Wisconsin.[4] One organization—Witness
to Innocence—serves all death row exonerees, no matter their location,
and the Innocence Project has two social workers who assist DNA
exonerees, regardless of location. These organizations do their best
to provide services for exonerees but struggle with staying fiscally viable,
especially during difficult economic times. Despite their best efforts
and intentions, they often are unable to fully meet the array of needs
presented by exonerees. And, of course, many exonerees are excluded
because they do not live in a state in which such an organization is
available.

This, then, is the patchwork quilt of services and compensation
made available to the wrongly convicted, a quilt inadequately stitched
and still full of holes. Such an ineffective and incomplete response to a
problem of the state's own making makes clear the degree to which the

state resists taking full responsibility for the damage caused to the lives of our participants (Westervelt and Cook 2010). This resistance is fully felt by exonerees and, in many cases, produces their most vehement reactions.

EXONEREES' PERSPECTIVES ON ASSISTANCE

All of our participants were released prior to 2004, when approximately sixteen states had compensation statutes in place, and eleven were released prior to 1999, when even fewer states (approximately thirteen) had statutory provisions. It should not, then, be surprising that the most common response to our question about what they received from the state upon release was a simple, but resolute, "nothing!" Even the comments from those few who received compensation reveal the problems with believing that money is a cure-all. Exonerees explain, from their own perspectives and experiences, what they believe would have been most helpful to them the day they walked out of prison.

What They Got

The most common response to our inquiry about what they got from the state upon release was, as noted above, simply, "nothing." Alan Gell says, "No state help. No federal help. No nothing. I had to pay out of my pocket every step of the way." Sabrina Butler echoes this: "No money. No nothing. They didn't give me jack! They just took the handcuffs off me and sent me out the door." Gary James makes it clear in the following exchange:

INTERVIEWER: Did the state give you anything? Did you get . . . bus fare, did you get clothes, did you get . . . anything?

JAMES: No.

INTERVIEWER: Services?

JAMES: No.

INTERVIEWER: Any assistance from the state whatsoever?

JAMES: No.

INTERVIEWER: In finding a job? Nothing?

JAMES: No.

INTERVIEWER: So, you didn't even get what a lot of parolees get?

JAMES: Yeah. I mean, I didn't get none of what they got.

James's codefendant Tim Howard drills the point home one last time when he says, "The State actually didn't give me nothing. . . . As far as giving me something for being wrongfully incarcerated? No. No. No, no, no, no, no, no! They gave me nothing. No. They gave me nothing." Charles Fain laughs and offers a slight concession to the state when describing what he left prison with: "A new pair of jeans . . . some shirts and underwear, a T-shirt." But aside from that, he received, well, nothing.

As to compensation, ten of our participants received no compensation. Two received compensation via statutory provisions. Kirk Bloodsworth received $300,000 from Maryland in 1993 upon receiving his pardon in December (after his release in June). Perry Cobb was acquitted and released in January 1987; however, he received his compensation of $140,000 from Illinois in June 2000, almost fourteen years later, after receiving a pardon from Governor George Ryan. Their experiences illuminate the variability of current compensation statute provisions. First, even though both served about the same amount of time in prison, Bloodsworth received more than double what Cobb received. Bloodsworth spent about eight years in prison, while Cobb spent about seven years in prison, although during their sentences Cobb spent more time on death row itself (about four years) than Bloodsworth (about one and a half years). Cobb also points out this variation in award amounts when comparing the amount he received for his wrongful conviction to that of fellow Illinois exoneree Dennis Williams (Protess and Warden 1998). Williams and his three codefendants received approximately $36 million from the litigation they pursued after release (Taylor 1999), litigation made possible by the notoriety of their cases. Cobb, whose case did not draw as much public attention, estimates Williams's personal award at around $12.8 million for his seventeen years of wrongful incarceration: "They give Dennis Williams $12.8 million. How's, why, how's a $140,000 gonna be compensation to me, and he gets $12.8 million?"

Second, both exonerees required a gubernatorial pardon to receive compensation. Although Bloodsworth waited six months for this process to be completed to be eligible for compensation, Cobb did not receive a pardon until 2000 and thus waited fourteen years for compensation. As discussed earlier with the North Carolina case of Scott Pierpoint, a pardon can be a sticky political issue, opening compensation claims up to political manipulation. Tough-on-crime governors may deny a pardon, regardless of legitimate claims of innocence, out of fear of political backlash from constituents, or governors in financially strapped states may deny a pardon to avoid paying out legitimate compensation claims. A pardon also is a costly process and requires legal expertise to file a successful application, resources typically in short supply for newly released exonerees. Finally, some exonerees are philosophically opposed to applying for a pardon to receive compensation. They simply do not understand why they must ask the state to pardon *them* when the state is the offending party. Alan Gell explains this position:

> I waited five plus on death row for something to happen. I waited another year and some change for my second trial to come. And I finally heard the truth. I finally heard "not guilty, free to go." To learn that you later have to ask the governor to forgive you or ask the governor to pardon you, it just, I think they've got that whole process backwards. It's not supposed to be me go to him and say, "Will you please pardon me for not doing what y'all said I did." It should be him coming forward on his own free will and saying, "Mr. Gell, our system don't normally do this. We're so sorry that you got caught up in it. That a bunch of different things could've contributed to it. But, I just want you to know, we're sorry for what happened." . . . I feel that's the way it should go. I don't foresee myself asking them to give that pardon.

Finally, the compensation received by Bloodsworth and Cobb also highlights, by contrast, those exonerees who received no compensation because such statutes were not available in their states or they were provisionally excluded, such as Shabaka Brown, Sabrina Butler, and Charles Fain. Butler's case is a good example of exonerees released prior to the establishment of a compensation statute who are now faced with steep start-up costs and statutes of limitation to file under newly established guidelines. While she has been actively trying to fulfill the necessary requirements, she has struggled to find competent representation and the financial resources to "motivate" an attorney to actively pursue the case on her behalf.[5]

Six of our participants used litigation as a mechanism to receive compensation and have been awarded varying amounts through this process. Alan Gell, for example, was awarded $3.9 million in a settlement with the state of North Carolina in 2009, five and a half years after his acquittal and release (Neff 2009). Ray Krone settled for $3 million from the city of Phoenix and an additional $1.4 million from Maricopa County, Arizona, both settlements coming about three years after his release (DeFalco 2005). Tim Howard and Gary James received $2.5 million and $1.5 million, respectively, for their twenty-six years in prison in Ohio (Price 2007), almost four years after their release. Several others reached settlements as well, though the amount was not made public. On average, these lawsuits took four years and substantial legal fees to settle, much of which was reimbursed from the awards themselves. Thus, while in the end they were successful, they did not have these awards available to them when they first left prison, or for several years thereafter. With the exception of Walter McMillian, all of our participants who were successful using this process were exonerated after 2002, possibly indicating that such litigation may be a more viable remedy now that a more widely accepted innocence framework has been established. With the exception of McMillian, none of them had been compensated at the time of our interview.

Whether they received compensation via statute or litigation, several exonerees noted that money did not solve all of their reintegration problems. Bloodsworth argues that while compensation is an essential piece of the reintegration puzzle, it is not a cure-all, and those who receive compensation, especially if the award is made public, should be aware of some pitfalls they may encounter. He describes how "new friends" and romantic partners may appear, wanting to take advantage of the exonerees' new fortune. As Bloodsworth says, "Try not to have any new friends if you can help it because that's not very good for you. You don't need no new pals. You just need some of the ones that have been sticking by you." He reveals how quickly his $300,000 whittled away as he spent money repaying debts to his father, paying back taxes, buying expensive cars, and supporting the buying habits of new friends and companions. He argues that exonerees need assistance in managing the compensation they receive. Many have never had substantial amounts of money and are not skilled at budgeting, investing, and saving. In our conversation with Tim Howard and his attorney Jim Owen, we found ourselves witness to a dispute between the two over how best to manage the money that Howard hoped to win in his lawsuit (which eventually settled for $2.5 million). Through personal conversations with his wife after his untimely death, we learned that Howard indeed struggled with the money once he received it.

Finally, several exonerees reiterated throughout the interview that while compensation is important, it cannot restore the years they lost to their wrongful conviction, the relationships that were damaged or destroyed, the family celebrations they missed, the jobs they could have had, the lives they could have lived. No amount of money can fully compensate for what was taken from them the day they were convicted: "The truth? I don't care about it [compensation] because they cannot pay me. They can put a billion dollars right there . . . that cannot pay me. I [am] more satisfied them owing me than them paying me because they *cannot pay me!* The only way they can pay me is by giving me my eighteen years back. And that's impossible" (Juan Melendez, his emphasis).

Compensation, then, is not the only resource exonerees need to assist in their reintegration, and states that establish compensation provisions should not see this as their sole responsibility to the wrongly convicted. Only a handful of exonerees reveal receiving assistance of any other kind, aside from compensation, such as assistance with housing and mental health or legal services. None of our participants received these services from the state. In several cases, an exoneree's appellate attorney was instrumental in assisting him immediately after release, as when Shabaka Brown lived with his attorney for several months and Scott Taylor's attorney helped him expunge his record. Friends and family often also fill this gap with whatever resources they may have available, which vary by exoneree. In several cases, exonerees paid for necessary services out of pocket. Bloodsworth, for example, recognized his need for mental health services: "You're gonna need just rehab, period! You're gonna need some therapy. You're gonna have to go talk to somebody like I did. [I told the psychologist], 'I gotta talk to you about everything. . . . I've been in prison for ten years. I was on death row for two. I haven't had sex for nine years. Where do you wanna start? I've got these issues with that, and I've got issues with being there, and I've got intimate issues with females. Start somewhere.' And that really helped me a whole lot." When asked who paid for those services, he responds quickly, "I did. Fifty dollars a session. . . . Once a week for six months."

In the immediate period after release, our participants were left on their own—no compensation, no emergency start-up funds, no transitional housing, no employment assistance. While compensation was available for two, their award was dependent upon the state they lived in and their ability, eventually, to secure a gubernatorial pardon as required by their state's statute. For others, compensation came many years later after an extended legal battle. In every case, the message heard loud and clear by our participants was that their needs were not important, the damage to their lives was theirs alone to undo, and they were most definitely on their own.

What They Need

Exonerees' discussions about what they would have liked to have had waiting for them upon release range from the very practical, such as a job, to the more abstract, such as acknowledgment or acceptance. Most everything they mention along this wide range is aimed in some way at assisting them in fitting back into their families and their communities. The overarching element they wish for is restoration, a restoration of the components of their financial, familial, and emotional lives that they believe were destroyed by their wrongful convictions.

STATE ASSISTANCE OR STATE RESISTANCE? What underlies most of their discussions of what they need after release is a strong belief that they should be given something *by the state* to repair the damage done to their lives. They firmly believe the state should be held accountable for their wrongful convictions and that an essential element of that accountability is voluntarily offered reparation (not forced out of the state by lawsuits). They believe that such good-faith offers of support would not only aid them with transition and reintegration but also, possibly more importantly, decrease their feelings of and experiences with rejection and stigmatization. However, for most, these forms of reparation have not been forthcoming. Instead, they believe their circumstances and needs have remained invisible to the state for a long time.

Alfred Rivera sums up this frustration over the state's inability to take responsibility for the damage caused to his life: "Seeing or hearing my case mentioned always reminds me of how the system can destroy a life anytime it get[s] ready. And how the system has no remorse after it prove[s] to itself that it is wrong and made a mistake." Tim Howard makes clear his feeling of invisibility when he says, "I feel that the state owes me. There's no doubt in my mind. Now, how much is another story. But, they don't reach out to you. I know that much. As soon as you get out, you have to make it on your own." Alan Gell again points out the paradox of the situation; if he had hurt someone, society would expect him to make amends, but the same is not required of the state: "It's not really somebody owes me, but it just seems like the right thing to do. You know? If I, after all, hurt one of my fellow human beings, maybe I can kinda do something to make amends. Nothing. They never did." Charles Fain notes the same irony: "If I go to court, I gotta . . . admit it, so why shouldn't they?"

Exonerees frequently express hostility and frustration over the state's lack of recognition of their needs and lack of accountability for its role in creating their situations. For example, Tim Howard argues that exonerees should automatically receive some type of compensation but explains why he thinks that will never happen by saying, "The state ain't never gonna take the blame for keeping a prisoner wrongfully incarcerated." Shabaka Brown agrees when he recognizes that he will never get the one thing he wants from the former governor of Florida, "to admit that he made a mistake." When asked if anyone had admitted that yet to him, he responds, "No one would do that. To do so would be a blanket indictment of the system of capital punishment in Florida." Juan Melendez gets so agitated during this part of our conversation that he gets up to walk around. He raises his voice when recounting the state's inability to own its mistakes:

> You talking about men that know I was innocent before going to trial and *still* wanted to kill me. Why?! . . . If he say, "Hey, I was wrong," then . . . I would embrace him, shake his hand . . . because it take a man to do that. It's that simple. But these people, they don't admit it when they do wrong. They cannot afford to admit that they do wrong. How the hell are they gonna say that, "We almost killed an innocent man in there," and they for the death penalty. It's political! (his emphasis)

This failure to admit responsibility ensures that mistakes will continue and exonerees will remain invisible.

The most agitated and hostile responses, however, came when exonerees expressed disgust not only over the state's resistance to recognizing its mistakes but also over its claims that their exonerations are evidence of the efficiency and efficacy of the system. Nothing makes an exoneree angrier than for a state official to claim that his or her exoneration is evidence that the system works (in spite of years of active resistance by the state to that same exoneration). A sampling of the retorts we received when we asked, "What do you say to people who argue that your case is an example that the system works?" includes the following:

> I knew that was coming. Baloney! I'm sorry. (Greg Wilhoit)

> No sir! No ma'am! No way! No how! The system didn't work! *I* worked. I got myself out. . . . I had a smart attorney . . . he's a judge now, who believed in me. But, even he did what I told him to do. He said, "You're either crazy or you're innocent." And I said, "Well, I'm both. Go do it!" (Kirk Bloodsworth)

> Because I'm free, the system works? If the system work[ed], I never would've been locked up. If it worked, if the police did they job, I never would've been locked up. If the State's Attorney did their job, they never would've tried me. If the judge was doing his job, I never would be found guilty. So how is the system work? The system is working for who? For the system? It's not working for me. You done took me away and put me away for all these years, and you done let me go out here and didn't give me anything to help myself, but you say the system work? (Perry Cobb)

In the end, they uniformly agree with Juan Melendez: "They got the nerve to tell me that because of what happen to me, it show that the system works. They got to be crazy! They got to be crazy! The system works . . . I was saved in spite of the system!"[6]

Our participants firmly believe that the state has a responsibility to provide at least a minimal amount of compensation and assistance to help them get back on their feet in the immediate aftermath of release, a responsibility exonerees feel is currently not being met. To add salt to their wounds by claiming that the state's handling of their cases is an example of the state at its best is simply the last straw.

PRACTICAL NEEDS. Exonerees discuss various practical needs that went unmet in the weeks, months, and years after release. Because they so often are starting completely over with nothing to their name (no money, no clothing, no place to live, no job . . .), it is not difficult for them to list a bundle of services that would have been helpful in those early days. Alan Gell lists off an array of services he had hoped to find waiting for him: "Health insurance. You know? Possible education. Checking to see if I have housing. An apology definitely would've helped. A legitimate effort to compensate for, to help you get a start. You know? . . . I think there should be at least some kind of start-up money to get you back into a normal life." Shabaka Brown mentions an even broader range of assistance:

> Some place to live because people get out, they don't have any-
> where to go. They've been locked up for so long . . . give them a
> place to live. Give them a job. Give them a chance . . . you know,
> where they can get started. And to take care of themselves again.
> And give them some type of counseling and rehabilitation to help
> them transfer back into the community, because see, like me, when
> I was locked up, I was a child. So, therefore, I didn't have no job
> skills, no nothing, you know what I'm saying? And if they get out,
> they need something like that. Give them a chance . . . maybe if
> they didn't get their GED while they was locked up, give them a
> chance to get that.

Given the wide array of practical needs often noted by exonerees, we grouped discreet types of needs together into three larger groupings—health care needs, financial needs, and legal needs—and discuss each of these three below.

Among these three larger groupings, our participants cited health care needs most frequently. This includes discussions of needed mental health services and rehabilitation, decompression time, resocialization assistance, and medical and dental health care. Among these, exonerees mentioned the need for mental health services far more frequently than any of the others. Given the incredible emotional and psychological trauma attendant upon being wrongly accused and convicted of a crime (Campbell and Denov 2004; Grounds 2004; Simon 1993) added to the daily stress of living in prison and on death row (Cohen and Taylor

1972; Haney 2003a, 2003b; R. Johnson 1981, 1998; Sykes 1958), it is not surprising that exonerees agree that they need mental health care to manage life after release. As Alfred Rivera so clearly articulates, "One who is sentenced to death and later relieved from such mental anguish should have outlets that can minimize the chances of stress or depressive type occurrences." He goes on to say, "The one thing I wish the state would have done was offer me avenues to get my life on track and give me access to clinical rehab to treat mental/psychological disorders that resulted from such an ordeal." Greg Wilhoit agrees, using his unique brand of humor to drive the point home: "I think everybody would do well to speak with a mental health professional. . . . Even if you're not nuts, I mean, you gotta be scarred by this experience somehow, whether you know it or not. And I probably am more screwed up than I'm willing to admit or maybe even know." Gary Beeman encourages service providers to include drug and/or alcohol rehabilitation services within the larger array of mental health services that should be made available to exonerees. He readily admits that after years of addiction both in and out of prison, "I needed help with substance abuse."

An additional component of mental health care advocated by several exonerees is what Shabaka Brown calls a "decompression period," a period of time immediately after release during which exonerees simply readjust to the daily routines of life—socializing, driving, grocery shopping, learning new technologies—free from the worries of finding a job, paying bills, or finding a permanent home. Because they so often leave prison with none of their material needs accounted for, they find that the immediate realities of providing for their food, clothing, and shelter rush in on them, only compounding the emotional and psychological stress of basic readjustment to living in a free society. A decompression period is something provided to parolees in the form of transition periods in a halfway house or supervised living facility (Petersilia 2003). However, these are not services made available to exonerees.

As Brown argues,

> What I'd like to see for the next guy that get out, I would like to see a system in place so he or she will have a chance to decompress. . . . You know, that they will be able to just chill and not have to worry about making a living, not worry about housing. There's so many

people that are walking out don't have families, don't have nowhere to go, don't have that support network. They're just out there. . . . A place where they could feel relaxed, so they could get their mind together.

Kirk Bloodsworth and Walter McMillian agree. They both argue that an initial period of decompression is essential to reintegration in that it allows exonerees a period simply to get used to living life again. About the first few months after release, Bloodsworth says, "Do nothing at all. Go home . . . go home to wherever you wanna call home now. Make it wherever you want it to be, but go there and do absolutely nothing. Relax. Smell the coffee. Don't do anything." McMillian echoes this sentiment: "For a while . . . [don't] be out in the world so much. And take it easy for a while, until you kind of get back in . . . the flow, until you get used to people and stuff." Thus, a period of readjustment free from the worries and burdens of everyday living is a key component to mental health.

Several exonerees noted that resocialization into the basic patterns of life should be the focus of the decompression period. This aspect of readjustment is often overlooked by those who have never been deprived of the ability to drive where they want, shop for groceries, go to a clothing store to buy a shirt of their choosing, talk to their friends, and the like. Yet, it is this freedom of choice that is most basic to everyday living. Thus, before exonerees can reapproach the workplace, family or intimate relationships, or community engagements, they must relearn these fundamentals of living a free life. As Bloodsworth explains, "I forgot how to use a fork and knife when I got out or to socialize. Ten years ago [when I first got out], I was a different fella. I would not have even come here to talk to you in your room because I couldn't socialize with you as just people." Ray Krone continues this same idea when he says,

You're not an adult [when you come out of prison]. You don't mature in prison. I mean, there's things that just can't happen in there because you don't have the same interactions, the same social goings-on and stuff that you had out in life. I mean, even just being capable of being a consumer. And you know that America's a consumerist country. You know what's a good brand to buy, what's a good deal, what's a bad deal. What to stay away from in the grocery store, what to avoid. When you're getting cheated, and when you're not. . . . Some of these other guys [exonerees] have no knowledge of what it is to be . . . a man, be a person, be living in this . . . free again.

Even though discussions of the mental health care they needed dominated most of their comments regarding health care services, some also did discuss their need for medical and dental care after release. They often discuss the array of medical problems they leave prison with, including asthma, digestive disorders, skin rashes, hepatitis, and arthritis. They reveal a number of medical and dental problems that have gone unattended while in prison, either due to a lack of adequate care in prison or fear on their part to allow prison medical staff to attend to them: broken bones that went unset, kidney stones treated with ibuprofen, tooth abscesses left to fester, tooth decay that goes without filling. So, upon release, they argue that they need, at the very least, a medical and dental checkup to assess their needs moving forward:

> Clearly, one of the biggest things that everybody's gonna need is medical. They need someone . . . whether it's a doctor or a dentist, whatever's willing to do a one-time checkup . . . you don't have to fix anything, but at least identify your needs. Most of the guys that come out of prison are gonna have some serious health issues. I mean, they're gonna have something because you don't get health care. . . . You get a toothache in there, and you finally get to see a dentist, they just pull them. But you gotta sign a waiver first, in case they break your jaw. . . . That's the kind of service you get. So a lot of these guys just avoid the medical issues to begin with, avoid teeth issues, or any of it. But that's the one thing they're gonna need. (Ray Krone)

The problem, of course, is that mental and health care services are expensive. While most people have medical insurance, via their place of employment, exonerees do not since their options for employment are so limited. Thus, without assistance from the state with their health care needs, they most likely go unmet.

The second largest grouping of needs discussed by exonerees revolves around their financial needs. They most often discuss their desires for compensation and immediate start-up funds, assistance with job training and finding meaningful employment, and a range of other services such as help with housing and educational expenses. Surprisingly, while compensation was the most often cited financial need they discussed, it was not the most often cited practical need in general. They were much more likely to note their need for mental health services than compensation. However, they do say that compensation from the state for their years of wrongful conviction would have greatly aided their transition back into society, as well as symbolically representing that the state recognizes their needs and its own responsibility for assisting them. Alfred Rivera addresses this quite directly when he says, "Financial compensation would have also been a responsibility that the state should have take[n] up," or as Bloodsworth sums up, "Although I think they [exonerees] need more than just money, they do need a lot of money." However, as noted earlier, exonerees are first to point out that compensation often comes with a set of management issues that many are unprepared to deal with. Compensation then should include assistance of some kind in handling the money.

Included in their discussions of compensation, many address the need for funds immediately after release to fill the gap while they await the processing of larger compensation packages: "I think there should be at least some kind of start-up money to get you back into a normal life" (Alan Gell). Such start-up funds could be used to pay for clothes, food, rent, and transportation in the immediate days and weeks after release, thus providing some degree of stability early on. Relief from these immediate burdens of material need also would provide the financial and emotional space required for the decompression period discussed earlier.

The second most often noted financial need was the need for employment and/or employment-related training and skills. Six of our participants (one-third of our total) were incarcerated for over ten years, and eight for over eight years. Considering the additional time they spent in jail awaiting trial, which in several cases totaled two to three years, over half of our participants have been out of the job market for ten years or more. The amount of technological change in that period of time can be staggering. Job skills they had going into prison may no longer be relevant or may have deteriorated to the extent of being useless. Entire new industries dominated by new technologies emerged

while many of them were incarcerated. They are unprepared for the job
market they confront after release. Yet they need a job. They need a way
to support themselves and, in some cases, begin to provide again for their
families and children. They need the benefits and health insurance coverage often attached to employment. They also need the positive identity that employment provides and the meaningful way that employment
structures daily life. Employment provides a way to feel a part of things
by making positive contributions to their families and communities.
The need for employment goes deeper than the paycheck it affords,
though the paycheck is, of course, quite significant in its own right.

Codefendants Gary James and Tim Howard both explain that assistance finding a job would have been helpful to them after release. James
says, "The only thing they really would have had . . . to do, just . . . get
me a job. Ya know, I would have been satisfied with that." And Howard
reiterates this: "Help with employment would have been nice." But
Delbert Tibbs believes that just any job will not suffice. He recognizes
that the value of a job for exonerees is only partly related to the financial
need it meets. Employment, according to Tibbs, more essentially provides a mechanism for exonerees to get reinvested in a meaningful life:
"They [exonerees] need to be occupied constructively. You oughta be
doing something that's going to reach a life or many of the lives of somebody around you. But to go to work in a paper clip factory, counting
paper clips, so that they will give you six dollars an hour ain't . . . that's
all you're gonna get outta that, is the six bucks. There's not going to be
any life enrichment." Tibbs understands that the value of employment
for exonerees extends beyond the money they earn and reaches into
their need for reconnection with self, others, and community.

Finally, exonerees mention other financial needs they face, including help with housing and educational costs. While some do have family
or friends willing to shelter them in the days immediately following
release, others do not. And even among those who do have a home to
go to, they often find that quarters are cramped, relationships get strained
quickly, and their welcome is easily worn thin. Living with an exoneree
in the days following release, after all, cannot be an easy task. The
decompression period for which so many exonerees advocate is made
more complicated when it is lived out in someone else's home or space.
Families usually are as ill prepared to meet an exoneree's needs as the

exoneree himself or herself; thus, families also need support and guidance. Assistance finding housing, even if for a transitional period, would be helpful and provide exonerees with the physical and emotional space they need to rediscover their way in the world. Alan Gell, for example, says that while he was grateful to be able to return to his mother's home after release, if for no other reason than to provide her with comfort and relief, he did long for a place of his own. Eventually, he purchased a small trailer that he parked near a small pond near her house. This way, she could see him, but he could have his own room to grow. Gell also discussed his struggles with going back to school. Because he was arrested and held for trial in his early twenties, he was not able to complete his education and wanted to go back to school after release. He thought this also would improve his employability. However, he did not have the resources to pay for tuition. Although he attended a local community college for a semester or two, he had to drop out because he could not pay the bills: "I always felt like, it seemed like somebody would offer to help me pay it some way. You know, just making amends for all the things that had happened. . . . [But], they never did."

The third grouping of practical needs mentioned by exonerees revolves around the legal services they still need after release but have few, if any, resources to pay for. If, for example, the compensation statute in their state requires a gubernatorial pardon, they must apply for that pardon, a process requiring legal expertise to complete. If their state has no compensation statute and they want to pursue compensation through litigation, they must hire an attorney to file the lawsuit. To reduce stigma and increase employability, many would like to have their records expunged of their wrongful capital convictions. The state does not automatically expunge this information from their records. Again, however, this is a legal process requiring exonerees to hire an attorney. While two or three of our participants had appellate attorneys who completed this process for them, the majority were not so lucky, and the record of their wrongful conviction is there for anyone who does a criminal records check to see. In a recent conversation with Shabaka Brown, he discussed his difficulty in finding a job this past year because even now, almost twenty-five years after his exoneration, his wrongful capital conviction still appears on his record and was flagged by a potential employer. Exonerees often are approached with offers to lend their

names to causes, participate in conferences and presentations, and sometimes have their cases written about for books or television. Sometimes
these offers require them to enter into complicated contracts. Again,
for this, they need legal advice. To the extent that they do not have the
resources to pay for legal services, this becomes one more barrier to
compensation, employability, and visibility. Alan Gell sums up the
frustration many exonerees feel regarding this need:

> In order to do the pardon process, one thing is you got like this
> much paperwork to fill out. And, one, I don't know how to fill it
> out. A lawyer has to. . . . And that means hiring the lawyers to do it.
> Sorry. I don't think that it's right, you know, to have to pay the
> money to get them to say, "Oh, We're sorry. We shouldn't have
> done that." . . . I think that the governor should come forward on
> his own free will and pay his lawyers to do the paperwork to explain
> why he's done it. I don't think that it should be that way. . . . You
> got to hire a lawyer to do an expungement. And you know,
> again I'd like to have it done. But the truth of the matter is,
> is if I had fifty million dollars, I wouldn't pay a damn lawyer a
> penny to do it. I think the governor should expunge it on his own.
> It shouldn't cost me to expunge . . . to expunge what should've
> never been there.

The list of practical needs noted by exonerees is extensive—mental,
medical, and dental health care, health insurance, decompression time
funded by emergency start-up funds to allow for resocialization and
adjustment, compensation, job assistance, housing, educational aid,
and legal services to remove remaining barriers to compensation and
employment. To the extent that these needs go unaddressed, exonerees
are impeded from full reparation and repair of their lives and relationships. To the extent that these needs go unrecognized, the state fails to
acknowledge its responsibility to doing justice for exonerees.

RESTORATION

More often than compensation or mental health services, employment or record expungement, the category of need most often mentioned by exonerees is their need for an apology. More often than not,
this was the first response we received when we asked exonerees what

they needed after release. But not any halfhearted, forced expression of culpability would do; they want a personal, meaningful, heartfelt apology offered by someone directly involved in the production of their wrongful conviction. In the simplest of terms, they wanted someone who did this to them to say, "I'm sorry." But, like most of the needs they have discussed thus far, this too is a need that typically goes unmet.

Ray Krone makes clear that anything short of a face-to-face expression of regret directly from someone responsible for his wrongful conviction is not enough: "You might be the head of the DA's office, but until that piece of shit prosecutor who did this to me comes and apologizes and looks at me and basically, you know, acts as almost bows his head and kneels down, it's like, what good is his [the figurehead official] apology? It's the people who are responsible are the ones who . . . should owe an apology, not somebody else that's taking the blame for it." Shabaka Brown ranks an apology as most important among the services he mentions needing after release: "I don't care about pardoning. I don't care about the press. I don't care about none of that. We [he and the other exonerees] want a public, 'Look, we're sorry we made a mistake.' That's what I want." He recognizes the impact such a public statement of responsibility would have on the public and thus on alleviating the stigma that exonerees often carry: "You see that public apology would erase from the mind of those that think that I just had a smart lawyer that got me off by coming up with some legal technicality." Krone agrees, "[An apology] carries a lot of weight right there to the public [so] that it would be something you could hold out as a proof of your innocence."

They rarely get the personal apology they want so much. The following exchange with Scott Taylor is reflective of the frustration they feel over being overlooked in this way:

INTERVIEWER: . . . You never got any kind of apology?

TAYLOR: None.

INTERVIEWER: Anything like that?

TAYLOR: None.

INTERVIEWER: From anybody? Prosecutor, police officer?

TAYLOR: Nobody.

INTERVIEWER: Victim survivors?

TAYLOR: Nope.

INTERVIEWER: What would that mean to you?

TAYLOR: It would mean a lot, actually to come from the court. . . . Just for the court to say, "Hey. We sorry."

One of the many times Perry Cobb made us laugh during our interview with him was when we asked if he had received an apology from anyone in the system. His reply: "Did the bear cook biscuits in the woods?" Many exonerees would no doubt agree that the prospect of receiving an apology from anyone involved in their case seems equally ridiculous.

Three of our participants did come close to receiving an apology, though each attempt fell short in some meaningful way. In Ray Krone's case, the DA held a press conference prior to Krone's final evidentiary hearing in which he said that *if* an injustice had been done in this case, Krone would deserve an apology. However, Krone was not at that press conference or asked to attend that event. He, in fact, did not learn about this statement until immediately after the hearing at which he was released when reporters confronted him with it. Krone describes that he responded angrily to the reporters, noting that no one from the district attorney's office had extended a hand to him or offered him a personal apology. The reporters used Krone's response to goad a representative from the DA's office, who had attended the final evidentiary hearing, into offering Krone a face-to-face, public "apology" on the spot. But Krone's analysis of the apology is as follows:

When I finally got released, when they actually dropped all the charges, they had sent a little gofer, a little geeky dude from the DA's office into represent their side. . . . He comes over and again, this little geeky dude won't look up, and he says, "I'm not sure if you're aware of it but [the DA] did offer you an apology in a press conference today." And that's all he did. All he did was reiterate that there was this press conference. He wouldn't even look at me. You know, he wouldn't say he apologized, but he would say, "Well, [the DA] did apologize to you. [He] did offer you an apology in a press conference today." But that's all he'd say. All he had to do is say, "On behalf of the DA's office . . . the city . . . it's a terrible thing that happened. Sorry." Anything like that, but no, this was again, this was this roundabout . . . convoluted. . . . "Well, we did say something. You deserve to have an apology. . . ." Just a simple apology, [but] he couldn't even look up at me.

The state had their moment but could not come through with the straightforward, meaningful apology that Krone needed to hear.[7] Scott Taylor similarly felt left out in the cold, as is obvious from his quote noted above. He did receive a deeply felt and clearly articulated expression of regret from the governor during the speech in which he pardoned Taylor. However, Taylor never received any apologies from those most directly responsible for his wrongful conviction, something that was important to him.

Finally, Kirk Bloodsworth eventually received a personal, meaningful apology from the DA who prosecuted his case, though it came over ten years after his exoneration and release. At the time of his actual release in 1993, the state's representative said in a press conference that while the DNA evidence revealed she no longer had the evidence to prosecute him, she was not prepared to say he was innocent (Junkin 2004). For ten years, the prosecutor in his case resisted submitting the DNA in his case to the DNA data bank, in spite of Bloodsworth's urgings. More than ten years later, she finally did. After receiving a cold hit on the actual offender in his case, the prosecutor finally offered the apology that Bloodsworth had so longed to hear, and the impact on him was life altering: "[She said,] 'There is nothing I can say to give you back . . . I am so sorry.' And then, just like water off a duck's back, my pain disappeared. My anger, it was all gone. . . . And I told her, I said, 'I'm not . . . I hated you for so long and I'm tired of hating' . . . and I hugged her before she left." He finally had the acknowledgment he had wanted since his release. At that moment, his healing began.

Interestingly, while those most directly responsible for our participants' wrongful convictions were not forthcoming with apologies, family members of the victims in their cases, as well as other case participants, often were. About half of our participants received expressions of regret from victim survivors or others involved in the case (e.g., jurors, family members of witnesses), even though, as the exonerees themselves note, these individuals had nothing to apologize for. Exonerees express how meaningful these acknowledgments have been to them in the years after their release and how grateful they are to those who offered them. As Tim Howard says about an apology he received from the family members of the bank security guard killed in his case: "It was real pleasant to hear . . . it's nice to know that they realize that James and I got railroaded. It's nice for them to; their eyes have [been] open enough to see this." James also found the apology meaningful: "That's the only thing that really that used to bother me, that they [the victim's family] thought . . . you know, that I did it. And now that he [a family member] wrote that letter [apologizing], I see what his family really thinks. . . . They didn't have nothing to apologize for." Alan Gell also finds solace in his meeting with the son of the murder victim in his case:

> It felt real good because I was, all the time, I had known all about the victim's family hating me and wanting me dead. And, I just wanted somehow to let them know that I didn't do it, and they got the wrong person, and you might want to pursue it too because, because they got me and not the right person, that means you're not getting justice. And that's just, was really important to me for them to not hate me, and for him talking about hating me and then not to think that I done it but I didn't. To find it out [that he doesn't blame me] is definitely, definitely a good experience.

Ray Krone's description of the apology he received from the mother of the victim in his case was particularly poignant. Krone points out that even though he was the one wrongly convicted and incarcerated, she too had been sentenced to a life of misery:

> That sweet old lady . . . and now she's gotta sit up here in this other trial [of the actual offender identified through DNA]. This will never be over. She'll probably die before this is over. She went through ten years with me. He hasn't even gone to trial yet . . . this has been made a tragedy for life, that she can never heal. And whose fault is that? . . . She was crying when she said it [her apology to him]. And I told her, "Look, I accept your apology though there's no need for it. I understand your anger was addressed at the person that killed your daughter. I knew that wasn't me." . . . She was just a poor, depressed, little withered up . . . I mean, just hurt inside so

deeply. I mean, what could she do. And you just wanna hug somebody like that. You wanna give them some reason to look up and smile and say, "Everything will be all right."

In the very moment that Krone had longed for the most, the day of his release and vindication, he found the most comfort in extending himself to this woman whose apology was so deeply felt though so unnecessary. For the state officials who were most responsible for his own suffering and who failed so miserably in extending themselves to him, he harbored nothing but anger and disrespect.

EXONEREES' EXPLANATIONS of what they needed most upon release from prison make clear that what they needed and wanted was simply a chance, a fresh start, a way to get up to speed and back on their feet after such an abrupt life disruption. They wanted a more equal playing field in which to begin putting the pieces of their lives back together, and they wanted the state to assist in that process. They wanted simple gestures of acknowledgment of the wrongs done to them and honest attempts at helping them restore their lives to something akin to normal. They wanted inclusion rather than exclusion, recognition rather than rejection. This is at the heart of what they want and need: "The community should welcome them back" (Shabaka Brown). Restoration of identity and community comes in many forms, of the financial self, the physical self, the psychological self, and the spiritual self. Restoration requires acknowledgment of the exoneree as a person of worth and value, a person who is no longer invisible, no longer expelled from humanity.

CHAPTER 12

Moving Forward

That was what I wanted more than anything. I wanted
to be loved again. I wanted people to respect me.
And I didn't want people to think I was a child killer
anymore. . . . I wanted love and acceptance.

—Kirk Bloodsworth

OUR PARTICIPANTS have conveyed the contours and
dimensions of their experiences with wrongful capital convictions.
Drawing from these experiences and from the work of other scholars
and advocates, we provide here our thoughts and proposals regarding
trauma recovery and structural reforms for life after exoneration from
death row. According to Judith Herman (1997), recovering from trauma
occurs in three stages: establishing safety, mourning and remembrance,
and reconnecting in daily life. We have revealed their experiences with
establishing safety and security; we have heard their voices of mourning
and remembrance for the losses they have endured; and we have examined their efforts to reconnect in their daily lives with their families
and communities and in the wider world. Herman (1997, 196) writes,
"Having come to terms with the traumatic past, the survivor faces the
task of creating a new future." What kind of future can the exonerated
pursue? What remedies are appropriate? Among the options, of course,
is to pursue redress from and reforms in the criminal justice system. Like
other trauma survivors, our participants understand the political dimension of their experiences and believe their ordeals illuminate broader
public policy debates. For some, this becomes a survivor mission
(Herman 1997). In this regard, our participants make their experiences
"a gift to others" who might benefit by learning the broader lessons from
our participants' experiences (Herman 1997, 207).

Not surprisingly, our participants advocate for reforms to the system. Surprisingly, however, this is a topic about which they are least vocal. Although their lived realities reveal how essential reforms are, some were not able to articulate the specifics of such reforms when asked directly. But, for others, their experiences inspire them to suggest big-picture reforms, systemwide changes in procedures, accountability from system officials who erred in their cases, and outright abolition.

Big-Picture Reforms

The big-picture reforms they advocate include reducing racial discrimination and honoring the intentions of the U.S. Constitution. Problems of racial bias in the criminal justice system were painfully real to our participants. Alfred Rivera, for example, sees his experiences as a direct consequence of racism in the United States, especially within the criminal justice system. He comments that "this country will never be as 'great' as it should be until it stops living in 'black and white.' The systems that defendants who are minorities have to face are already operating on preconceived notions and condemnation. What chance do we have to do better in our lives when everywhere we turn we are frowned upon? People should know these things and work to correct them." To remedy racism, therefore, would be to remedy, at least in part, the racist conditions contributing to their wrongful capital convictions: tunnel vision, rush to judgment, inadequate representation, police and prosecutorial misconduct, as well as broader social conditions such as poverty, poor educational opportunities, limited economic options, and inadequate political representation (see K. Parker et al. 2001).

Related to racial bias, the U.S. Constitution provides for equal protection under the law and protection against cruel and unusual punishment. These enshrined legal values are not realized, according to our participants, as evidenced by their experiences with wrongful capital convictions. Gary Gauger says, "I'd love to see an end to the hypocrisy in this country, and I'd like to see people live up to the ideals in the Constitution." Alfred Rivera offers this view:

The brightest, smartest country on the planet, and she can't figure out how to mold her inhabitants into productive citizens? They place police in the sectors of community they don't understand, and are [as] foreign to them as a human being living on Pluto. This causes police brutality and racial profiling. This causes a black man in the Bronx to be shot nineteen times because he tried to flash his identification, or a black man to have a broom handle rammed up his anus in Brooklyn, or a black man in California to be beat near to death for a traffic violation. This causes so many to be placed in handcuffs for nothing other than who they are and how they look. The governing body of this country . . . must not continue to turn a blind eye to the realities that exist.

Our participants see their predicaments as a direct consequence of broader social conditions such as racism, not as aberrations or rare errors, as a logical outcome of a society marred by inequality and discrimination.

Systemwide Changes

Our participants advocate for systemwide changes to criminal justice procedures to prevent wrongful convictions, focusing in particular on restricting the use of snitches and providing better defense representation at trial. Informant testimony and jailhouse snitch testimony were key factors in the wrongful convictions of several of our participants, and many complained about their inadequate representation at trial. This might be why they focused on these two aspects of the system. Juan Melendez believes a "prosecutor is doing business with the devil" by using snitch testimony. Alan Gell sees snitch testimony as "manipulation" by snitches and prosecutors: "[T]hink about what our goals are in the system, think what they're doing; [snitches are] manipulating it too. I'm trying to get legislators to cut out testimony by known coconspirators to the degree of giving them a plea bargain." Charles Fain suggests that in order to improve the system, it is going to cost money, especially for better defense representation: "The public defender's office is overworked and understaffed." Kirk Bloodsworth says, "I had really slipshod attorneys in the beginning" who failed to object at key moments in the original proceedings. In a darkly humorous moment, Bloodsworth recalls a meeting with his original trial attorney:

He comes in [to the jail] . . . and he says, "Kirk! You're in big trouble!" He's pretty bright, I'm thinking [sarcastically]. I said,

"Yeah, I'm in big trouble. What are you gonna do for me, man? Can you help me with this thing?" He says, "Oh, I know my way around the courtroom. I know my way around the criminal justice system, and I'm gonna find our way out of this." . . . The final thing he says to me, "Kirk, take care. You're in good hands." . . . He got up, turned around, and ran right into the wall. True story!

No doubt, our participants would be supportive of many, if not most, proposed remedies to prevent wrongful convictions, including changes to informant/snitch handling, improved defense services, interrogation reforms, improved forensic techniques and evidence handling, revised eyewitness identification procedures, and open discovery for prosecutors, to name just a few (Bernhard 2001; www.innocenceproject.org; Leo 2001; Northwestern Center on Wrongful Convictions 2004; Turtle et al. 2003; Zimmerman 2001).

Our participants also advocate for improvements to state compensation statutes. Foremost, they firmly believe that substantive compensation should be provided, but not simply for the financial benefits. They also see compensation as a means for the state to "own up to [their error]" as Gary James phrases it, recognizing that money alone cannot repair the harms they endured. Exonerees understand that financial compensation is a gesture toward reparations, and they interpret reluctance to provide compensation as an ongoing insult that results in continued "reputational harm" (Lawrence 2009, 395).

They also advocate for reform of compensation statutes to reduce barriers to full compensation. For example, some state provisions carry restrictive eligibility requirements, such as requiring a gubernatorial pardon, or disqualifiers, such as denying compensation to those said to have "contributed" to their wrongful conviction or who have other, unrelated felony convictions. Some statutes have high burdens of proof and short statutes of limitation (Avery 2009; Bernhard 2009; Norris 2011). Greg Wilhoit's experience is illustrative of how such barriers can impede an exoneree's ability to receive compensation. He applied for compensation in Oklahoma and was denied:

You ought to see this application for compensation! And, the first hoop you gotta jump through to be eligible for this money . . . is you gotta be pardoned by the governor, get an official pardon.

So [my attorney Mark Barrett] went in front of this board and all this stuff. And they said that they don't have the authority to pardon somebody who hasn't been convicted of anything. See I got acquitted in mine; I got a directed verdict. I'm not eligible for a pardon because I'm not guilty of anything. Now what kind of shit is that? See fortunately, I got a good sense of humor, otherwise I'd go crazy. It's a catch-22, you know. I'm convinced they did it on purpose; they knew what they were doing.

Even though Wilhoit had been wrongly convicted once, he was later acquitted at a second trial when the judge entered a directed verdict of "not guilty." The governing committee used this against him, claiming he was not eligible for a gubernatorial pardon because of his acquittal. In other words, they claimed they could not pardon him because he was no longer thought to be guilty of anything. Since the compensation law requires such a pardon, he was not eligible for compensation. Thus, while Oklahoma has a compensation statute, its provisions serve only as roadblocks to full reparation. Our participants argue for a variety of systemwide changes to procedures to prevent wrongful convictions and better provide for exonerees after release.

Accountability

As important as financial reparations are to our participants, holding public officials accountable also is a central remedy they would like to pursue. Juan Melendez suggests, "[Y]ou got to hold them [police and prosecutors] *accountable*. That way the next one will think twice. But, they got immunity, by law they got immunity. They can do all this violence and get away with it" (his emphasis). Scott Taylor agrees: "We should be able to hold corrupt cops, judges, state's attorneys accountable when we find out they framed me or planted false evidence and knew and intentionally tried to kill me. Until then, who knows how many innocent people we're gonna execute. How many innocent people are actually in prison right now, because they get away with those things?" Lacking official acknowledgment of the harms inflicted by the state and punishment of wrongdoers, our participants sometimes satisfy themselves by speaking out. Doing so exposes the true nature of their "perpetrator" to the public, revealing that they understand an aspect of the perpetrator's identity that perhaps the general public has not seen (Herman 1997). As victims of state harm (Westervelt and Cook 2010), death row exonerees often seek ways to expose the flaws of the system of criminal and capital prosecutions.

Abolition

Our participants are quite vocal in their desire to abolish the death penalty in the United States. Greg Wilhoit voices his belief that the system is beyond repair: "It's broken. Not just the capital murder system, the whole system." Juan Melendez agrees: "It cannot be reformed because the justice system is always going to be subject to human error. It's that simple, and some innocent people are gonna be messed up." Shabaka Brown wants "to remove the death penalty, to stop killing people and to start treating them like people. You can't make laws that say it's not right to commit murder and turn right around in the same breath and [execute] a person. It's the same thing; it's premeditation. It's malice. They know they're going to kill you, and they think about it; they plan it! Premeditation. They got all the factors they need to convict the state." Ray Krone sees the trend toward eroding capital punishment as an extension of our "evolving public standards" where it is now unconstitutional to execute juveniles and the mentally ill. He says, "Okay, it's not socially acceptable to kill the mentally retarded, and okay, we're not killing kids anymore either, and [eventually] we're not killing anybody 'cause people aren't going to stand for it." Their near-death experiences demonstrate the mechanisms by which errors happen and what those mistakes mean for them and their supporters. To leave the system functioning so poorly risks harming other innocents, which, according to Ray Krone, is unacceptable. He says, "I don't want it [the death penalty] to happen to anyone; I don't even want it to happen to a guilty person, to be in a system [that] promotes itself to be the best there is. So, if this is the best there is; we are sorely lacking."

REPARATION

Remedies discussed by advocates and experts include many of those recommended by exonerees, such as financial compensation and official acknowledgment by the state of its errors. But these discussions include additional proposals for an array of transitional services, postrelease support systems, and even media management (Illinois Criminal Justice Information Authority 2002; Innocence Project 2009; Lawrence 2009; Lonergan 2008; Weigand 2009). Based on our findings, we support much of what has been proposed to assist exonerees as they rebuild after release, and we extend these proposals further to more fully address needs we think have been overlooked.

Compensation typically is the remedy that draws the most attention. And, certainly, every state should adopt compensation statutes that provide substantive and timely relief after exoneration. We support the compensation provisions proposed by the Innocence Project (2009). They recommend minimum compensation of $50,000 (untaxed) per year of wrongful imprisonment and $100,000 (untaxed) per year for time served on death row. However, as Frederick Lawrence (2009, 391) warns, "Compensation is just one of the necessary means for helping to fully restore the exonerated to society." According to Judith Herman (1997, 190), the "quest for fair compensation is often an important part of recovery. However, it also presents a potential trap. Prolonged, fruitless struggles to wrest compensation from the perpetrator or from others may represent a defense against facing the full reality of what was lost. Mourning is the only way to give due honor to loss; there is no adequate compensation."

Thus, compensation is a good beginning, but it is only a beginning for establishing meaningful remedies for exonerees. The Innocence Project (2009) also provides a rich and detailed set of recommendations for postrelease social services, which include appropriate attorneys' fees associated with filing for compensation; transitional assistance with housing, transportation, education, workforce development, and physical and mental health care; an official acknowledgment of the wrongful conviction; automatic record expungement; and assistance with child support or child custody, if necessary. We also endorse these proposals as they would provide significant steps toward reparation and remedy for exonerees.

Craig Haney (2003b, 2006) offers a similar set of reforms aimed at addressing the impact of incarceration on all former prisoners, not just exonerees. After an exhaustive exploration of the damage done by incarceration, Haney (2003b, 58) suggests that released prisoners need transitional services to adjust to their new homes, such as "effective decompression programs . . . occupational and vocational training . . . pre-release assistance [for resuming family roles], . . . [and] specialized transitional services to facilitate their reintegration into the free world." Furthermore, Haney (2003b, 58) cautions against a direct and unassisted release from supermax or solitary confinement into free society due to the "adverse effects of long-term isolation" so that ex-prisoners can "reacquaint themselves with the social norms of the world to which they will return." These recommendations affirm what exonerees have told us about the need for a period of decompression immediately after release when they can adjust and get resocialized.

The Innocence Project (2009) also recommends that exonerees develop a "release plan" for returning to their communities and families by assessing available resources for immediate assistance. Jessica Lonergan (2008, 440–446) further develops this idea into a detailed framework for service delivery to exonerees after release. She calls for the use of individualized reentry plans (IRPs), similar to individualized education programs for students with special needs. Each plan follows ten steps, from evaluation of needs to delivery of services and progress measures. Lonergan advocates that an IRP be crafted as soon as possible after an exoneree's release to address each individual's unique circumstances. She recommends the IRPs include many elements also identified by the Innocence Project (2009): financial compensation, mental and medical health care, reintegrative services, education, employment assistance, housing assistance, and legal assistance. According to her model, the state would be responsible for delivering some significant components of the plan, thus addressing exonerees' desires for the state to acknowledge its role in their wrongful conviction. As a result, exonerees would not be "kicked to the curb," as several of our participants experienced. Specifically, each ten-step IRP would include (Lonergan 2008, 440–446) the following:

1. Exonerated individual is identified as possibly needing reentry and related services.
2. Exoneree is evaluated.
3. Eligibility is decided.
4. Exoneree is found eligible for services.
5. Individual Reentry Plan (IRP) meeting is scheduled.
6. IRP meeting is held and the IRP is written.

7. Services are provided.
8. Progress is measured.
9. IRP is reviewed.
10. Exoneree is reevaluated for continuing eligibility.

While we think this model holds great potential for providing substantial assistance to exonerees upon release, a few additional components should be considered. First, Lonergan does not include an apology from state officials to the wrongly convicted. As our participants have revealed, an apology is an essential need they identify. As we have argued, an apology is significant to exonerees and can play a key role in promoting healing, reducing stigma, and increasing community acceptance. Second, Lonergan does not include a place for community participation in assisting with reintegration, outside of professional service providers. Other community members who could participate would be leaders in civic life, such as mayors, civic and relief organization leaders, faith leaders, journalists, and others deemed appropriate by exonerees and their team of supporters. Soliciting assistance from community members more broadly can build bridges between the community and the exoneree, reducing their experiences of rejection and disconnection. Third, the IRP involves the exoneree as a key member of the team, though the later steps of establishing "benchmarks" for review, assessment of goals, and "progress measures" risk treating the exoneree as a "subject" of control and therefore may be experienced by him or her as paternalistic. We caution service providers to resist establishing goals and progress measures without the clear endorsement and understanding of the exonerated individual. Finally, we encourage the IRP to include contact with and support from other exonerees when possible, as our participants have noted the significance of such support to their own postrelease adjustment. We endorse Lonergan's framework with these items modified and spell out more clearly how to integrate this model into our own proposals for reintegration in the next section.

When evaluating exonerees' needs after release, Heather Weigand and Tuere Anderson (2007) argue that it is essential to remember that exonerees' situations change over time as they encounter different dimensions of life after release. Working closely with exonerees through LAEP, they identify four transitional stages after release: stage 1 is the "celebrity phase" (zero to six months); stage 2 is the "process stage" (six months to one year); stage 3 is "life on life's terms" (one year to eighteen months); and stage 4 is "finding a niche" (after eighteen months and for years beyond). Consistent with our findings, exonerees' postrelease needs emerge in stages from practical, immediate needs to larger, more existential needs as they find ways to make sense of their experiences. This model makes clear what we find in our own examination of life after exoneration: reintegration is a process, and any release plan should account for these changes over time.

Weigand (2009, 434) goes on to argue that, in addition to the array of transitional services identified by the Innocence Project and Lonergan, exonerees and their advocates should develop a plan for managing media coverage after exoneration and release:

> The mass attention exonerees often receive raises hopes that society will help them in some way. When the cameras go away and the limelight dims, however, exonerees are left with broken promises of assistance, including job offers that are rarely, if ever, fulfilled. . . . While the media sells the story the public is left frustrated—wanting to help, but not knowing how. If we could find a way for journalism to be more pro-active with their story beyond print, then perhaps this would facilitate better outcomes for the exonerated and their personal exposure to the community. This approach would build human and social capital for the exonerees and his or her community.

Weigand also cautions against too much media exposure since overexposure can trigger posttraumatic stress reactions. While we agree that the media can be a positive influence on community attitudes toward exonerees, we caution that media coverage does not always favor the exoneree's side of the story. In an effort to appear fair and balanced, media may cover police and prosecutors' claims that the exoneree is actually guilty, thus heightening rather than reducing community hostilities. Finding the right balance of coverage is necessary for individual exonerees as they confront their transition.

Finally, we agree with Frederick Lawrence (2009, 397), who advocates for an "official declaration of innocence" as a necessary component of redress for the wrongly convicted. He suggests that the exonerated should "have a right to sue for a declaration of innocence" since there "is no other remedy that is aimed directly at the restoration of their damaged reputations." This official declaration from the state should be released publicly to ensure exonerees can use it for employment, education, and social reintegration purposes as needed. Though Lawrence does not specifically include an official apology as a component of this declaration of innocence, we advocate including an official and public apology directly to exonerated individuals. Efforts to declare actual innocence, we believe, would aid significantly in preventing the isolation and rejection many of our participants experience when returning to their communities.

REINTEGRATION AND RESTORATIVE JUSTICE

Building on the proposals for reform discussed thus far, we take perhaps a surprising turn toward restorative justice as a basis for our concluding recommendations. John Braithwaite's (2002, 15–16) work in restorative justice informs our vision for reparations and reintegration. Braithwaite outlines restorative justice values that should guide official responses to injustices and that are enshrined in international human rights agreements, including (but not limited to) restoration of human dignity, restoration of damaged relationships and communities, emotional restoration, compassion and caring, peace, freedom, and empowerment or self-determination. Restorative justice practices provide opportunities for those injured and their perpetrators to meet in a safe and facilitated process to make amends and develop a plan for redress. Such practices have been utilized in cases ranging from juvenile crime to homicide and sexual assault as well as in postconflict societies using Truth and Reconciliation inquiries. Elements of this approach that make it attractive to us include the opportunities for injured persons to be heard by those who inflicted the injury, opportunities for supporters to share their experiences with the impact of the injury, and opportunities for perpetrators to take responsibility, genuinely apologize, and make amends, which can empower and liberate survivors. Braithwaite (2002, 157) writes, "An underestimated way restorative justice might confer power upon the disenfranchised is simply by listening to their stories and taking them seriously." Because our participants have been severely silenced by courts, the media, prison officials, and others, providing them with an opportunity to be heard is crucial for their recovery. But who will listen, and for what purpose should they voice their experiences?

Participants in restorative remedies for exonerated death row survivors—those listening—might include the exonerees and their family members, attorneys, and supporters; social service providers; criminal justice system officials, mainly prosecutors, police investigators, and sheriffs; and other community and civic leaders, such as mayors, city council members, local representatives, business leaders, faith leaders, and nonprofit organizers who might provide assistance. The purpose of exonerees sharing their experiences would be to reclaim their innocence, shed stigma, discuss publicly how the injustice harmed them and their families, hear system officials take responsibility and offer apologies for their errors, and build a plan for making amends.

By adapting a restorative justice framework (J. Braithwaite 2002; K. J. Cook 2006; K. J. Cook and Powell 2006), we prioritize the voices and experiences of the wrongly condemned to develop our recommendation for "reintegration networks" to support and provide for exonerees after release. Reintegration networks draw from the social and legal service provision models emphasized by the Innocence Project (2009) and Lonergan (2008) while incorporating a focus on restorative justice ideals and practices. At a minimum, reintegration networks would include much, if not most, of what is recommended by the Innocence Project and Lonergan. In the short-term, this would include immediate monetary assistance to support a decompression period that includes housing in a safe and comfortable environment without pressure to be self-supporting for the first year, initial medical and psychological evaluations to establish baseline needs, a reintegration mentor or coach (perhaps another exoneree) to assist in relearning the skills of independent living (e.g., driving, managing bank accounts, using technology, shopping for groceries and clothes), support services for family members to assist with reunification and transition, and vocational or occupational skill development. Longer term services would include substantive and meaningful compensation to include help with financial planning and assistance with housing, employment, health care (mental and physical), educational expenses, and transportation. Long-term services also would address legal needs: assistance with automatic expungement of the wrongful conviction, filings for compensation, a gubernatorial pardon, if required, or other official certifications of innocence, and child support or child custody issues.

We envision these reintegration networks as similar to "circles of support" (Spagnolo et al. 2011).[1] Circles of support are consistent with the values of restorative justice as they are "person centered planning techniques" that "[consist] of a group of people willing to support an individual in working toward achieving their future vision" (Spagnolo et al. 2011, 234). A typical product for a circle of support is a visual representation, or map, that identifies multiple resources and people who can provide assistance in various arenas of need identified above. For exonerees, participants in the circles of support, represented on this map, would include the service providers (social, health care, financial), attorneys, supporters, and advocates who come together to help exonerees meet the demands of rebuilding their lives after prison. In addition, we strongly encourage this map to include other exonerees and/or death row survivors as mentors because they best understand the struggles new exonerees will encounter and can provide empathic assistance and advice. We also emphasize, as does Lonergan (2008), the importance of the role of the state, most probably in partnership with nonprofit organizations, in providing many of these services. Exonerees see the state as the "perpetrator" of the injustice done to them and firmly believe the state should take responsibility for making amends.

Reintegration networks, then, would be responsible for addressing the array of practical financial and transitional needs exonerees face after release. However, drawing from the restorative justice tradition, they also would confront the broader issues of community stigma and rejection exonerees encounter more fully than models proposed thus far in the literature. Thus, in addition to the circles of support recommended above, we also recommend that reintegration networks afford each exoneree the opportunity to participate in a community reintegration forum. Psychosocial healing may be accomplished, in part, by giving voice to their injuries in an authentic community forum where the injured person—the exoneree—speaks and an interested audience listens. Healing also involves the public identification of the injured person, providing opportunities to shed negative stigma and reclaim his or her innocent identity by integrating the experiences of trauma, as appropriate. Ideally, participants in this forum would include those who are responsible for the injury so they could hear, firsthand, how the harm has affected the person injured and his or her companions. In the case of exonerees, this would mean bringing together criminal justice officials who participated in the investigation and prosecution of their case. This would be one opportunity for accusers to listen carefully to exonerees, help restore them to their innocent status through a public apology and/or other offers of support, and encourage community members to welcome them into free society again.

We recognize, however, that many officials may be resistant to participating in such a forum. Given how often criminal justice representatives continue to insist on guilt well after exoneration, we understand that full participation by those parties that exonerees see as responsible for their wrongful convictions may not be possible. But the community reintegration forum need not hinge on their participation or presence and can be conducted in their absence. Other representatives from community and civic life can participate and provide many of the same benefits of acknowledgment, acceptance, and understanding to exonerees. It is true, though, that the failure of criminal justice officials to participate in the forum denies exonerees the opportunity to hear directly from those they hold most responsible for their wrongful capital conviction.

We also encourage, to the extent possible, the victim survivors of the original crime to participate in the reintegration forum. Having heard our participants describe their relief when victim survivors have offered their support and understanding, we are convinced that victim survivors who are willing to participate should be encouraged to do so, provided their participation is predicated on accepting that the exoneree was, indeed, wrongly convicted. If the victim survivors continue to believe the exoneree is the person responsible for the death of their loved one, other restorative justice mechanisms should be explored and provided to them as appropriate.

Additional participants in the forum would include family members of the exoneree who can speak to their own trauma and needs moving forward. Other exonerees can help illuminate the difficulties the exoneree may confront and guide discussions about their needs. Service providers and prospective employers (most likely from the circle of support) would be present to explain what they have to offer and show their support for the exoneree's reintegration. The audience would include representatives from the community and media members, who would have an opportunity to ask questions and receive detailed answers to help bridge the gap between the exoneree and the community. Additional audience members could include representatives from faith communities, local higher education, and local and/or state legislators or government officials.

Naturally, this approach would require careful planning by a trained restorative justice facilitator, preferably with an emphasis on victim-driven techniques, who would work with forum participants to arrive at a specific set of goals to be accomplished by the forum for each exoneree. The facilitator would be responsible to maintain decorum during the forum and ensure that all voices are heard while preventing additional injuries from being inflicted. We do not envision this community forum as automatically peaceful and congenial; substantial preparation work would be devoted to identifying key participants, securing their respectful involvement, and facilitating the dialogue.[2] It is possible, maybe even likely, that significant emotional distress and uncertainty remain percolating through the communities where the original crimes occurred and where the wrongful convictions were tried, especially if the actual offender remains unknown. Our hope is that providing public, positive support for exonerees from community and criminal justice representatives both through service provision and the community reintegration forum will help diminish any lingering hostilities and increase community acceptance and acknowledgment.

Our final recommendation for reform is for abolition of the death penalty. Maintaining capital punishment in the United States continues to risk the execution of innocents, given that some scholars and activists fear it already has happened (Radelet et al. 1994). Facing execution for a crime one did not commit is an unimaginable horror, profoundly traumatizing and irreversible. However, should capital punishment continue, every effort should be made to maintain mandatory state and federal appeals for all condemned prisoners as well as to provide meaningful appellate representation. Our participants' experiences outline vividly the crucial role that postconviction review and substantive defense services played in saving their lives. We recommend that post-conviction state and federal review be extended to all prisoners serving life without parole sentences despite the increased costs this would incur.

Our participants are death row exonerees, though hundreds more wrongly convicted prisoners have been released from long-term incarceration and life sentences, many because of the services provided by pro bono representation from specialized attorneys determined to help them. If nothing else, the reality of the growing numbers of exonerees should make clear that our system is flawed, not merely by a few "bad apples" (Westervelt and Cook 2010). The state makes mistakes. It should be incumbent upon the state to rectify those mistakes when they occur. We do not believe this postconviction review should fall to nonprofit organizations alone to provide; state and federal governments should offer options for the wrongly convicted to have their cases reviewed.

ACKNOWLEDGMENT, ACCEPTANCE, AND RESTORATION

In her analysis of the needs of trauma survivors, Judith Herman (1997, 7) says, "Traumatic events are of human design, those who bear witness are caught in the conflict between victim and perpetrator. It is morally impossible to remain neutral in this conflict. The bystander is forced to take sides." As such, we take sides with our participants by prioritizing their voices, their experiences, and their perspectives in shaping reforms and remedies. Our research does not include the voices of prosecutors, defense attorneys, or victim survivors whose ideas about remedy and reform may be quite different. In prioritizing the needs of exonerated death row survivors, we have identified four core dimensions of their needs for reintegration into life after death row, as adapted from Herman (1997).

- A place to call home
  - Material support (e.g., food, clothing, shelter)
  - Practical support (e.g., driving, banking, shopping, technology)
  - Emotional support (e.g., affection, understanding, compassion, patience)
- Safety and freedom
  - Safety from any real threat of death or other potential injuries from the state
  - Freedom to explore and define oneself in the world, to incorporate their experiences into a new definition of self

- Recognition and understanding
  - Recognition of the trauma inflicted on them, often through telling their stories, to make visible their circumstances and needs
  - Understanding by those who hear their stories
  - Acknowledgment of the injustice they have suffered, through provision of an apology, compensation, and support services (most particularly by the state)
  - Acceptance into society as factually innocent and reputable people
- Reconnection
  - With self, having integrated the lessons of experience
  - With primary-group others, e.g., family, close friends, attorneys, associates
  - With the wider world, as a person of consequence whose life experience matters to larger public issues of prosecution, persecution, and prevention

Meeting these needs throughout the postrelease adjustment period helps counteract, and perhaps heal, the damage done by the wrongful capital conviction. Effective healing from this ordeal is unlikely to succeed unless and until exonerees connect with others who are sensitive and compassionate to their experiences. Knowing that someone else in the world understands and cares about what they have endured provides comfort and acknowledgment. Still, "resolution of the trauma is never final; recovery is never complete" (Herman 1997, 211). Recovery is a grueling process that includes major advances and significant setbacks that are unpredictable and require support. Recovery is not linear, nor developmentally steady; it is more like a roller coaster, with highs and lows, and sometimes long plateaus. Recovery requires more than counseling and compensation; it requires a safety net of complex transitional social supports. It requires acceptance and acknowledgment of the trauma they have endured. To combat the dislocation from self and community exonerees have experienced, recovery requires reestablishing their place in the world and restoring their self to a place where their innocence is no longer in question.

Epilogue

HERE, WE PROVIDE brief summaries of the lives our participants have led since their exonerations and our interviews with them.[1] We thank Casey Strange for her contributions to early drafts of this section.

Gary Beeman

Throughout the 1980s and 1990s, Gary Beeman was in and out of jail on drug and alcohol-related charges.[2] As of 2007, Beeman had been sober and clean for five years and was actively involved in the anti–death penalty movement through organizations such as Witness to Innocence and Journey of Hope. He often speaks about his experiences at colleges and universities and public forums. After becoming clean and sober, he was able to repair his strained relationship with his parents and developed a stable relationship with a woman with whom he fell in love. Sadly, between 2006 and 2009, he suffered three traumatic losses of close family members, including his partner, his brother, and his father. These were difficult times, though he remained sober through the help of several organizations and support systems.

Kirk Bloodsworth

The murder of Dawn Hamilton was solved in 2003.[3] After ten years of urging by Bloodsworth, who wanted desperately to clear his name, the prosecutor submitted the DNA to the national DNA data bank. Kimberly Shay Ruffner was identified and had been incarcerated for a different offense at the same facility as Bloodsworth. They knew each other. Ruffner was a known sex offender who lived near the area where Hamilton had been brutalized. In May 2004, Ruffner was convicted of raping and murdering Dawn Hamilton and sentenced to life in prison.

Life after prison was initially difficult for Bloodsworth. He received $300,000 in compensation from the state of Maryland; however, legal fees, repayment of old debts, taxes, and generosity with friends and family quickly ate away at the money. He soon had nothing left, was homeless, was jobless, and survived by trapping animals to sell for food. During this time, Bloodsworth struggled with depression and stigma. In 1998, he attended a conference for exonerees hosted by the Center on Wrongful Convictions at Northwestern University School of Law, where he spoke publicly for the first time about his experience. This was a catalyst for him, and since then he has been a vocal, nationally known anti–death penalty advocate. In 2004, President George W. Bush signed the Innocence Protection Act that provided federal funding for the Kirk Bloodsworth Post-Conviction DNA Testing Grant Program, to increase access to DNA testing for those incarcerated. He served on Maryland's Commission on Capital Punishment in 2008 and advocates nationally and internationally for justice reform, innocence issues, and abolition of capital punishment. On a personal note, Bloodsworth and his wife were divorced during his incarceration. He married again after release, though he is recently divorced after eleven years. In the winter of 2011, he moved out of the state of Maryland for the first time since his release.

Joseph Green "Shabaka" Brown

Since his release over two decades ago, Shabaka Brown has led a quiet life with his wife, whom he married after release.[4] He has enjoyed being more involved in the lives of his children and grandchildren. Brown lectures publicly against capital punishment but keeps his family and private life shielded from the public. He has never received a public apology or compensation from the state of Florida. For a while, he worked at a drop-in shelter, feeding and counseling the homeless in Washington, D.C.; however, he and his wife have recently moved, and he is currently looking for employment, which is difficult since his record has not been expunged, and thus his wrongful capital conviction appears whenever a potential employer does a background check.

Sabrina Butler

Since her exoneration in 1995, Butler has continued to live in her hometown in Mississippi with her husband, Joe, whom she married soon after her release.[5] In addition to her eldest son, who was taken from her after Walter Dean's death, she and Joe now have two younger children. Life for Butler has been quite difficult. Many in her small town still believe she is guilty, which has affected her ability to find steady work. She has spent much of her time as a stay-at-home mom relatively isolated from her community. More recently, Butler has been writing a memoir about her experience with the criminal justice system to be published in 2012. She has not been very active in the wrongful conviction and anti–death penalty movements, although recently we have been able to connect her with Witness to Innocence and she has done a few events for them. Unlike with her male counterparts, her ability to travel widely is limited by her role as the primary caregiver to three children. She recently filed for compensation under new statutes passed in Mississippi in 2009. As of September 2011, she has been told that the state is willing to settle with her for an undisclosed amount, and the money will arrive in 2012, seventeen years after her exoneration.

Perry Cobb

In 1993, after Cobb and Tillis were exonerated, their trial judge was convicted on corruption charges, including taking bribes to acquit defendants.[6] Federal prosecutors alleged that the judge was biased against defendants who did not offer him bribes. Cobb was reincarcerated on attempted arson charges in the early 1990s, for which he spent three years in prison. Since his release in 1995, he has left Chicago and settled in another state, where he has enjoyed reconnecting with his children and grandchildren. His wrongful conviction took a toll on his first marriage, and they divorced. He did remarry, but more recently has divorced again. Over ten years after his exoneration, on June 15, 2000, Cobb received a "pardon based on innocence" from Illinois governor George Ryan. After his pardon, Cobb received approximately $140,000 in compensation for his wrongful conviction. He has struggled to reignite his singing career, which was his primary source of work before his wrongful conviction; however, he finds that he is uncomfortable performing as crowds and strangers make him wary. He has been an outspoken advocate for innocence issues and against the death penalty. Since May 2010, he has been recovering from triple bypass surgery and a series of small strokes, but he is feeling better and has a positive outlook for his future.

Charles Fain

Since exoneration, Charles Fain has continued to live in Idaho and harbors little animosity toward prosecutors or the justice system, though he has never received compensation for the nearly two decades he spent wrongly incarcerated.[7] Fain does wish for the victim's family's sake that authorities will find the true identity of the killer, and as recently as February 2011, the local news station has continued to report on the case, asking members of the public to come forward with new information. Fain worked for a box-making company after his release and felt welcomed by his manager and coworkers. Fain finds comfort in his Christian faith and calls the church he attends regularly his "second home." Most of his friends and social activities are directed through his congregational membership. Among exonerees, many have told Fain that he seems to be the most well adjusted to life after death row, something that he attributes to his deep faith.

Gary Gauger

In 1997, a Milwaukee federal grand jury indicted James Schneider and Randall Miller, members of the Outlaw motorcycle gang, for the murder of Gauger's parents.[8] By 2000, both had been convicted for these crimes. Immediately after release, Gauger lived with his sister and brother-in-law on the family farm where his parents were murdered, but now he and his wife, Sue, live on an adjacent farm, which they operate as a certified organic farm. In 2002, Gauger sued three sheriff's deputies and the county for false imprisonment and malicious prosecution, but the case was dismissed in favor of the defendants. However, that same year, he received a pardon from Illinois governor Ryan. Gauger continues to be adamantly opposed to the death penalty and all violence and frequently speaks at conferences and abolitionist events around the country. As a farmer, he enjoys the busy pace of his nine-month intensive growing season, but he admits to some depression during the winter months when he slows down. Gauger has completed a book about his journey through the criminal justice system, titled *In Spite of the System*.

Alan Gell

After release, Gell returned to live with his mother and stepfather in a small town in North Carolina and began attending a local community college.[9] In 2004, the prosecutors in Gell's case received an official reprimand from the North Carolina Bar Association for their roles in his wrongful conviction. One year later, Gell and his lawyer, David Rudolf, filed a lawsuit against state prosecutors and investigators, based on the claim that his civil rights had been violated because of the evidence and testimonies withheld by police and prosecutors in his case. The lawsuit settled in 2009 for $3.9 million, to be paid to Gell in monthly checks for the rest of his life. Also in 2005, Gell (age thirty-one) began an intimate relationship with a fifteen-year-old girl, who became pregnant with his child. When paternity of the unborn child became known, Gell was prosecuted on statutory rape charges. He eventually pled guilty to indecent liberties with a minor and was sentenced to five years in state prison. Gell was released in August 2011 after serving his full sentence. He now enjoys spending time with his son and family and hopes to move out of North Carolina as soon as his parole stipulations allow.

Tim Howard and Gary James

When Howard first got out of prison, he worked with his son in his barber shop.[10] At the time of our interview, he was working in a hospital and talked about how much he enjoyed his work. He seemed also to be enjoying getting to know his children again as well as his grandchildren, who were born while he was incarcerated. He was living with his girlfriend, Denise, at whose house we completed our interview. In 2004, Howard's criminal record was completely expunged by his attorney, Jim Owen, and in 2006 Owen helped him win a $2.5 million settlement for his twenty-six years of wrongful incarceration. The day after his award settlement, he and Denise were married. However, life for Howard seemed to spiral out of control after receipt of the financial settlement. He got involved with drugs and was arrested on gun and drug charges. He attempted drug rehabilitation but was not successful. Howard died on March 19, 2007, of a heart attack partially related to his drug habit.

While in prison, both of James's parents and his grandmother passed away. Thus, upon release, he moved in with his sister. He worked as a short-order cook and in a bar while delivering papers and cleaning carpets on the side. James and his attorney, Jim Owen, both admit that he has struggled with alcohol problems since his release as well as having persistent conflicts with women. At the time of our interview, he had several outstanding warrants for disorderly conduct related to a domestic incident and various traffic violations. Owen also pursued a lawsuit on James's behalf and was awarded $1.5 million in a settlement with the state in 2007. At the time of our last contact, James was still living in Ohio.

Dave Keaton

Since his exoneration and release almost four decades ago, Keaton's story has been told and retold in several popular and academic press forms.[11] The history of the Quincy Five was told in the book *David Charles: The Story of the Quincy Five*, and Keaton became one whose story was featured in the off-Broadway play *The Exonerated*. He continues to live in Quincy, Florida, as most of his close relatives and friends live next door and down the street. Keaton periodically participates in anti–death penalty rallies in Florida and occasionally speaks about his wrongful conviction. Over the years, he has had problems with drugs and alcohol and more recently has had health problems that have tempered his ability to travel to such engagements.

Ray Krone

Four years after Krone's exoneration, Kenneth Phillips pled guilty to Ancona's murder and was sentenced to fifty-three years to life in prison.[12] Since his exoneration and release, Krone has moved home to Pennsylvania near his parents. His life is largely built around his status as an exoneree. He frequently participates in conferences to speak about wrongful convictions and is an outspoken anti–death penalty activist. Krone was instrumental in forming the organization Witness to Innocence, which provides various forms of assistance to death row exonerees and works to abolish the death penalty. In 2005, he received free dental work courtesy of the ABC reality show *Extreme Makeover*, straightening the crooked teeth that were at the root of his wrongful capital conviction. That same year, Krone was awarded a total of $4.4 million in settlements with the city of Phoenix and Maricopa County, Arizona.

Walter McMillian

Since his release, McMillian has settled with the county and sheriff's department for an undisclosed amount for their part in withholding evidence and pressuring witnesses to give false testimony against him.[13]

At the time of our interview with him, McMillian still lived a serene life in Monroeville, running his own small business as a handyman and selling used auto parts. Since then, he lost part of his home to a fire and lived temporarily with his daughter in another town. He also has suffered some health problems. However, it is our understanding through conversation with others who know him that he is now back in Monroeville. He occasionally participates in anti–death penalty events, usually through his relationship with Bryan Stevenson's Equal Justice Initiative.

Juan Melendez

Since his exoneration, Juan Melendez has become an outspoken abolitionist advocate.[14] Though he dislikes politicians, he often has had the ear of governors and other lawmakers in his quest to abolish the death penalty. Melendez has traveled extensively in the United States and abroad telling his painful story of wrongful capital conviction and eighteen-year incarceration. Advocacy work is his primary vocation. Although he initially returned to Puerto Rico to live with his beloved mother, he now lives in the southwestern United States.

Alfred Rivera

Rivera's first act as a free man was to hug his three-year-old son who had been born while he was incarcerated.[15] Rivera initially worked as a landscaper in Lexington, North Carolina, after he was released while he tried to make up for lost time with his son. Within a year of his release, Rivera was finding it difficult to maintain himself and support his son as work opportunities became sparse. In late 2000, he was again arrested in Winston-Salem, North Carolina, where police detectives had told him they would be on the lookout for him. He was tried on drug-trafficking charges and sentenced to life in prison, a sentence he is currently serving in a federal prison in South Carolina.

Scott Taylor

During his incarceration, Taylor met his current wife, and they married while he was still on death row.[16] Since his exoneration, he has successfully sued the city where his wrongful conviction occurred and the detectives involved in his case and received a settlement. One of the former detectives in his case was found guilty of lying under oath as well as of the abuse and torture of suspects in criminal investigations, including Taylor's. After his mother's death in early 2008, Taylor and his family relocated to another state, where he prefers to remain anonymous. He no longer participates in public events related to his wrongful conviction. He and his wife have two young boys.

Delbert Tibbs

Tibbs has had a difficult time with employment since his exoneration, but now works with Witness to Innocence as their assistant director of communications and training.[17] He has long been a strident anti–death penalty activist in the United States and abroad and has written extensively about his life and experiences through poetry. Tibbs was one of the exonerees featured in Blank and Jensen's off-Broadway play The Exonerated, which also toured the country in the mid-2000s. In 2010, he participated in the World Congress for Abolition in Switzerland, and more recently he spoke at the Illinois statewide campaign to abolish the death penalty. He maintains a website that chronicles his activism work and showcases his poetry.

Greg Wilhoit

Since his exoneration in 1993, Wilhoit has struggled with PTSD and intermittently with drug and alcohol abuse caused by his experience.[18] He received no compensation despite the Oklahoma legislature having passed a bill that should have guaranteed him $200,000. After his release, Wilhoit worked with his attorney Mark Barrett to exonerate his best friend Ron Williamson from death row. Williamson's journey is chronicled in John Grisham's The Innocent Man. Wilhoit has been very involved in the anti–death penalty movement and finds speaking engagements to be therapeutic as he copes with his experiences. Because of lingering hostilities over how he was treated by the state of Oklahoma, he moved to California for many years. In 2009, he was hit by a truck while riding his bicycle and sustained severe injuries that required extensive rehabilitation. Early in 2010, his health problems were so serious that his family had concerns for his survival. They brought him back to Oklahoma to participate in his convalescence. By April 2010, his recovery was well under way, and in September he married his fiancée and now enjoys spending time with his new wife, parents and sisters, daughters and grandchildren.

NOTES

CHAPTER 1 LIVING THE AFTERMATH OF A WRONGFUL CONVICTION

1. Information about the Life After Exoneration Program can be found at www.exonerated.org.
2. One notable exception is the oral history provided by Vollen and Eggers (2005) in *Surviving Justice*, based on transcriptions of interviews with exonerees. We applaud their efforts to give voice to exonerees' accounts of their experiences. While the transcriptions do include some discussion of life after exoneration, they focus primarily on the wrongful conviction process. In addition, the book is focused on oral histories and provides little analysis of the interviews.

CHAPTER 2 RESEARCHING THE INNOCENT

1. See the Death Penalty Information Center at www.deathpenaltyinfo.org and the Innocence Project at www.innocenceproject.org.
2. For a discussion of the debate about what constitutes "innocence," "exoneration," or an "exoneree," a discussion beyond the scope of this analysis, see Burnett (2010), Forst (2004), Markman and Cassell (1988), Poveda (2001), Radelet and Bedau (1987), Risinger (2007), Westervelt and Humphrey (2001), and Zalman et al. (2008).
3. The literature on the effects of incarceration on ex-prisoners after release is quite limited. The literature on the effects of incarceration primarily focuses on the experiences, psychological reactions, and coping strategies of inmates during their time in prison. See, for example, Cohen and Taylor (1972), Haney (2006), R. Johnson and Toch (1982), Liebling and Maruna (2005), Porporino and Zamble (1984), Sykes (1958), Wormith (1984), and Zamble and Porporino (1988).

CHAPTER 3 INTRODUCING THE EXONEREES

1. To prepare for each interview, we developed in-depth summary narratives that provided as many details about each case as possible, including the crime itself, the primary "players" in the case, evidence used toward conviction, appellate and exoneration processes, retrial information (when applicable), and dates of arrest, adjudication, conviction, death sentencing, and exoneration. We gathered this information from newspaper and magazine articles, academic journal articles, book chapters, websites, and appellate case

decisions. Some of this information was then supplemented by the interviews themselves and from other personal communications with our participants. For each case overview provided in chapter 3, we note the primary sources used for each case. While not an exhaustive list of sources (which in some cases number in the dozens), each note includes those sources that contributed most significantly to the development of the summary narrative on that case.

2. *Ohio v. Beeman* (1978); Death Penalty Information Center (www.deathpenalty info.org); Northwestern Center on Wrongful Convictions (www.law.north-western.edu/cwc/); personal communication, Michael Radelet (2002); personal communication, Gary Beeman (May 11, 2006; September 29, 2006; December 27, 2009).

3. *Bloodsworth v. Maryland* (1986); Dao (2003); Junkin (2004); Northwestern Center on Wrongful Convictions (www.law.northwestern.edu/cwc/).

4. *Brown v. Florida* (1980); *Brown v. Florida* (1983); *Brown v. Florida* (1986); Anderson (1997); Freedberg (1999); Northwestern Center on Wrongful Convictions (www.law.northwestern.edu/cwc/).

5. *Butler v. Mississippi* (1992); Amnesty International (1998); Mitchell (1995a, 1995b); Pratt (1990a, 1990b).

6. *People v. Cobb* (1983); *United States v. Maloney* (1995); Mandell (2001); Northwestern Center on Wrongful Convictions (www.law.northwestern .edu/cwc/).

7. *Idaho v. Fain* (1988); Bonner (2001); Weinstein (2001a, 2001b); Northwestern Center on Wrongful Convictions (www.law.northwestern.edu/cwc/).

8. *Gauger v. Hendle et al.* (2002); Keeshan (2002); Northwestern Center on Wrongful Convictions (www.law.northwestern.edu/cwc/).

9. Neff (2002a, 2002b, 2002c, 2002d).

10. A. Johnson (2002a, 2002b, 2003a, 2003b, 2003c).

11. *Keaton v. Florida* (1973); Blank and Jensen (2005); Lickson (1974).

12. *Arizona v. Krone* (1995); Dodd (1995); Laughlin (1996, 2002); Nelson (2003).

13. *McMillian v. Alabama* (1993); Earley (1995); "Johnny D," *60 Minutes*, CBS News (November 1992); written summary provided by Angie Setzer, Equal Justice Initiative (www.eji.org).

14. *Melendez v. Florida* (1998); *Melendez v. Florida* (2001); Associated Press (2003); Word (2003); Canadian Coalition Against the Death Penalty (www.ccadp.org/juanmelendez.htm).

15. *North Carolina v. Rivera* (1999); Hinton (1999); Ziegenbaig (1999).

16. To respect Taylor's request for confidentiality, we do not cite any documents here that could link him to his actual identity.

17. *Tibbs v. Florida* (1976); McClory (1983); Radelet et al. 1994; Terkel (2001); Northwestern Center on Wrongful Convictions (www.law.northwestern .edu/cwc/).

18. *Wilhoit v. Oklahoma* (1991); Juozapavicius (2001); Saletan (2003); Vollertsen (2004).

PART TWO   STRUGGLING WITH LIFE AFTER EXONERATION

1. See, for example, the following: the four-part investigative series on the Alan Gell case written by Joseph Neff in the Raleigh *News & Observer* between December 8 and December 11, 2002; the eight-part series on the Darryl

Hunt case written by Phoebe Zerwick in the *Winston-Salem Journal* during November 2003 (see "Murder, Race, Justice: The State vs. Darryl Hunt" at http://darrylhunt.journalnow.com/frontStories.html); *Thin Blue Line* written by Errol Morris (1988); "Johnny D," *60 Minutes*, CBS News (November 1992); "The Man of Her Nightmares," *20/20*, ABC News (February 1998); "Falsely Accused," *The Twentieth Century with Mike Wallace*, A&E (July 1998); "The Case for Innocence," *Frontline*, PBS (2000).

2. "What Jennifer Saw," *Frontline*, PBS (1997); see also Rob Hiaasen's (2000) article on Kirk Bloodsworth in the *Baltimore Sun*.

Chapter 4   Facing Practical Problems

1. Disrupted sleep and/or reliving of traumatic events during sleep are symptoms of posttraumatic stress disorder (PTSD) (see American Psychiatric Association 2000). Exonerees describe a variety of problems symptomatic of PTSD, including but not limited to difficulty envisioning the future, apathy and problems connecting emotionally to others, and survivor guilt. Many of these also are noted by Adrian Grounds (2004) in his psychiatric assessment of eighteen wrongly convicted individuals and by Robert Simon (1993) in his case study of three people falsely arrested and jailed. These are symptoms common among survivors of life-threatening trauma in various forms (see, e.g., Brashers et al. 1999; Brison 2002; Grounds and Jamieson 2003; Herman 1997; Shevlin and McGuigan 2003; M. Smith et al. 2003). We point out the similarities between these experiences of our participants and noted symptoms of PTSD; however, we cannot state that exonerees suffer from PTSD. As sociologists, we are not trained as diagnosticians. It would be inappropriate and unethical for us to draw such conclusions.

Chapter 5   Managing Grief and Loss

1. An in-depth discussion of the wide-ranging literature on grief and mourning is beyond the scope of this analysis. For an overview of this literature, see Sharp (2005).
2. The Innocence Project reports that the average time of incarceration for their 273 DNA exonerees is 13 years (www.innocenceproject.org). According to the Death Penalty Information Center, the average time of incarceration for death row exonerees is 9.8 years (www.deathpenaltyinfo.org).

Chapter 7   Negotiating Emotional Terrain

1. *The Hurricane* (1999), produced by Azoff Entertainment and Beacon Communications, distributed by Universal Pictures; see also the books on which the film is based, *Lazarus and the Hurricane* (Chaiton and Swinton 1999) and *The 16th Round* (Carter 1991).

Chapter 9   Coping with Life after Death Row

1. Some helpful review materials about core concepts in the coping literature are Bonanno (2004), Boss (1999), Fullerton and Ursano (1997), Gist and Lubin

(1999), Herman (1997), Lazarus (1999), Lazarus and Folkman (1984), E. Miller (2003), C. Miller and Major (2003), and Neimeyer (2001).
2. Information about Witness to Innocence can be found at www.witnessto innocence.org.
3. Information about Death Penalty Focus can be found at www.deathpenalty .org.
4. The Justice Project appears to have been disbanded, as we can no longer find information about them online. Bloodsworth is no longer employed by them.
5. For information about the National Conference on Wrongful Conviction and the Death Penalty, the first Northwestern School of Law conference in 1998, see Bendavid (1998), K. Davis (1998), and Zuckoff (1998). For information about the National Gathering of Death Row Exonerees, the second Northwestern conference in 2002, see Guerrero (2002).
6. We are purposefully not naming the title of the book here because we believe it provides a biased and inaccurate account of Butler's case.

CHAPTER 10   RECLAIMING INNOCENCE

1. Compare Butler's experience with the church to that of Tim Howard, who says, "[I've had] a good community response and churches and everything. Denise's church [his girlfriend] took up a collection for me. Pastor and them recognize I come to church. . . . Pastor say something good [about me] . . . and make me stand up. . . . No, I haven't had a negative response."
2. We have chosen not to provide a citation for this speech in deference to Taylor's request to remain anonymous.
3. In four cases (Bloodsworth, Gauger, Keaton, and Krone), the actual offender or offenders were convicted of those crimes. In two cases (Gell and Rivera), the actual offenders were convicted on lesser charges related to the case but not recharged with the primary crimes after the exonerations. The actual offenders in Gary Beeman's and Perry Cobb's cases were never charged. The actual offender in Juan Melendez's case was dead by the time of his exoneration (see table 3.1 in chapter 3).
4. Weigand (2009) argues that sometimes media attention can do more harm than good.

PART FOUR   DOING JUSTICE

1. See Bernhard (2009) and Norris (2011).
2. See Bernhard (1999, 2004, 2009), Lonergan (2008), and Norris (2011).
3. See Innocence Project (2009) and Weigand (2009).
4. See Bernhard (2009) and Norris (2011).
5. See the Innocence Project website at www.innocenceproject.org and Norris (2011).
6. Through our personal networks and online searches, we were able to find ten organizations that appear to be, at least in part, dedicated to providing services for exonerees (the dates of establishment are noted in parentheses): the Darryl Hunt Project for Freedom and Justice in North Carolina (2005), the Exoneree Project at the University of Texas–Arlington (2008), FocuzUp in California (2006), the Life After Exoneration Program in California (2003), Life After Innocence in Illinois (2008/2009), the Life Intervention for

Exonerees Foundation in California (2009), Proving Innocence in Michigan (2008), Resurrection After Exoneration in Louisiana (2007), Wisconsin Exoneree Network in Wisconsin (2008), and Witness to Innocence in Pennsylvania (2005). The degree of involvement in service provision no doubt varies by organization. It also should be noted that in 2006 the Innocence Project added to their staff two social workers who provide social service assistance to their clients (see Innocence Project 2009).

7. Bernhard (2004, 711) notes that when she explains to the media that most exonerees receive no compensation, they often are shocked. We agree that most in the "lay" public commonly believe exonerees receive immediate and substantial compensation. We have had numerous conversations with friends, students, and the public in general who firmly believe in the myth of substantive compensation. In fact, after writing this chapter, Saundra went to a wedding the following weekend, where someone noted to her this very myth. She was sorry to have to disabuse them of their misperception.

CHAPTER 11 SEARCHING FOR REINTEGRATION AND RESTORATION

1. See the case of John Thompson in Louisiana as an example of how difficult it is to pursue a lawsuit based on the misconduct of system officials (Savage 2011).
2. Some examples of exonerees who won significant awards from lawsuits include $36 million awarded to Dennis Williams, Verneal Jimerson, Kenneth Adams, and Willie Raines (the Ford Heights Four) (Protess and Warden 1998; Taylor 1999); $5 million to Alberto Ramos (A. Elliott 2003); $20 million to Aaron Patterson, Leroy Orange, Stanley Howard, and Madison Hobley (Babwin 2007); $4.4 million to Ray Krone (DeFalco 2005).
3. Note that according to Norris (2011), no state has instituted provisions in full compliance with the model proposed by the Innocence Project, though Texas comes the closest.
4. See note 6 of part 4 for a list of these ten organizations.
5. Personal communication with Butler throughout 2009 and 2010. More recently (May 2011), Butler told us that the state has agreed to settle her claim for a yet-to-be disclosed amount. However, they have put payment of her award on hold until 2012. If she receives payment, she will have waited around seventeen years for compensation.
6. Gary Gauger so adamantly agrees with this statement that he titled the autobiographical account of his case *In Spite of the System* (Gauger and Von Bergen 2008).
7. Krone eventually did receive a more heartfelt public apology, but still not from the actual police and prosecutors in his case. In February 2006, nearly four years after his exoneration and release, Krone received a standing ovation from both houses of the Arizona legislature in a public attempt by policy makers to apologize to him for his wrongful conviction. Seven legislators individually apologized (Davenport 2006a).

CHAPTER 12 MOVING FORWARD

1. We are grateful to Terry Rumsey, interim executive director of Witness to Innocence, for making us aware of "circles of support."

2. We envision this forum as similar to victim–offender dialogues structured around a restorative justice framework. For more information, see www .restorativejustice.org.

Epilogue

1. The updates provided in the epilogue are based on published materials as well as personal communications maintained with participants since our interviews. When possible, we have noted the exact dates of those communications; however, in many cases, our conversations by phone and email have been relatively persistent over that period.
2. Fox (2007); Journey of Hope (www.journeyofhope.org/pages/); personal communication, Gary Beeman (September 29, 2006; December 13, 2006; December 27, 2009).
3. Justice for All Act (H.R. 5107, Pub. L. No. 108–405, October 30, 2004), *Congressional Record*, vol. 150; personal communication, Kirk Bloodsworth (periodically between 2004 and 2010).
4. Personal communication, Shabaka Brown (periodically between 2004 and 2011).
5. Personal communication, Sabrina Butler (periodically between 2005 and 2011).
6. Clemency petition, filed by MacArthur Justice Center (1999); Northwestern Center on Wrongful Convictions (www.law.northwestern.edu/cwc/); personal communication, Perry Cobb (January 10, 2011).
7. Grey (2011); personal communication, Charles Fain (periodically between 2004 and 2006).
8. *Gauger v. Hendle et al.* (2002); Gauger and Von Bergen (2008); Northwestern Center on Wrongful Convictions (www.law.northwestern.edu/cwc/); personal communication, Gary and Sue Gauger (periodically between 2003 and 2009).
9. Neff (2004, 2006, 2009); Neff and Beckwith (2007); personal communication, Alan Gell (periodically between 2006 and 2009).
10. A. Johnson (2004); Price (2007); personal communication, Jim Owen (August 14, 2006) and Denise Ruth (June 2007).
11. Blank and Jensen (2004, 2005); Lickson (1974).
12. Boccella (2005); Davenport (2006b); DeFalco (2005).
13. *McMillian v. Monroe County, Alabama* (1997); Equal Justice Initiative (www.eji.org); personal communication, Angie Setzer, Equal Justice Initiative (periodically between 2005 and 2010).
14. Personal communication, Juan Melendez (periodically between 2003 and 2009).
15. Associated Press (2001); personal communication, Alfred Rivera (periodically between 2006 and 2007).
16. Again, we have chosen not to provide any bibliographic references for this information to maintain anonymity; personal communication, Scott Taylor (April 14, 2011).
17. Blank and Jensen (2004); Witness to Innocence (www.witnesstoinnocence.org); Delbert Tibbs's website (www.delberttibbs.com/Speaking%20Engagements.html); personal communication, Delbert Tibbs (periodically between 2004 and 2011).
18. Grisham (2006); personal communication, Greg Wilhoit's sister Nancy Vollertsen (periodically between 2004 and 2010).

References

Books and Articles

American Psychiatric Association. 2000. *Diagnostic and Statistical Manual of Mental Disorders*. 4th ed., text revision. Washington, DC: American Psychiatric Association.

Amnesty International. 1998. "Fatal Flaws: Innocence and Death Penalty in the USA." November.

Anderson, G. 1997. "Fourteen Years on Death Row: An Interview with Joseph Green Brown." *America* 176:17–20.

Apel, R., and G. Sweeten. 2010. "The Impact of Incarceration on Employment during the Transition to Adulthood." *Social Problems* 57:448–479.

Appleton, C. 2010. *Life after Life Imprisonment*. Oxford: Oxford University Press.

Associated Press. 2001. "Freed Death-Row Inmate Accused of Cocaine Trafficking." *Herald-Sun*, January 1.

Associated Press. 2003. "Former Death Row Inmate Supports CCR, Holton." January 30.

Atkinson, R. 1998. *The Life Story Interview*. Thousand Oaks, CA: Sage.

Austin, J., and P. Hardyman. 2004. "The Risks and Needs of the Returning Prisoner Population." *Review of Policy Research* 21:13–29.

Avery, M. 2009. "Obstacles to Litigating Civil Claims for Wrongful Conviction: An Overview." *Public Interest Law Journal* 18:439–451.

Ayalon, L., C. Perry, P. Arean, and M. Horowitz. 2007. "Making Sense of the Past—Perspectives on Resilience among Holocaust Survivors." *Journal of Loss & Trauma* 12:281–293.

Babwin, D. 2007. "Chicago Pays $20M to Settle Lawsuits Alleging Police Tortured Death-Row Inmates." Associated Press, December 7.

Bahr, S., L. Harris, J. Fisher, and A. H. Armstrong. 2010. "Successful Reentry: What Differentiates Successful and Unsuccessful Parolees?" *International Journal of Offender Therapy and Comparative Criminology* 54:667–692.

Beck, E., S. Britto, and A. Andrews. 2007. *In the Shadow of Death*. Oxford: Oxford University Press.

Becker, H. 1963. *Outsiders*. London: Free Press.

Beech, N. 2011. "Liminality and the Practices of Identity Reconstruction." *Human Relations* 64:285–302.

Bendavid, N. 1998. "Former Death Row Inmates Honored at NU Conference." *Chicago Tribune*, November 15, sec. 1, 4.

Bernhard, A. 1999. "When Justice Fails: Indemnification for Unjust Conviction." *University of Chicago Law School Roundtable* 6:73–112.

———. 2001. "Effective Assistance of Counsel." In *Wrongly Convicted*, ed. S. Westervelt and J. Humphrey, 220–240. New Brunswick, NJ: Rutgers University Press.

———. 2004. "Justice Still Fails: A Review of Recent Efforts to Compensate Individuals Who Have Been Unjustly Convicted and Later Exonerated." *Drake Law Review* 52:703–738.

———. 2009. "A Short Overview of the Statutory Remedies for the Wrongly Convicted: What Works, What Doesn't, and Why." *Public Interest Law Journal* 18:403–425.

Blank, J., and E. Jensen. 2004. *The Exonerated: A Play*. New York: Dramatists Play Service.

———. 2005. *Living Justice*. New York: Atria Books.

Blieszner, R., K. Roberto, K. Wilcox, E. Barham, and B. Winston. 2007. "Dimensions of Ambiguous Loss in Couples Coping with Mild Cognitive Impairment." *Family Relations* 56:196–209.

Boccella, K. 2005. "Wrongly Convicted Pa. Man Gets a New Reason to Smile." *Philadelphia Inquirer*, February 10, B01.

Bocknek, E., J. Sanderson, and P. Britner. 2009. "Ambiguous Loss and Posttraumatic Stress in School-Age Children of Prisoners." *Journal of Child & Family Studies* 18:323–333.

Bonanno, G. 2004. "Loss, Trauma, and Human Resilience: Have We Underestimated the Human Capacity to Thrive after Extremely Aversive Events?" *American Psychologist* 59:20–28.

Bonner, R. 2001. "Death Row Inmate Is Freed after DNA Test Clears Him." *New York Times*, August 24, A11.

Borchard, E. 1932. *Convicting the Innocent*. New Haven, CT: Yale University Press.

Boss, P. 1999. *Ambiguous Loss*. Cambridge, MA: Harvard University Press.

Bowker, L. 1982. "Victimizers and Victims in American Correctional Institutions." In *Pains of Imprisonment*, ed. R. Johnson and H. Toch, 63–76. Beverly Hills, CA: Sage.

Boyle, J. 2011. "After Almost 18 Years in Prison, Exonerated Felon from Madison County Denied Compensation from State." *Asheville Citizen-Times*, April 9.

Braithwaite, J. 2002. *Restorative Justice and Responsive Regulation*. New York: Oxford University Press.

Braithwaite, V. 2004. "The Hope Process and Social Inclusion." *Annals of the American Academy of Political and Social Science* 592:128–151.

Brashers, D. E., J. L. Neidig, L. W. Cardillo, L. K. Dobbs, J. A. Russell, and S. M. Haas. 1999. "'In an Important Way, I Did Die': Uncertainty and Revival in Persons Living with HIV or AIDS." *AIDS Care* 11:201–219.

Brison, S. 2002. *Aftermath*. Princeton, NJ: Princeton University Press.

Budd, P., and D. Budd. 2010. *Tested*. Dallas, TX: Brown Books.

Burnett, C. 2010. *Wrongful Death Sentences*. Boulder, CO: Lynne Rienner.

Cabana, D. 1996. *Death at Midnight*. Boston: Northeastern University Press.

Campbell, K., and M. Denov. 2004. "The Burden of Innocence: Coping with a Wrongful Imprisonment." *Canadian Journal of Criminology and Criminal Justice* 46:139–163.

Carter, R. 1991. *The 16th Round.* New York: Penguin.

Chaiton, S., and T. Swinton. 1999. *Lazarus and the Hurricane.* New York: St. Martin's Griffin.

Charmaz, K. 2005. *Constructing Grounded Theory.* Thousand Oaks, CA: Sage.

Cherlin, A., and P. B. Walters. 1981. "Trends in United States Men's and Women's Sex-Role Attitudes, 1972 to 1978." *American Sociological Review* 46:453–460.

Chiricos, T., K. Barrick, W. Bales, and S. Bontrager. 2007. "The Labeling of Convicted Felons and Its Consequences for Recidivism." *Criminology* 45:547–581.

Clear, T., D. Rose, and J. Ryder. 2001. "Incarceration and the Community: The Problem of Removing and Returning Offenders." *Crime & Delinquency* 47:335–351.

Coen, J. 2004. "In Limbo, Exonerees Must Navigate Uncertain Path to Restart Lives." *Chicago Tribune,* April 1.

Cohen, S., and D. Hastings. 2002. "For 110 Inmates Freed by DNA Tests, True Freedom Remains Elusive." Associated Press, May 28.

Cohen, S., and L. Taylor. 1972. *Psychological Survival.* New York: Pantheon.

Collins, P. H. 1991. *Black Feminist Thought.* New York: Routledge.

Cook, K. J. 1998. *Divided Passions.* Boston: Northeastern University Press.

———. 2006. "Doing Difference and Accountability in Restorative Justice Conferences." *Theoretical Criminology* 10:107–124.

Cook, K. J., and C. Powell. 2006. "Emotionality, Rationality, and Restorative Justice." In *Advancing Critical Criminology,* ed. W. DeKeseredy and B. Perry, 83–100. New York: Lexington Books.

Cook, K. M. 2008. *Chasing Justice.* New York: Harper.

Dallaire, D. 2007. "Incarcerated Mothers and Fathers: A Comparison of Risks for Children and Families." *Family Relations* 56:440–453.

Dao, J. 2003. "In Same Case, DNA Clears Convict and Finds Suspect." *New York Times,* September 6, A7.

Dardis, F., F. Baumgartner, A. Boydstun, S. De Boef, and F. Shen. 2008. "Media Framing of Capital Punishment and Its Impact on Individual's Cognitive Responses." *Mass Communication & Society* 11:115–140.

Davenport, P. 2006a. "Arizona Lawmakers Apologize to Exonerated Man." Associated Press, February 21.

———. 2006b. "Man Gets Prison in Slaying Previously Pinned on Wrong Man." Associated Press, August 18.

Davis, C. 2001. "The Tormented and the Transformed: Understanding Responses to Loss and Trauma." In *Meaning Reconstruction and the Experience of Loss,* ed. R. Neimeyer, 137–155. Washington, DC: American Psychological Association.

Davis, K. 1998. "Hope Sought for Innocents Sentenced to Die." *USA Today,* November 13, 14A.

———. 2011. "After Years, Even Decades, the Exonerated Leave Prison Walls Behind—Only to Find New Barriers." *ABA Journal* 97:50–55.

DeFalco, B. 2005. "Phoenix to Pay $3 Million for Framing Ray Krone for Murder and Jailing Him 10 Years." September 27. Retrieved from http://arizona .indymedia.org/news/2005/09/31030.php.

Dodd, S. 1995. "Guilty Until Proven Innocent." *York Daily Record,* May 24.

Donnelly, D., K. J. Cook, D. Van Ausdale, and L. Foley. 2005. "White Privilege, Color Blindness and Services to Battered Women." *Violence Against Women* 11:6–37.

Earley, P. 1995. *Circumstantial Evidence*. New York: Bantam Books.

Ehrenreich, B. 1983. "After the Breadwinner Vanishes." *Nation* 236:225–242.

Elliott, A. 2003. "City Gives $5 Million to Man Wrongly Imprisoned in Child's Rape." *New York Times*, December 16.

Elliott, G., H. Ziegler, B. Altman, and D. Scott. 1982. "Understanding Stigma: Dimensions of Deviance and Coping." *Deviant Behavior* 3:275–300.

Ely, M., with M. Anzul, T. Friedman, D. Garner, and A. M. Steinmetz. 1991. *Doing Qualitative Research*. New York: Falmer.

Endler, N., and J. Parker. 1999. *CISS: Coping Inventory for Stressful Situations Manual*. 2nd ed. North Tonawanda, NY: Multi-Health Systems.

Erikson, K. 1976. *Everything in Its Path*. New York: Simon & Schuster.

Fearday, F., and A. Cape. 2004. "A Voice for Traumatized Women: Inclusion and Mutual Support." *Psychiatric Rehabilitation Journal* 27:258–265.

Ferraro, K., J. Johnson, S. Jorgensen, and F. G. Bolton. 1983. "Problems with Prisoners' Families: The Hidden Costs of Imprisonment." *Journal of Family Issues* 4:575–591.

Fishman, S. H. 1981. "Losing a Loved One to Incarceration: The Effect of Imprisonment on Family Members." *Personnel & Guidance Journal* 59:372–375.

Forst, B. 2004. *Errors of Justice*. Cambridge, UK: Cambridge University Press.

Fox, R. J. 2007. "Anti-Death Penalty Crusader Tells Story." *Dayton Daily News*, March 29.

Frankl, V. 1984. *Man's Search for Meaning*. New York: Pocket Books.

Freedberg, S. 1999. "'Yes, I'm Angry. . . . Yes, I'm Bitter. I'm Frustrated.'" *St. Petersburg Times*, July 4.

Freud, S. [1917] 1984. "Mourning and Melancholia." In *The Pelican Freud Library: On Metapsychology: The Theory of Psychoanalysis*, vol. 11, 245–268. London: Penguin.

Fullerton, C., and R. Ursano, eds. 1997. *Posttraumatic Stress Disorder: Acute and Long-Term Response to Trauma and Disaster*. Washington, DC: American Psychiatric Press.

Gaes, G., and N. Kendig. 2003. "The Skills Sets and Health Care Needs of Released Offenders." In *Prisoners Once Removed*, ed. J. Travis and M. Waul, 105–153. Washington, DC: Urban Institute Press.

Garrett, B. 2008. "Judging Innocence." *Columbia Law Review* 108:55–141.

Gauger, G., and J. Von Bergen. 2008. *In Spite of the System*. Lake Geneva, WI: Fourcatfarm Press.

Gibbs, J. 1982. "The First Cut Is the Deepest: Psychological Breakdown and Survival in Detention Setting." In *Pains of Imprisonment*, ed. R. Johnson and H. Toch, 97–114. Beverly Hills, CA: Sage.

Gil, A., M. Johnson, and I. Johnson. 2006. "Secondary Trauma Associated with State Executions: Testimony Regarding Execution Procedures." *Journal of Psychiatry & Law* 34:25–35.

Gilligan, C. 1982. *In a Different Voice*. Cambridge, MA: Harvard University Press.

Gist, R., and B. Lubin, eds. 1999. *Response to Disaster*. Philadelphia: Brunner and Mazel.

Glaser, B. G., and A. Strauss. 1967. *The Discovery of Grounded Theory*. New York: Aldine de Gruyter.

Goffman, E. 1963. *Stigma*. New York: Simon & Schuster.

Goldman, M., and J. Whalen. 1990. "From the New Left to the New Enlightenment: The Methodological Implications of Public Attention to Private Lives." *Qualitative Sociology* 13:85–107.

Goodley, D. 1996. "Tales of Hidden Lives: A Critical Examination of Life History Research with People Who Have Learning Difficulties." *Disability and Society* 11:333–348.

Grey, J. 2011. "Detectives Still Searching for 1982 Murderer." KTVB TV, February 24. Retrieved from http://www.ktvb.com/news/Searching-for-a-killer-29-years-later-116892838.html.

Grisham, J. 2006. *The Innocent Man*. New York: Bantam Dell.

Gross, S., and B. O'Brien. 2008. "Frequency and Predictors of False Conviction: Why We Know So Little, and New Data on Capital Cases." *Journal of Empirical Legal Studies* 5:927–962.

Gross, S., K. Jacoby, D. Matheson, N. Montgomery, and S. Patel. 2005. "Exonerations in the United States, 1989 through 2003." *Journal of Criminal Law and Criminology* 95:523–553.

Grounds, A. 2004. "Psychological Consequences of Wrongful Conviction and Imprisonment." *Canadian Journal of Criminology and Criminal Justice* 46:165–182.

Grounds, A., and R. Jamieson. 2003. "No Sense of an Ending: Researching the Experience of Imprisonment and Release among Republican Ex-prisoners." *Theoretical Criminology* 7:347–362.

Guerrero, L. 2002. "40 Off Death Row Push End to Executions." *Chicago Sun-Times*, December 16, 7.

Haney, C. 2003a. "Mental Health Issues in Long-Term Solitary and 'Supermax' Confinement." *Crime & Delinquency* 49:124–156.

———. 2003b. "The Psychological Impact of Incarceration: Implications for Postprison Adjustment." In *Prisoners Once Removed*, ed. J. Travis and M. Waul, 33–66. Washington, DC: Urban Institute Press.

———. 2005. *Death by Design*. Oxford: Oxford University Press.

———. 2006. *Reforming Punishment*. Washington, DC: American Psychological Association.

Harding, D. 2003. "Jean Valjean's Dilemma: The Management of Ex-Convict Identity in the Search for Employment." *Deviant Behavior* 24:571–595.

Harding, S. 1986. *The Science Question in Feminism*. Ithaca, NY: Cornell University Press.

Henry, V. 2004. *Death Work*. New York: Oxford University Press.

Herman, J. L. 1997. *Trauma and Recovery*. New York: Basic Books.

Hiaasen, R. 2000. "Life after Death Row." *Baltimore Sun*, July 30, F1, F8–F9.

Hinton, J. 1999. "Rivera Is Acquitted in Two Killings Once under a Sentence of Death, He Walks Free for First Time in 2 Years." *Winston-Salem Journal*, November 23.

Hirschfield, P., and A. Piquero. 2010. "Normalization and Legitimation: Modeling Stigmatizing Attitudes towards Ex-Offenders." *Criminology* 48:27–55.

Hones, D. 1998. "Known in Part: The Transformational Power of Narrative Inquiry." *Qualitative Inquiry* 4:225–248.

Huff, C. R., A. Rattner, and E. Sagarin. 1996. *Convicted But Innocent*. Thousand Oaks, CA: Sage.

Hughes, E. 1945. "Dilemmas and Contradictions of Status." *American Journal of Sociology* 50:353–359.

Ibañez, G., C. Buck, N. Khatchikian, and F. Norris. 2004. "Qualitative Analysis of Coping Strategies among Mexican Disaster Survivors." *Anxiety, Stress, and Coping* 17:69–85.

Illinois Criminal Justice Information Authority. 2002. "The Needs of the Wrongfully Convicted: A Report on a Panel Discussion." Report to the Governor's Commission on Capital Punishment, March 15.

Innocence Project. 2009. "Making Up for Lost Time: What the Wrongfully Convicted Endure and How to Provide Fair Compensation." Retrieved from http://www.innocenceproject.org/docs/Innocence_Project_Compensation_Report.pdf.

Irwin, J., and B. Owen. 2005. "Harm and the Contemporary Prison." In *The Effects of Imprisonment*, ed. A. Liebling and S. Maruna, 94–117. Portland, OR: Willan.

Jacobs, D., Z. Qian, J. T. Charmichael, and S. Kent. 2007. "Who Survives Death Row? An Individual and Contextual Analysis." *American Sociological Review* 72:610–632.

Jamieson, R., and A. Grounds. 2005. "Release and Adjustment: Perspectives from Studies of Wrongly Convicted and Politically Motivated Prisoners." In *The Effects of Imprisonment*, ed. A. Liebling and S. Maruna, 33–65. Portland, OR: Willan.

Johnson, A. 2002a. "Convicts May Be Wrong Guys." *Columbus Dispatch*, December 10, 1A.

———. 2002b. "Were They Wrongly Convicted?" *Columbus Dispatch*, February 10, 1A.

———. 2003a. "Polygraph Test Frees Prisoner." *Columbus Dispatch*, July 16, 1A.

———. 2003b. "Prisoner Hopeful He'll Be Freed Too." *Columbus Dispatch*, May 1, 1B.

———. 2003c. "26 Years in Hell." *Columbus Dispatch*, April 18, 1A.

———. 2004. "2 Wrongfully Convicted Men Ask State to Pay for Mistake." *Columbus Dispatch*, March 11, 1A.

Johnson, R. 1981. *Condemned to Die*. New York: Elsevier.

———. 1982. "Life Under Sentence of Death." In *Pains of Imprisonment*, ed. R. Johnson and H. Toch, 129–145. Beverly Hills, CA: Sage.

———. 1998. *Death Work*. Belmont, CA: Wadsworth.

Johnson, R., and H. Toch, eds. 1982. *The Pains of Imprisonment*. Beverly Hills, CA: Sage.

Junkin, T. 2004. *Bloodsworth*. Chapel Hill, NC: Algonquin.

Juozapavicius, J. 2001. "The Scars of Justice." *Abolish*, April 23. Retrieved from http://venus.soci.niu.edu/~archives/ABOLISH/apr01/0311.html.

Kahn, D. 2010. "Presumed Guilty Until Proven Innocent: The Burden of Proof in Wrongful Conviction Claims Under State Compensation Statutes." *University of Michigan Journal of Law Reform* 44:123–168.

Kaniasty, K., and F. Norris. 1999. "The Experience of Disaster: Individuals and Communities Sharing Trauma." In *Response to Disaster*, ed. R. Gist and B. Lubin, 25–61. Philadelphia: Brunner and Mazel.

Kean, S. 2010. "The Experience of Ambiguous Loss in Families of Brain Injured ICU Patients." *Nursing in Critical Care* 15:66–75.

Keeshan, C. 2002. "Gauger Lawsuit Against County Tossed, but Judge Criticizes Handling of Murder Case." *Chicago Daily Herald*, September 27, F1, F2, F3, M1.

King, R. 2005. *Capital Consequences*. New Brunswick, NJ: Rutgers University Press.

Kupers, T. 2008. "What to Do with the Survivors? Coping with the Long-Term Effects of Isolated Confinement." *Criminal Justice and Behavior* 35:1005–1016.

Laughlin, L. 1996. "Judge Lets Krone Live." *York Daily Record*, December 10.

———. 2002. "Apology Accepted." *York Daily Record*, April 30.

Lawrence, F. 2009. "Declaring Innocence: Use of Declaratory Judgments to Vindicate the Wrongly Convicted." *Public Interest Law Journal* 18:391–401.

Lazarus, R. 1999. *Stress and Emotion*. New York: Springer.

Lazarus, R., and S. Folkman. 1984. *Stress, Appraisal, and Coping*. New York: Springer.

Leary, M., and L. Schreindorfer. 1998. "The Stigmatization of HIV and AIDS: Rubbing Salt in the Wound." In *HIV and Social Interaction*, ed. V. Derlega and A. Barbee, 12–29. Thousand Oaks, CA: Sage.

Lee, H. 1999. *To Kill a Mockingbird*. New York: HarperCollins.

Lee Hyer, J., M. Woods, E. McCraine, and P. Boudewyns. 1990. "Suicidal Behavior among Chronic Vietnam Theatre Veterans with PTSD." *Journal of Clinical Psychology* 46:713–721.

Leo, R. 2001. "False Confessions: Causes, Consequences, and Solutions." In *Wrongly Convicted*, ed. S. Westervelt and J. Humphrey, 36–54. New Brunswick, NJ: Rutgers University Press.

———. 2005. "Rethinking the Study of Miscarriages of Justice: Developing a Criminology of Wrongful Convictions." *Journal of Contemporary Criminal Justice* 21:201–223.

Leo, R., and J. Gould. 2009. "Studying Wrongful Convictions: Learning from Social Science." *Ohio State Journal of Criminal Law* 7:7–30.

Lewis, D. 2008. "Using Life Histories in Social Policy Research: The Case of Third Sector/Public Sector Boundary Crossing." *Journal of Social Policy* 37:559–578.

Lickson, J. 1974. *David Charles: The Story of the Quincy Five*. Tallahassee, FL: Mockingbird Press.

Liebling, A., and S. Maruna, eds. 2005. *The Effects of Imprisonment*. Portland, OR: Willan.

Lifton, R. J. 1967. *Death in Life*. New York: Random House.

———. 1970. "The Hiroshima Bomb." In *History and Human Survival*, 114–155. New York: Random House.

———. 1985. *Home from the War*. New York: Basic Books.

———. 2001. "History of Trauma." In *Beyond Invisible Walls*, ed. J. Lindy and R. J. Lifton, 213–223. New York: Brunner-Routledge.

Link, B., and J. C. Phelan. 2001. "Conceptualizing Stigma." *Annual Review of Sociology* 27:363–385.

Lisak, D., and S. Beszterczey. 2007. "The Cycle of Violence: The Histories of 43 Death Row Inmates." *Psychology of Men & Masculinity* 8:118–128.

Locke, M. 2011. "Freedom Is Sweet, but New Problems Set In." *News & Observer*, September 4.

Lonergan, J. 2008. "Protecting the Innocent: A Model for Comprehensive, Individualized Compensation of the Exonerated." *Legislation and Public Policy* 11:405–452.

Luster, T., D. Qin, L. Bates, D. Johnson, and M. Rana. 2009. "The Lost Boys of Sudan: Coping with Ambiguous Loss and Separation from Parents." *American Journal of Orthopsychiatry* 79:203–211.

Mandell, A. 2001. "Innocent on Death Row: An Interview with Perry Cobb." *Cornerstone* 30:10–19.

Markman, S., and P. Cassell. 1988. "Protecting the Innocent: A Response to the Bedau-Radelet Study." *Stanford Law Review* 41:121–160.

McClory, R. 1983. "Justice for Mr. Tibbs." *Reader* 12:1, 14–15, 18–20, 22, 24–25.

Messerschmidt, J. 2000. *Nine Lives*. Boulder, CO: Westview Press.

———. 2004. *Flesh and Blood*. Lanham, MD: Rowman & Littlefield.

Metraux, S., and D. Culhane. 2004. "Homeless Shelter Use and Reincarceration Following Prison Release." *Criminology and Public Policy* 3:139–160.

Miller, C., and B. Major. 2003. "Coping with Stigma and Prejudice." In *The Social Psychology of Stigma*, ed. T. Heatherton, R. Kleck, M. Hebl, and J. Hull, 243–272. New York: Guilford.

Miller, E. 2003. "Reconceptualizing the Role of Resiliency in Coping and Therapy." *Journal of Loss and Trauma* 8:239–246.

Mills, C. W. 1959. *The Sociological Imagination*. New York: Oxford University Press.

Mitchell, A. 1995a. "Butler Found Not Guilty." *Commercial Dispatch*, December 17, 1A, 12A.

———. 1995b. "Jury Selection Underway for Butler Retrial." *Commercial Dispatch*, December 11, 1A.

Mumma, C. 2004. "The North Carolina Actual Innocence Commission: Uncommon Perspectives Joined by a Common Cause." *Drake Law Review* 52:647–656.

Murray, J. 2005. "The Effects of Imprisonment on Families and Children of Prisoners." In *The Effects of Imprisonment*, ed. A. Liebling and S. Maruna, 442–462. Portland, OR: Willan.

Neff, J. 2002a. "Chapter 1: Who Killed Allen Ray Jenkins?" *News & Observer*, December 8, A1.

———. 2002b. "Chapter 2: A Witness, a Tangled Web." *News & Observer*, December 9, A1.

———. 2002c. "Chapter 3: Gell Defense Left in Dark." *News & Observer*, December 10, A1.

———. 2002d. "Chapter 4: Evidence Points to Innocence." *News & Observer*, December 11, A1.

———. 2004. "NC Bar Hearing Provokes More Anger." *News & Observer*, October 21, B1.

———. 2006. "Alan Gell Charged with Statutory Rape." *News & Observer*, April 13, A1.

———. 2009. "State Pays $3.9 Million for Wrongful Conviction." *News & Observer*, October 2, A1.

Neff, J., and R. T. Beckwith. 2007. "Ex-Girlfriend, Son Barred from Visiting Gell." *News & Observer*, December 27, B5.

Neimeyer, R., ed. 2001. *Meaning Reconstruction and the Experience of Loss*. Washington, DC: American Psychological Association.

Nelson, R. 2003. "Death Road, Ray Krone Is America's New Anti-Death-Penalty Poster Boy." *Phoenix New Times*, May 22.

Norris, R. 2011. "Assessing Compensation Statutes for the Wrongly Convicted." *Criminal Justice Policy Review*. Online First. doi:10.1177/0887403411409916.

Northwestern Center on Wrongful Convictions. 2004. *The Snitch System*. Chicago: Northwestern University.

Oakley, A. 1981. "Interviewing Women: A Contradiction in Terms." In *Doing Feminist Research*, ed. H. Roberts, 30–61. London: Routledge & Kegan Paul.

O'Brien, M. 2007. "Ambiguous Loss in Families of Children with Autism Spectrum Disorders." *Family Relations* 56:135–146.

Oyserman, D., and J. Swim. 2001. "Stigma: An Insider's View." *Journal of Social Issues* 57:1–14.

Parker, K., M. DeWees, and M. Radelet. 2001. "Racial Bias and the Conviction of the Innocent." In *Wrongly Convicted*, ed. S. Westervelt and J. Humphrey, 114–131. New Brunswick, NJ: Rutgers University Press.

Parker, R., and P. Aggleton. 2003. "HIV and AIDS-Related Stigma and Discrimination: A Conceptual Framework and Implications for Action." *Social Science & Medicine* 57:13–24.

Patton, M. Q. 2002. *Qualitative Research and Evaluation Methods*. 3rd ed. Thousand Oaks, CA: Sage.

Persky, A. S. 2011. "North Carolina's Death Row Inmates Let Statistics Back Up Bias Claims." *ABA Journal* 97 (May). Retrieved from http://www.abajournal.com/magazine/article/north_carolinas_death_row_inmates_let_statistics_back_up_bias_claims/.

Petersilia, J. 2003. *When Prisoners Come Home*. New York: Oxford University Press.

Petrie, M., and J. Coverdill. 2010. "Who Lives and Dies on Death Row? Race, Ethnicity an Post-Sentence Outcomes in Texas." *Social Problems* 57:630–652.

Phillips, L., and M. Lindsay. 2010. "Prison to Society: A Mixed Methods Analysis of Coping with Reentry." *International Journal of Offender Therapy and Comparative Criminology* 20:1–19.

Pierce, G., and M. Radelet. 2002. "The Law and Politics of the Death Penalty: Abolition, Moratorium, or Reform?" *Oregon Law Review* 81:39–96.

Pittaway, E., L. Bartolomei, and R. Hugman. 2010. "Stop Stealing Our Stories: The Ethics of Research with Vulnerable Groups." *Journal of Human Rights Practice* 2:229–251.

Porporino, F., and E. Zamble. 1984. "Coping with Imprisonment." *Canadian Journal of Criminology* 26:403–422.

Poveda, T. 2001. "Estimating Wrongful Convictions." *Justice Quarterly* 18:689–708.

Pratt, M. 1990a. "Jury Sentences Butler to Death by Injection." *Commercial Dispatch*, March 14, 1A, 10A.

———. 1990b. "Sentencing Today for Defendant." *Commercial Dispatch*, March 13, 1A, 8A.

Presser, L. 2005. "Negotiating Power and Narrative in Research: Implications for Feminist Methodology." *Signs: Journal of Women in Culture and Society* 30:2067–2090.

Price, G. 2007. "At Long Last, a Win for Gary James." *Columbus Call and Post*, May 23–29, 1A.

Protess, D., and R. Warden. 1998. *A Promise of Justice*. New York: Hyperion.

Radelet, M. 1981. "Racial Characteristics and the Imposition of the Death Penalty." *American Sociological Review* 46:918–927.

———. 1989. "Introduction and Overview." In *Facing the Death Penalty*, ed. M. Radelet, 3–15. Philadelphia: Temple University Press.

Radelet, M., and H. A. Bedau. 1987. "Miscarriages of Justice in Potentially Capital Cases." *Stanford Law Review* 40:21–179.

Radelet, M., and G. Pierce. 1985. "Race and Prosecutorial Discretion in Homicide Cases." *Law and Society Review* 19:587–621.

———. 1991. "Choosing Those Who Will Die: Race and the Death Penalty in Florida." *Florida Law Review* 43:1–34.

Radelet, M., H. A. Bedau, and C. Putnam. 1994. *In Spite of Innocence*. Boston: Northeastern University Press.

Radelet, M., M. Vandiver, and F. Berardo. 1983. "Families, Prisons, and Men with Death Sentences: The Human Impact of Structured Uncertainty." *Journal of Family Issues* 4:593–612.

Reinharz, S. 1979. *On Becoming a Social Scientist*. San Francisco: Jossey-Bass.

———. 1992. *Feminist Methods in Social Research*. New York: Oxford University Press.

———. 2011. *Observing the Observer*. New York: Oxford University Press.

Richards, A. 2001. "Spiritual Resources Following a Partner's Death from AIDS." In *Meaning Reconstruction and the Experience of Loss*, ed. R. Neimeyer, 173–190. Washington, DC: American Psychological Association.

Richardson, G. 2002. "The Metatheory of Resilience and Resiliency." *Journal of Clinical Psychology* 58:307–321.

Risinger, D. M. 2007. "Innocents Convicted: An Empirically Justified Factual Wrongful Conviction Rate." *Journal of Criminal Law and Criminology* 97:761–806.

Roberts, J., and E. Stanton. 2007. "A Long Road Back after Exoneration, and Justice Is Slow to Make Amends." *New York Times*, November 25, 38; see also the multimedia interactive presentation at http://www.nytimes.com/interactive/2007/11/25/nyregion/20071125_DNAI_FEATURE.html.

Robins, S. 2010. "Ambiguous Loss in a Non-Western Context: Families of the Disappeared in Postconflict Nepal." *Family Relations* 59:253–268.

Saletan, I. 2003. "My Nightmare of a Journey through the Criminal Justice System—An Interview with Greg Wilhoit." *FCL Newsletter*, June. Retrieved from http://www.ocadp.org/news/stories/wilhoit_fcl.html.

Savage, D. 2011. "Supreme Court Rejects Damages for Innocent Man Who Spent 14 Years on Death Row." *Los Angeles Times*, March 30.

Scheck, B., and P. Neufeld. 2001. "DNA and Innocence Scholarship." In *Wrongly Convicted*, ed. S. Westervelt and J. Humphrey, 241–252. New Brunswick, NJ: Rutgers University Press.

Scheck, B., P. Neufeld, and J. Dwyer. 2000. *Actual Innocence: Five Days to Execution, and Other Dispatches from the Wrongly Convicted*. New York: Doubleday.

Schneider, G. 1975. "Survival and Guilt Feelings of Jewish Concentration Camp Victims." *Jewish Social Studies* 37:74–83.

Schnittker, J. 2007. "Working More and Feeling Better: Women's Health, Employment, and Family Life, 1974–2004." *American Sociological Review* 72:221–238.

Schnittker, J., and A. John. 2007. "Enduring Stigma: The Long-Term Effects of Incarceration on Health." *Journal of Health and Social Behavior* 48:115–130.

Schoenfeld, E. 2005. *My Life Reconstructed*. Kennesaw, GA: Kennesaw State University Press.

Scully, D. 1988. "Convicted Rapists' Perceptions of Self and Victim: Role Taking and Emotions." *Gender & Society* 1:61–84.

Seccombe, K. 2002. "'Beating the Odds' versus 'Changing the Odds': Poverty, Resilience, and Family Policy." *Journal of Marriage and the Family* 64:384–394.

Sharp, S. 2005. *Hidden Victims*. New Brunswick, NJ: Rutgers University Press.

Shevlin, M., and K. McGuigan. 2003. "The Long-Term Psychological Impact of Bloody Sunday on Families of the Victims as Measured by the Revised Impact of Event Scale." *British Journal of Clinical Psychology* 42:427–432.

Shih, M. 2004. "Positive Stigma: Examining Resilience and Empowerment in Overcoming Stigma." *Annals of the American Academy of Political and Social Sciences* 591:175–185.

Shillingford, M., and O. Edwards. 2008. "Application of Choice Theory with a Student Whose Parent Is Incarcerated: A Qualitative Case Study." *International Journal of Reality Therapy* 28:41–44.

Shivy, V., J. J. Wu, A. Moon, S. Mann, J. Holland, and C. Eacho. 2007. "Ex-Offenders Reentering the Workforce." *Journal of Counseling Psychology* 54:466–473.

Siegel, K., H. Lune, and I. Meyer. 1998. "Stigma Management among Gay/Bisexual Men with HIV/AIDS." *Qualitative Sociology* 21:3–24.

Simon, R. 1993. "The Psychological and Legal Aftermath of False Arrest and Imprisonment." *Bulletin of the American Academy of Psychiatry and the Law* 21:523–528.

Slevin, P., and K. Lydersen. 2008. "Exonerated Ex-Inmates Struggle to Shed Stigma." *Washington Post*, April 28, A1.

Smith, E., and A. Hattery. 2011. "Race, Wrongful Conviction & Exoneration." *Journal of African American Studies* 15:74–94.

Smith, M., D. Lees, and K. Clymo. 2003. "The Readiness Is All: Planning and Training for Post-Disaster Support Work." *Social Work Education* 22: 517–528.

Sosulski, M., N. Buchanan, and C. Donnell. 2010. "Life History and Narrative Analysis: Feminist Methodologies Contextualizing Black Women's Experiences with Severe Mental Illness." *Journal of Sociology & Social Welfare* 37:29–57.

Spagnolo, A., J. Dolce, M. Roberts, A. Murphy, K. Gill, L. Librera, and W. Lu. 2011. "A Study of Perceived Barriers to the Implementation of Circles of Support." *Psychiatric Rehabilitation Journal* 34:233–242.

Stoll, M., and S. Bushway. 2008. "The Effect of Criminal Background Checks on Hiring Ex-Offenders." *Criminology and Public Policy* 7:371–404.

Sykes, G. 1958. *The Society of Captives*. Princeton, NJ: Princeton University Press.

Tak, Y. R., and M. McCubbin. 2002. "Family Stress, Perceived Social Support and Coping Following the Diagnosis of a Child's Congenital Heart Disease." *Journal of Advanced Nursing* 39:190–198.

Taylor, G. F. 1999. "The Case of the Ford Heights Four." *Police Misconduct and Civil Rights Law Report* 6:37–46.

Terkel, S. 2001. *Will the Circle Be Unbroken?* New York: New York University Press.

Tewksbury, R., and D. McGaughey. 1997. "Stigmatization of Persons with HIV Disease: Perceptions, Management, and Consequences of AIDS." *Sociological Spectrum* 17:49–70.

Thornton, A., and L. Young-DeMarco. 2001. "Four Decades of Trends in Attitudes toward Family Issues in the United States: The 1960s through the 1990s." *Journal of Marriage and the Family* 63:1009–1037.

Tierney, W. 1998. "Life History's History: Subjects Foretold." *Qualitative Inquiry* 4:49–70.

Travis, J., and M. Waul, eds. 2003. *Prisoners Once Removed*. Washington, DC: Urban Institute Press.

Turner, V. 1967. *The Forest of Symbols*. Ithaca, NY: Cornell University Press.

———. 1969. *The Ritual Process*. Chicago: Aldine.

Turtle, J., R.C.L. Lindsay, and G. Wells. 2003. "Best Practice Recommendations for Eyewitness Evidence Procedures: New Ideas for the Oldest Way to Solve a Case." *Canadian Journal of Police and Security Services* 1:5–18.

Uggen, C., J. Manza, and M. Thompson. 2006. "Citizenship, Democracy, and the Civic Reintegration of Criminal Offenders." *Annals of the American Academy of Political and Social Sciences* 605:281–310.

U.S. Department of Justice. 1996. *Convicted by Juries, Exonerated by Science*. Washington, DC: National Institute of Justice.

Vandiver, M. 1989. "Coping with Death: Families of the Terminally Ill, Homicide Victims, and Condemned Prisoners." In *Facing the Death Penalty*, ed. M. Radelet, 123–138. Philadelphia: Temple University Press.

Vandiver, M., and F. Berardo. 2000. "'It's Like Dying Every Day': The Families of Condemned Prisoners." In *Families, Crime and Criminal Justice*, vol. 2, ed. G. L. Fox and M. Benson, 339–358. New York: Elsevier.

Vollen, L., and D. Eggers. 2005. *Surviving Justice*. San Francisco: Voice of Witness.

Vollertsen, N. 2004. "Condemned to Die: The Story of Greg Wilhoit." Death Penalty Focus. Retrieved from http://www.deathpenalty.org/index.php?pid=Greg.

Warden, R. 2003. "The Revolutionary Role of Journalism in Identifying and Rectifying Wrongful Convictions." *University of Missouri Kansas City Law Review* 70:803–846.

Wayment, H., R. C. Silver, and M. Kemeny. 1995. "Spared at Random: Survivor Reactions in the Gay Community." *Journal of Applied Social Psychology* 25:187–209.

Weigand, H. 2009. "Rebuilding a Life: The Wrongfully Convicted and Exonerated." *Public Interest Law Journal* 18:427–437.

Weigand, H., and T. Anderson. 2007. "Life After Exoneration Program: Case Services Provision Model." Retrieved from http://www.innocencenetwork.org/docs.

Weinstein, H. 2001a. "Condemned Man Could Go Free after DNA Testing." *Los Angeles Times*, August 19.

———. 2001b. "DNA Tests Give Idahoan Freedom after 17 Years on Death Row." *Los Angeles Times*, August 24.

Weitz, R. 1990. "Living with the Stigma of AIDS." *Qualitative Sociology* 13:23–38.

Westervelt, S., and K. J. Cook. 2007. "Feminist Research Methods in Theory and Action: Learning from Death Row Exonerees." In *Criminal Justice Research and Practice*, ed. S. Miller, 21–38. Lebanon, NH: University Press of New England.

———. 2008. "Coping with Innocence." *Contexts* 7:32–37.

———. 2010. "Framing Innocents: The Wrongly Convicted as Victims of State Harm." *Crime, Law and Social Change* 53:259–275.

Westervelt, S., and J. Humphrey, eds. 2001. *Wrongly Convicted*. New Brunswick, NJ: Rutgers University Press.

Williams, N., M. Davey, and K. Klock-Powell. 2003. "Rising from the Ashes: Stories of Recovery, Adaptation and Resiliency in Burn Survivors." *Social Work and Health Care* 36:53–77.

Winnick, T., and M. Bodkin. 2007. "Anticipated Stigma and Stigma Management among Those to Be Labeled 'Ex-Con.'" *Deviant Behavior* 29:295–333.

Word, R. 2003. "25 Inmates Freed from Florida Death Row." Associated Press, July 2.

Wormith, J. 1984. "The Controversy over the Effects of Long-Term Incarceration." *Canadian Journal of Criminology* 26:423–438.

Yates, S., D. Axsom, and K. Tiedman. 1999. "The Help-Seeking Process for Distress after Disasters." In *Response to Disaster*, ed. R. Gist and B. Lubin, 133–165. Philadelphia: Brunner and Mazel.

Zalman, M., B. Smith, and A. Kiger. 2008. "Officials' Estimates of the Incidence of 'Actual Innocence' Convictions." *Justice Quarterly* 25:72–100.

Zamble, E., and F. Porporino. 1988. *Coping, Behavior, and Adaptation in Prison Inmates*. New York: Springer-Verlag.

Ziegenbaig, D. 1999. "Death Row Inmate Gets a New Trial, Supreme Court Says Judge Erred by Excluding Evidence That Might Prove Defendant Was Framed." *Winston-Salem Journal*, April 10.

Zimmerman, C. 2001. "Back from the Courthouse: Corrective Measures to Address the Role of Informants in Wrongful Convictions." In *Wrongly Convicted*, ed. S. Westervelt and J. Humphrey, 199–219. New Brunswick, NJ: Rutgers University Press.

Zuckoff, M. 1998. "Death-Row Survivors Tell How Justice Errs." *Boston Globe*, November 15, A01.

CASES

Arizona v. Krone (1995), 182 Ariz. 319; 897 P.2d 621.

Bloodsworth v. Maryland (1986), 307 Md. 164; 512 A.2d 1056.

Brown v. Florida (1980), 381 S0.2d 690.

Brown v. Florida (1983), 439 S0.2d 872.

Brown v. Florida (1986), 785 F.2d 1457.

Butler v. Mississippi (1992), 608 S0.2d 314.

Gauger v. Hendle et al. (2002), U.S. Dist. LEXIS 18002 (Case No. 99 C 50322).

Idaho v. Fain (1988), Ida. LEXIS 135 (Sup.Ct. Idaho).

Kansas v. Marsh (2006), 126 S.Ct. 2516, 2538; 165 L.Ed. 429, 456–457.

Keaton v. Florida (1973), 273 S0.2d 385.

McMillian v. Alabama (1993), 616 S0.2d 933.

McMillian v. Monroe County, Alabama (1997), 88 F3d 1573.

Melendez v. Florida (1998), 718 S0.2d 746.

Melendez v. Florida (2001), Case No. 88,961 (not published).

North Carolina v. Rivera (1999), 350 N.C. 285; 514 S.E.2d 720.

Ohio v. Beeman (1978), Ohio App. LEXIS 10670 (Case No. 894).

People v. Cobb (1983), 97 I11.2d 465, 455 N.E.2d 31.

Tibbs v. Florida (1976), 337 S0.2d 788.

United States v. Maloney (1995), 71 F.3d 645.

Wilhoit v. Oklahoma (1991), 1991 OK CR 50, 816 P.2d 545.

FILMS AND VIDEOS

"The Case for Innocence." *Frontline*, PBS (2000).

"Falsely Accused." *The Twentieth Century with Mike Wallace*, A&E (1998).

The Hurricane. Azoff Entertainment, Beacon Communications, Universal Pictures (1999).

"Johnny D." *60 Minutes*, CBS News (1992).

"The Man of Her Nightmares." *20/20*, ABC News (1998).

Thin Blue Line. Errol Morris, Miramax (1988).

"What Jennifer Saw." *Frontline*, PBS (1997).

WEBSITES

www.ccadp.org/juanmelendez.htm (Canadian Coalition Against the Death Penalty).

www.deathpenalty.org (Death Penalty Focus).

www.deathpenaltyinfo.org (the Death Penalty Information Center).

www.eji.org (Equal Justice Initiative).

www.innocencenetwork.org (the Innocence Network).

www.innocenceproject.org (the Innocence Project at Cardozo School of Law).

www.journeyofhope.org/pages/ (Journey of Hope).

www.exonerated.org (the Life After Exoneration Program).

darrylhunt.journalnow.com/frontStories.html ("Murder, Race, Justice: The State vs. Darryl Hunt").

www.law.northwestern.edu/cwc/ (Northwestern Center on Wrongful Convictions).

www.restorativejustice.org (Restorative Justice online).

www.nytimes.com/interactive/2007/11/25/nyregion/20071125_DNAI_FEATURE.html (Roberts and Stanton multimedia presentation on "A Long Road Back," 2007).

www.delberttibbs.com/Speaking%20Engagements.html (Delbert Tibbs website).

www.witnesstoinnocence.org (Witness to Innocence).

Index

About the Authors

SAUNDRA D. WESTERVELT lives in Greensboro, North Carolina, with her husband, Van, and their son, Drew. She is an associate professor of sociology at the University of North Carolina at Greensboro. Her broad areas of interest include criminology and the sociology of law, but her more recent work has focused on miscarriages of justice. Her earlier work includes *Shifting the Blame: How Victimization Became a Criminal Defense* (1998) and *Wrongly Convicted: Perspectives on Failed Justice* (2001, with John Humphrey), both with Rutgers University Press. In her spare time, she enjoys traveling with her family and chasing turtles with her son.

KIMBERLY J. COOK lives in Wilmington, North Carolina. She is a professor and chair in the Department of Sociology and Criminology at the University of North Carolina Wilmington. Her areas of interest include capital punishment, restorative justice, violence against women, and social justice. Her earlier work includes *Divided Passions: Public Opinions on Abortion and the Death Penalty* (1998), published by Northeastern University Press. In her spare time, she enjoys hanging out with her son, Greg, major domestic renovations, going to the beach, birding, pottery, shopping with Saundra, and chasing turtles with Drew, Saundra, and Van.

Robert H. Tillman and Michael L. Indergaard, *Pump and Dump: The Rancid Rules of the New Economy*

Mariana Valverde, *Law and Order: Images, Meanings, Myths*

Michael Welch, *Crimes of Power & States of Impunity: The U.S. Response to Terror*

Michael Welch, *Scapegoats of September 11th: Hate Crimes and State Crimes in the War on Terror*

Saundra D. Westervelt and Kimberly J. Cook, *Life after Death Row: Exonerees' Search for Community and Identity*